Insights

©2013 Norman D. Sorensen
All rights reserved
First Edition
ISBN: 978-1-304-23394-3

3 5 7 9 10 8 6 4

Book production by Keystroke Studios
16 Oliver St.
Watertown, MA 02472
www.keystrokestudios.com

www.insights-book.com

Insights

ONE MAN'S SPIRITUAL JOURNEY

Norman D. Sorensen

To my loving wife, Glorian

*Personal appreciation to my family
for their unending support.
With heartfelt thanks to Sis and Hank.*

*They will find a joyous reward as readers
actually discover the love found in Christ.*

Table of Contents

Introduction: Where We're Going xii

Part I: The Three Secrets of a Life of Biblical Faith

Secret Number 1 2
Nicodemus — A Man Who Looked for Answers 3
For Sure 8
I Responded 10
Calista 14
Melvyn 21
Saul: The Unusual Birth of a New Man 28
Cindy at the Fairgrounds 36
A Gift 44
The Certainty of a New Birth 46
The Holy Grail 53
Some Questions About the New Birth 60
Let's Plow Deeper into Secret Number 1 65
He Who Believes in Me — *Has* — He Possesses 69
The Father Testifies to the Validity of My New Birth 71
Secret Number 2 77
The Wellspring of Faith 78
My Words are Soldiers 86
The Power of the Scriptures 88
Built on Rock 92
I Bummed a Ride on Como Avenue 94
Someone Has To Stand Behind It 100
The Day the People Cried 106
After All, It Belongs to You 109
Walt Jensen: A Life in the Dark 114
Letter from Ted 125

Proof 128
A Letter 132
The Hidden Treasure of Faith 134
Secret Number 3 135
A Mirror 136
Catch of Fish 139
A Tree 144
Priscilla of Samaria 148
Children are the Products of Words 155
Mary 161
Prayer 166
Centurion 172
Already Prepared 176
God Looks on the Heart 182
I Act on What God Says 185
Tear Up the Roof 188
Reify — I See the Unseen 196
Mary Magdalene 199
Jesus Speaks to the Storm 206
Words 210
Five Thousand Fed 214
Anisa and the Pharisee 217
Transfiguration 222
Our First Baby — A Miracle 226
The Significance of David and Goliath 229
They Closed Their Ears 238
The One Who Sees Beyond 242
Why Me? 244
Practicing the Three Secrets 250
Thirty-One Personal Professions of My Faith 253

Part II: Collected Stories and Essays

A Great Man 262
John 274
Spend It, Baker Boy, Spend It 279

Galton	284
Self Pity	288
Widow of Nain	293
The Day I Ate What I Read	297
The Devil and Mr. Kanatha	303
The Quiet Time (QT)	307
Sarepta of Sidon	311
Headache	316
A Rich Man Finds True Riches	319
Romans 4:17	323
Lazarus	327
He's Not Here	333
Stephen	336
Pool of Bethesda	342
Hot Cross Buns	347
John The Baptist	350
Light of the World	357
To a Land	362
A Look at Parables	364
The Lady From Dallas	367
The Hidden Treasure of Faith	372
Letter to Ted	381
One Word Can Make Your Day	383
He Had Never Walked	387
I Need a Watchman	392
Singers Go Before the Army	396
Letter to Larry	402
A Soldier Learns About Real Authority	405
Illusions	413
About the Author	420

God's Love
makes our family a circle
of strength and love. What He says
overrules the circumstances of our lives,
so we speak of unseen things He has
promised as though they had
already taken place
in our lives.

Introduction

*"To know the road ahead,
ask those coming back."*
− Chinese Proverb

Where We're Going

I was meandering along a creek when a rock in the water caught my eye. I bent down to retrieve it from the water and rolled my find around in my hands. I marveled.

No, it wasn't an agate. Nor was it a diamond. It wasn't a gold nugget. It was just another gray rock, except for one thing: it was round like a golf ball. As I stood by the flowing creek I pictured the rock caught in a bowl-like depression at the bottom of the stream. There the current tumbled over and over and over, like in a washing machine. Years went by as the rock was tossed against the side of the bowl. Then I found it.

My round rock reminded me of understanding a verse of the Bible. It has to tumble around the bowl of my mind to be comprehended. I may not see the meaning of the verse with a single reading. Comprehension can be slow in coming to my spirit.

Isaiah, the Messianic prophet, wrote about the doorway to a clear picture of what is said:

> The word of the Lord was onto them precept upon precept, precept upon precept; line upon line, line upon line; here a little, and there a little *(Isaiah 28:10)*.

Nature worked diligently to shape my round rock in the bowl

Introduction

of the creek. So, also the Holy Spirit works tirelessly to unveil the riches found in the Lord Jesus Christ.

I've read a verse many times over the years, but one day I slap my forehead and exclaim, "Where'd *that* come from?! I never saw that before." I'm now in my tenth decade of life — evidently it had been tumbling around in my mind for a long time.

Paul, the disciple of faith, shares from personal experience the secret of seeing again, and again, and again. Look at what he confides with believers in Rome:

> Faith comes, and comes, and comes, by the hearing of the Word about Christ *(Translation from Greek, Romans 10:17).*

This promise guarantees faith will come if one hears, and hears, and hears the Word about Christ. That's some guarantee!

I return to the gushing creek. Once more my round rock tumbles around in my hands. With renewed clarity I comprehend the journey to faith in the Lord Jesus Christ. From time to time I have to remind myself to be patient in learning. With that patience, I have come to three great secrets I have learned — The Three Secrets of a Life of Biblical Faith — included among the *insights* of this book.

Here is a short preview of the Three Secrets, described and illustrated in Part I of this book:

In *Secret Number 1*, we see that *I can know with certainty that I have been born again.* When Jesus laid down the imperative, "You must be born again," He did not imply I needed a new beginning. He declared I required nothing less than a new life.

Secret Number 2 points to God's promise: *He always does what He says He will do.* The certainty I enjoyed in the first secret comes from God's faithfulness to always do what He says He will do.

Secret Number 3 takes us further: *I now know the Holy Spirit lives in me so I can experience for myself what God promises me in the Bible.* In 1 Corinthians 2:12, we learn that we have received the Spirit — Who is from God — so that we might enjoy the promises the Father has freely given to us in His Word.

The Three Secrets of a Life of Biblical Faith can guide you on your exciting journey to a surprising new life of faith. We are not born with faith, so we do not come by it naturally. We *learn* to believe. What can we learn in these secrets? Faith, the noun for "believe," gives us extraordinary access and awesome power to activate and live out what God has promised in the Bible.

Each secret is illustrated in Part I with stories and essays — both contemporary and from the Bible — that bring these promises to life. You can practice these three secrets using a set of professions of faith, included at the conclusion of Part I, based on Biblical promises with life-changing power. Part II of this book is a collection stories, essays and observations illustrating insights I have gained on my own journey.

It is my hope that these insights will help to guide you, too, on your journey of faith.

— *Norman D. Sorensen*
Minneapolis, Minnesota
July 2013

Part I

The Three Secrets of a Life of Biblical Faith

Secret Number 1

I CAN KNOW WITH CERTAINTY
I HAVE BEEN BORN AGAIN

When Jesus laid down the imperative, "You must be born again," He did not imply I needed a new beginning. He declared I required nothing less than a new life *(John 3:7)*.

Nicodemus — A Man Who Looked for Answers

Jesus enjoyed several days with His mother Mary, His brothers, and His disciples in the resort city of Capernaum. This town with mountainous views lay on the northwest coast of the Sea of Galilee. In this springtime of the year Jesus set out for Jerusalem, almost 100 miles due south, to be there for the Passover celebration. His disciples policed the crowds as the slow moving and often interrupted journey took several days. At thirty years of age His ministry was young, only months old, but already many believed in Him as He demonstrated His divinity in miracles. Once in Jerusalem, this powerful Man drove the money changers out of the temple, and the city buzzed with excitement over this rising charismatic leader.

Reports that Jesus worked miracles disturbed a man by the name of Nicodemus. Like Paul the apostle, he was a Pharisee, a sect noted for their strict observance of Jewish laws. He understood authority as a member of the Sanhedrin, the seventy-member council that ruled the Jewish nation.

"I am intrigued by this man."

"He turns water into wine."

"He threw our money changers out of the temple. (I have to admit they were a corrupt bunch)."

"If He is of God this will come out."

"If he is not of God this too will come to the surface."

"The only way to get answers is to visit Him."

Nightfall had taken over Jerusalem, but this influential man huddled in a robe traveled through darkened streets to secretly meet this Man from Nazareth face to face.

"One of His disciples arranged this meeting," Nicodemus thought. "I believe his name was John. I hope John keeps his word. I feel a little guilty ... some of my compatriots wouldn't approve ... but then again, where would I be if I always did what others told me to do?"

Nicodemus arrived at the home where Jesus was staying and knocked on the door. John greeted him with a smile and a handshake.

"Good to see you," spoke John, "I'm glad you made it in the dark." With warmth he introduced Nicodemus to Jesus. The coolness of the night forced them to draw up their robes as they seated themselves near the fire.

Nicodemus sized up the Man who sat four feet from him. What grabbed him right away was His youthfulness. He could have been his own son. So, this is the Man everyone is talking about. This is the Man who has a message that stirs the people. He felt drawn to this Man. How can that be? After all, I am a Pharisee, and a member of our Sanhedrin, Jerusalem's ruling council.

All day Jesus had been mobbed by large crowds which followed Him. Public ministry demanded much so He was appreciative when John brought Him a glass of fruit juice. He enjoyed this interlude with Nicodemus because it gave Him the opportunity to share a special teaching without any interruptions.

Nicodemus would be the first to speak. "I want to tell this Man," he thought to himself, "how much I admire Him." His words were measured and deliberate. Part compliment and part question, out of respect this man of high position, he addressed Jesus as Rabbi.

"Rabbi, I know you are a teacher Who has come from God. No man can do these miracles you have been doing, unless God is with Him." Nicodemus had moved right to the purpose of his visit — to find the truth about the Man. He had heard exaggerated stories. The Sanhedrin itself looked at second-hand reports. Rumors. "I sometimes wonder," mused Nicodemus to himself, "if I'm the only one in the Sanhedrin who asks silly questions."

Nicodemus performed all the religious duties which he hoped would earn him entrance into the kingdom of heaven. "God chose the temple in Jerusalem as His residence. I'll gain favor by doing all the works of the Law. How else can I please God?" Thoughts tumbled in the mind of Nicodemus. He had faith — plenty of faith — but it was all in what he did. If you used a spiritual stethoscope to listen inside, you would soon diagnose he was dead within.

Against this backdrop Jesus leaned toward His visitor and spoke, "I want to emphasize this to you personally, without a second birth — a birth from heaven — you cannot see the kingdom of God."

Jesus had made clear to Nicodemus that entry into God's family was by spiritual birth. Entrance into the human family came by birth; in like manner entrance into the family of God is impossible without birth.

The face of Nicodemus showed bewilderment. A second birth? A birth from heaven? Maybe He's saying I should start over as a baby. God knows that I have been a very religious man. He glanced from the Teacher to the fire and back again. Jesus could see that His visitor was at a loss for words.

"How?" Nicodemus repeated to himself, "How? Can I speak my thoughts; surely I will sound foolish."

"How can I be born a second time?" He had framed his question to Jesus. "Certainly this sounds ridiculous, am I supposed to reenter my mother's womb and be born a second time?"

Jesus elaborated. "This is all important, unless you are born of

Insights

water even the Spirit, you cannot enter the family of God."

"I'm in over my head," reflected Nicodemus to himself. "If I say anything it will only reveal my ignorance." Jesus set a piece of wood on the fire and the sparks flew. The Pharisee with the gracious demeanor appreciated the distraction.

The declaration by the young Teacher must have been very important to Him because He said it twice. Jesus had made it plain to Nicodemus that the only condition to see the kingdom of God was to be born a second time. Jesus explained two different worlds as He continued.

"What is born of the physical is physical and what is born of the Spirit is spirit."

Jesus saw the look of wonderment in the face of Nicodemus. He responded, "you shouldn't be so astonished at my telling you the need for a second, or spiritual, birth. This goes for everyone, not just you. Take the wind for an example. It blows where it pleases. You can hear the sound of the wind. But you have no idea where it came from, and where it's going. Like the wind, so is everyone who is born of the Spirit (unseen, personal, unique and of God)."

"I must confess that I have trouble understanding what you say."

"You're a teacher in Israel, a teacher," Jesus challenged, "yet these truths are strange to you. Let me say this with all seriousness, I am talking about what I know to be a fact. I have seen these truths with my own eyes, yet you refuse to receive the testimony I have given you, and the testimony of all those who have been born of the Spirit."

INSIGHT

Jesus could have preached this glorious revelation of the second birth to a crowd of fifteen thousand. He didn't. He shared this life-changing truth with one man — Nicodemus — this is appropriate. The Holy Spirit excludes others when He con-

fronts a person. His workshop is found in the individual's heart.

"I want pose a question to you." Jesus paused. "I have told you of things that happen here on earth, and no one believes, how can you believe if I tell you of heavenly things? No one has ever gone up to heaven, but there is One Who has come down from heaven — the Son of Man Himself."

As Moses lifted up a serpent on a pole so also must the Son of Man be lifted up on the cross, that everyone who believes in Him may live forever. For God so greatly loved mankind that He gave up His only begotten Son, so that whoever believes in Him will live forever.

Follow-up Thoughts

Nicodemus believed that the seat of worship was the temple in Jerusalem. Jesus said, no, the temple is not the seat of worship. He introduces a revolutionary truth. The seat of worship is the heart. God will now use the spirit — man's spiritual nature — as His workshop.

What about Nicodemus? Did his secret meeting with Jesus change him? Subsequent events proved that it did. The Sanhedrin council weighed the charges against Jesus *(John 7:50, 51)* and Nicodemus spoke up in His defense when he asked, "Does our Law convict a man without giving him a hearing and finding out what he has done?"

Nicodemus and Joseph of Arimathea, both members of the council of the Sanhedrin, both secret believers in Jesus, requested the body of Jesus after His crucifixion *(John 19:38)*. At a time when the twelve had fled these two men stepped forward to declare their faith in Christ.

See John 3:1-21.

For Sure

> VERIFY: *To prove by demonstration, evidence or testimony confirm or substantiate; to make true. What I believe is verified by what He says in the Bible.*

How can I know for certain that I have been born again? This is the question before you and me. No answer to this question will be found outside of the Bible, for this would only be something man invented. Paul the apostle writes:

> In whom you also trusted after you heard the Word of Truth, the Gospel of your salvation, in whom you believed and you were sealed with the Holy Spirit of promise *(Ephesians 1:13)*.

Our salvation, Paul writes, has been sealed by the Person of the Holy Spirit. He has taken up residence in the life of the believer (a glorious fact!).

So, what is a seal? If you look at a dollar bill you will see the seal of the United States. This seal verifies the authenticity of the paper. A seal confirms or guarantees a pledge made by one party to another party. In times past, letters were sealed with a wafer of molten wax into which was pressed the distinctive seal of the sender. A personal stamp or signet ring was used for making this personal impression. This seal attested to the authenticity of the document. Of course, the worth of such a seal rests on the trustworthiness of the guarantor.

As we have said, God also has a seal. He does not use a stamp or a signet ring. He seals the guarantee with a Person of the Godhead — the Holy Spirit Himself. Paul says that the Father has sealed your new life in Christ through the residence of the Holy Spirit. All believers are indwelt by the Person of the Holy Spirit.

How can I know for certain that I have been born again? My salvation has the seal of the indwelling Holy Spirit. But a reader raises his hand, "I have no awareness or consciousness of His presence, what do I do?" Faith. Faith steps up. It has a voice, and it declares:

> Father, You have given me the seal to my salvation, which is the Person of the Holy Spirit. I know for certain He lives in my spirit because You say so in Your word.

Why does the Father seal the believer with the person of the Holy Spirit? Grasp this: to those who are not in the family of Christ the Bible is a book in a language they cannot read. The Spirit indwells the believer to interpret spiritual truths. Look at the ministry of Jesus *(Matthew 13:10 – 17)*. His disciples wanted to know why He taught in parables. He replied: "To you it has been given to know the secrets and mysteries of the kingdom of heaven, but to them it has not been." *(see also 1 Corinthians 2)*

> A staggering truth: a Member of the Godhead personally indwells each believer!

Now I can say: "The person of the Holy Spirit actually lives in me." He stands as a witness to the authenticity of my new life. You can recall that the believer is an heir. He possesses an inheritance in the promises of the Word. The Holy Spirit activates these promises as the Christian believes them.

How can I know for certain that I have been born again? The child of God did not come about because of his lineage. Nor can he owe his birth to a natural father. He was born again not because of his own will, but of the will of God. *(John 1:13)*

I Responded

In the front of the church stood a bulletin board. A paper sign was posted twice a week. On Thursday the new sign would read:

>Sunday 10:45 am
>Reaching For The Stars
>Pastor Blake Preaching

On Sunday the sermon announcement came down and a saying went up:

>I cried when I had no shoes,
>till I met the man
>who had no feet.

I worked as a sign painter apprentice in a small shop so it fell to my lot to maintain the church sign board. One day pastor Blake said to me, "Norman, you're doing a fine job with the bulletin, but I'd like to see if you could take over one of my jobs."

"Sure, Pastor, what do you have in mind?"

"I'll keep on giving the Thursday copy, Ya' know, the sermon title, but would you figure out the quotations, ya' know, what you put up on Sunday?"

"Sure, I'll be happy to do that I'll do the best I can."

"Whatever ya' choose is fine with me." Little did I understand the ramifications of that moment.

When I received my new assignment, a question popped into my mind. What message belongs in front of a church? I thought about the saying, "I cried when I had no shoes, till I met the man who had no feet." I understood this quotation did not come from the Bible. I also knew these words were simply the thoughts of a man. So I wrestled in my new duty, and came to the conclusion the sign should quote the Bible. This didn't come as an epiphany. I didn't see a ball of fire on a clothes line. It added up that way, as simply as $2 + 2 = 4$.

So my obligation not only gave me practice in my trade of sign painting, but it also gave me a new mission studying the Bible once a week. I enjoyed the confidence that the pastor would be happy with my use of Bible verses. You could ask, as you studied for the first Bible verse, "what did you put up?" I selected:

The Lord is my Shepherd.
I shall not want.
Psalm 23:1

I didn't get any feedback from that sign, but later on when I looked back, it was one of the high water marks of my life. In those college age years I tried to find out which side of life was up now. You can picture a confused young man reading John 3:16. Here it lays down a spiritual law. Jesus says one has to be born a second time to see the kingdom of heaven. I scratched my head and tried to come up with an answer. None was there.

So I decided to see Pastor Blake.

"Norman, I'm afraid I can't help you, but I do have a book you can look at. It's called *The Way of Salvation in the Lutheran Church*. It's by John Gerberding." The book didn't answer my question. My confusion continued, but a friend suggested I try philosophy.

Under my bunk (I'm now in the army) was a cardboard box. It housed my books on philosophy — a half dozen or so. It's early summer. Again, you picture a young man sitting on his bunk seeking to absorb all the lofty thoughts of European philosophers. My heart was torn by the emptiness of these men and the stress of Basic Training.

So three players stood on the stage of my decision-making at this time: the challenge that came from my study of the Bible; the loneliness of the far-away philosophers; and a new visitor to my thinking — The Methodist Chaplain — who proclaimed that a right relationship with God was by faith. He took me back home to a signboard in front of a church. To John Chapter Three. To the new birth. He asked me to face myself. I knew I needed to cross this bridge.

One thing was clear to me. The philosophers were not cutting the mustard to alleviate the onslaught I faced. Another truth stared at me. The Father asked: what are you doing about My Son? I had been told that salvation was an external process, now I learned that my spirituality was an inward action. My inner man stood in a confrontation. I reflected back to the day I stood on the sidewalk and looked at the church bulletin board. I thought of the saying of the man without shoes. I had made a choice: say what the Bible says. Again I stood at a crossroads. Which road should I take?

Sunday evening. I had been in camp only a few weeks. It had been a day of catch up. Shower. Laundry. Letter writing. About a hundred yards west of our tent row lay a hill and a gully. It was a place where I could be alone. I walked over there and sat on a knoll. The setting sun signaled the close of a pivotal day in my life. Thoughts tumbled around in my mind like a clothes dryer. Voltaire. The chaplain. John Chapter Three was in the mix. I knew I had to make a decision. I saw the roads that were deadend. So I kneeled. Then I spoke.

"Father, I understand You sent Your Son to die for me. As best as I know how I invite the Lord Jesus into my life."

That's all I said. My faith said in the inner man that I had become a Christian. I was filled with gratitude for the new life I had received. I returned to a sitting position, and reflected on the experience that had brought me to this hour. One thought was for sure: the philosophy books had to go (that week I boxed them up and sent them home). The hours I had spent studying for the church sign came to mind. Being a soldier had brought a cataclysmic change to my life. The chaplain had clued me in on salvation being received by faith. It wasn't a process, it was an act. The gates to a new life as I walked back to the row of tents. On this Sunday evening no angels sang. No choir. No philharmonic symphony. No applause. I was enveloped in a total sense of well-being. I knew I had crossed a bridge that had to be crossed.

Many roads lead to Christ. One woman said, "I answered the altar call at an evangelistic meeting." A teenager testified, "I was nine when my mother made clear to me the way of salvation." "When I was a waitress," professed a college age girl, "I received Christ from a tract a customer gave me." One man dated his faith to a summer Bible camp. One lady said, "when I became a believer I grasped the fact it was not something I had concocted, God had revealed this to me." What road had I taken to bring me to this joyous Sunday evening? My trek consisted of a simple reading of the Bible. The nuggets I had posted on the signboard had also been written on my heart. So I read that those who wait on the Lord shall renew their strength *(Isaiah 40:31)*. This truth translated into being a valiant soldier in the inner man. My induction into the army had stripped me of most of my life, but now a New Life had been revealed to me. I was changed from a young man of despair to a young man of gratitude.

Calista

She Spoke of Her Healing Before She Received It

This story can be found in each of the first three Gospels. Mark 5:25-34 covers it best. I have named the main character "Calista" to enliven her person. The Gospel writers refer to her as "a certain woman".

Jesus calls her "daughter" because she had become a member of the family through her faith.

"Have you heard of Simon Peter?" Calista's mother posed the question.

"I think he's a fisherman," answered Calista.

"He was. That's until he joined up with the traveling Preacher. Ya' know, the young man from Nazareth."

"What's the point, Mom?"

"This I got from the tomato man at the market."

"This sounds like gossip," laughed Calista.

"No. No. I haven't told you what you should know."

"What might that be, Mom?" asked the daughter.

"The Preacher and His followers were at Simon Peter's house around dinner time. When the Preacher learned that Simon Peter's mother in law had been laid low by a severe fever, He went up to her room and took her by the hand. He took her by the hand, now listen to this; Calista, and had her stand. She was healed."

"I'm listening, Mom. I'm listening. That's something."

People like Calista's mom spread the joyful news of the miraculous work of this young man.

Calista, the young lady who said she was listening, suffered from a blood loss disease. For twelve agonizing years, since her teens, she had suffered from this debilitating malady.

"I see my sickness as a nightmare journey to a foreign land; no sunshine, no flowers, a story told through the lens of exhaustion." This was the tearful lament of this young woman.

"What you need, young lady is a change in diet." This was the first doctor she saw. Eat nothing but fruits and vegetables. This went on for two years, and at the end of that time she had not improved. She had spent much money only to see her health deteriorate.

"I can't wait to tell you the news," Calista's mother stood breathless with her groceries from the market. "This you have to hear."

"I love your stories, Mom."

"This one's about the soldier. A captain, no less. You know that captain who heads up the guard."

"I've seen him."

"He went to the teacher."

"But he is a Roman, he's not a Jew," observed Calista.

"I know, I know, that's what makes it bizarre."

"He told the teacher his servant boy was critically ill."

"All you have to do," he told the teacher, "is say the word and my servant will be healed."

"He sure had a lot of faith," commented Calista.

"Right. But to make a long story short, he healed the child to the great joy of the soldier." A tear appeared in the corner of the mother's eye.

"I know what you're getting at, Mom, but picture me in that stampeding crowd."

Mom advised, "He's too busy to come here. So the only out is for you to go to Him."

Night and day she dreamed of new health. The disease has to run its course. This was the prescription of the young intern who assured her he had the latest medical research.

Calista reported back to him after two years. "I've led the normal life you prescribe, but I'm worse off today than I was two years ago." Her years were going by as well as the little money she had, and she longed for citizenship in a new life of health vitality. Her last doctor was an advocate of meditation.

One hour a day. Seated. Cross legged. Eyes closed. Picture health. See yourself running. Learn to breathe properly. Calista traveled this road for eighteen months. Her conditioned had worsened. Her weekly visits ate up more money. Over and over she asked herself, is this some sort of a ruse?

"I give up. No more doctors, I've come to the end of that road. Besides, I'm broke."

"This young Preacher," her mother spoke. "He enjoys Capernaum. He's always coming back. He was at the synagogue this morning. The Sabbath, you know."

Calista pictured the young man everyone talked about. He was a man of many stories.

"Keep your eyes on him," whispered the Pharisees, "if he heals he breaks the law." This did not detour the Lord.

Mom related this story.

"'Stand up!' Jesus spoke to a man with a withered hand. He stood up. 'Now stretch out your hand,' commanded Jesus. He did, Calista, and his withered hand was healed. I can't tell you how long he'll be here. But I see something in your eyes. My daughter, it won't cost you a penny."

"But the crowd," insisted Calista.

"I know, I know, I'll take you. That's right. We'll go together. You hold my arm."

The stories her mother brought convinced Calista this man had the power of God. From her years of disappointments she found a new resolve. She would brave the crowds. She would take the chance of being trampled.

"You know, Mom, I do believe He could heal me. Could you picture that? Me, with all my strength for the first time in my adult life. If it takes my last ounce of strength we'll see him."

Calista had been robbed of her twenties. At the end of the day when all is said and done, her sickness was her life. Sure, she had girlfriends, a tight-knit group, who saw in her a fighter. She shivered with excitement at the thought of a life that could lead to dating, courtship and marriage. Her mother had said in encouragement, "Someday you'll have a family of your own. A husband. Children." For now these were only a sea of dreams leaving in their wake a focus of what lay ahead. Now the teacher. His name was an invocation. A holy Word.

She had to ask herself, "Am I simply desperate? Or am I persuaded?" She lost no time. "From what I've heard I know I have the faith to be healed."

"Are you ready, dear?" Her mother called to her with a brave voice.

"I think so." Calista's tone mirrored her apprehension of the trampling crowds. "I hope I can get close to Him."

"Take my arm," she said, "I'm told He's near the sea. It's been a long journey for you. Step by little step always downhill. Today will be a giant step. Right, Calista?"

Her dark and sunken eyes looked at her mother. She found herself unable to frame words. A faint smile crossed her closed lips.

Dust clouds choked the air as two huddled figures neared the crushing mass of humanity. The din made it riot. Calista covered her face with her scarf as she tried to make sense of the scene. She looked across the sea of heads, and thought to herself, "They remind me of waves of the ocean." She was propelled by the memory of the many dead-end streets she had traveled. She recalled the story of the man who had been lowered through the roof.

"Get back, Sister!" A large woman drove a wedge between Calista and her mother.

"Mom! Mom!" The pandemonium drowned out her cry. She searched the jostling crowd. "Mom!" No familiar face. She was on her own. She had nothing to say about where the crowd swept her. No one offered a hand, the very thing she had feared happened. Helpless, it took all her strength to stand. In a swarm of people she was alone. No one offered a hand to faltering Calista.

She spotted a tree a stone's throw away. "I'll find protection by that trunk. No one will knock me down there." She looked up to see people in her tree. Where did they come from? Why are they here? She knew some were hungry. Others wanted healing. There were the curious. After all, it was it was like a circus. A show. Then there were those who saw him as a potential king. He had his detractors: it's all magic. Hypnotism. "Am I in a dream? Where's Mom?"

In the swirling turmoil a phrase had framed itself on Calista's lips:

"I know he can heal me!"

"I know he can heal me!"

He had to come to her.

"I am too weak to claw my way through to him, I wonder what happened to Mom?"

"Hey lady!"

"Hey lady!"

A teenager in the tree hollered to Calista as she clung to the trunk. He pointed.

He's moving this way.

She stood on her tiptoes to look in the direction the young man pointed. Nothing but heads and dust clouds.

Again the excited teenager shouted. "His disciples are parting the crowd. Can you see Him?"

"For a moment," Calista confessed to herself, "I felt abandoned. But look! This young man sees my plight. Someone does care."

She weaseled herself to a spot where He appeared to be headed. She searched the undulating crowd. Her heart beat in expectation. Then she saw Him.

"This is Him!" shouted the teenager. She was frozen with fright. One of his disciples spoke to her.

"Move aside, Move aside."

Unable to move, she saw a man with an unmistakable aura of authority. "That's Him!" Dizzy. Disoriented. She lost him. But He turned to talk to one of His men. In the split second she reached out. Just the hem of His cloak. That's all she could do. But with the brush tears ran down her cheeks. She stood transfixed. Suddenly she realized she had been healed. "I'm healed! I'm healed!" The flow of blood had stopped. She felt it all through her body.

But Calista now heard His voice.

"Who touched me?"

"Who touched me?"

Jesus searched the faces of the crowd. "It wasn't me, babbled a scared old man."

His disciples laughed. "You gotta be kidding. Look at the people jostling and shoving you. Everyone's touching you." But Jesus persisted.

"I'm looking for one person. He moved His way back through the crowd." The crowd parted to expose Calista. With head bowed she raised a trembling arm in confession. She lifted her face to look into the eyes of love. She threw herself at His feet and poured out her story with childlike openness.

"I know her!" one woman claimed with her pride, "that's Calista, my neighbor."

Jesus took Calista by the hand. "Stand up," said Jesus. She finished her story.

"Daughter," he declared with explanation, "you have received your healing through the doorway of your faith. You are healed. Enjoy your new life."

"Master, master, we have to go to Jairus' house." The interruption from his disciples tore him away.

The crowd; the dust; the commotion; all disappeared. Calista stood alone. She felt stunned. She thought of others who had been touched by the Teacher. "Peter's mother-in-law; the servant boy of the soldier; the man with the withered hand. And the fellow they lowered through the roof. Step by little step; little step; line upon line her faith had come. Twelve years. Twelve long years. Now I can live life." She shuddered in thankfulness.

"Calista! Calista!"

"Mom! Mom!" I'm over here.

"Are you alright? You're not hurt?"

"I saw him! I talked to him! I'm healed!"

"Tell me about it."

Mother and daughter stood on the knoll. Tears flowed. They were engulfed in each other's arms.

Melvyn

"God loves you! Do you know that? God loves you!" The young preacher spoke with an eloquence that denied his years. Bradley, the preacher, had won top Preacher Boy awards at Houghton College. This was the first time I'd heard him and I was impressed. Gestures, pauses, inflection, delivery, just like an old pro.

The Preacher Boy's appearance belied his polish. A big man, I'd have to admit, he looked a size too large. He delivered his words on God's love with authority, but not "down" to the men at the mission; this night, I was certain, was a special night.

Darkness enveloped the skid-row area of downtown Dallas. An hour ago the six of us pulled out of the campus parking lot. With a week of classes behind us we were squeezed into Tom's rusty Plymouth. We were carrying out our requirement for "in the field" Christian service. Tonight we conducted the service at this gospel mission.

Ted assisted "Preacher Boy" on the platform. I was the greeter at the door. The others worked the streets — passing out tracts — encouraging people to come in. Bradley stopped. He stepped down from the platform. He could touch the men in the front row. His voice was a whisper, but he spoke with feeling and intimacy.

About one hundred and twenty-five men sat on folding chairs in this old furniture store. Many of them were waiting for the soup and sandwich, but when Bradley gave his "Altar Call," two men ambled forward.

I glanced out the store windows that faced toward the west. Downtown Dallas silhouetted the evening sky. The meal over, I stood at the front door and bade the shuffling men goodnight. One man, a few feet from me, appraised the tract rack. He alone dawdled. Why? He wasn't a down and outer. Thirtyish. Neat. About six feet tall. His face had an anxiety about it which said he had a little room for humor. What is he doing here? He doesn't fit.

I walked to him with outstretched hand.

"Hi, my name is Norm." His handshake was firm as he said a self-conscious "Hi." I tried to break the ice. "What did you think of the message?" He looked out the window into the night. The question fell to the floor. An invisible burden had taken his mind captive. An uncomfortable silence followed. He wanted out.

"I'd like a little fresh air." He took a step for the front door.

"I didn't catch your name," I countered his exit.

"Melvyn," he breathed. He talked to the floor. He avoided eye contact. This was no time to rush in. I patiently waited.

"Have a seat." I motioned to a folding chair. He sat down, I pulled up a chair to face him. He looked down at his hands which made fists in his lap. His shoulders were pulled up.

"Melvyn," I ventured, "you strike me as a man looking for an answer." My query got no answer. His mind was buried in a problem avalanche. He massaged his hands.

I was an eyewitness to an intense struggle in the spirit realm. I knew Melvyn needed a spiritual prescription to reach his spirit, and the only one to do that would be the Person of the Holy Spirit. So I picked up my Bible and spoke firmly to Melvyn.

"Here's a verse. This twelfth one. Oh, by the way, this is the Gospel of John, Chapter One. When you and I listen to this verse we understand this is God speaking."

His ears were open but his eyes were downcast.

I knew that this verse was alive with the divine power to give Melvyn new life.

So I read slowly, " ... as many as received Jesus into their heart, to them God gave them the right to become the sons of God, even to those who believe on his name."

I paused, Melvyn mirrored no comprehension. His eyes rested on the Bible in my lap. I knew the Spirit was working.

"In this verse God tells you and me how to become a child of God — a son of God." I sat quietly. Maybe he needs a little time to ruminate. The seconds ticked away. I knew the Holy Spirit could go through the impenetrable walls he had constructed around himself.

"As you listened to this verse," I placed my hand on his knee and asked, "can you tell me from this verse, how does one become a Christian?" He sat a little straighter with his hand over his mouth.

Then for the first time he spoke. "You're asking me who is a Christian?"

"That's right."

"Well I would say," he paused to reflect, "I would say a Christian is one who does good deeds."

I was jarred back for a moment. I could hear he had not heard what the verse said. The verse carried a gracious simplicity. A small child could understand it. It was this: invite Jesus into your life and God would make you his child — His son.

Don't lose Melvyn; make another run at his fortress. "That's true. A Christian is one who does good deeds." If I had said, "That is not what the verse says." I am sure he would have run out into the Dallas night, but he sat quietly. Where do I go from here? Again, quietness. I used the time to let the Holy Spirit work.

"Would you do something for me, Melvyn?"

"What is that?"

"Would you read this verse for me?"

He paused. "I guess I can."

I laid the Bible in his lap and pointed to the verse. "It's this twelfth one. Right here." I pointed to the verse. "This verse," I stated, "tells one how to become a Christian," Please read it out loud so I can hear it too.

Haltingly he read, "... as many as received Jesus ..." he paused. He was brave. He was doing a courageous deed for a stranger.

The Holy Spirit charged his embattlements.

"Go on Melvyn, you're doing fine."

His voice was above a whisper. "... to them God gave the right ... to become a child of God ... even to them who believe on His name."

I knew that his faith had to come from knowledge. Did he understand what the verse said? Like Bradley had intoned, God loved him. Jesus died for him. I thought this could well be the only time in his life that someone cared for his soul.

I leaned toward him. "Melvyn," I confided, "you've read the verse, and like I said, it tells you and me who is a Christian. So as you read the verse ask yourself ... how does one become a Christian?"

Melvyn looked at me. Uneasiness showed. He suppressed his smoldering anger. Should he cross this bridge or not?

He could say, "I think you're right," and leave. That was the last thing I wanted to happen. Mental assent was the easy way out. A truth came to me. The mind can think it. Only the heart lives it. The heart is the battle ground of the Holy Spirit.

The question lay on the table: How does one become a Christian? So I repeated. "From this verse, how does one become Christian?"

"You have already asked me that question, remember, and I answered it. I told you a Christian is one who does good. You didn't seem to get it."

He was now argumentative, his breathing quickened. I exposed the conflict within. There were those who said to Melvyn, "you don't have to listen to this guy. He doesn't know what he's talking about." I knew a great warfare was taking place in the spirit realm. I could see Jesus standing at Melvyn's heart door. "Melvyn, I want to come in. I'll give you a new life — my Own. You'll live by My power."

In the midst of this battle for Melvyn's life, I sat as a spectator. I pondered the words: no one is as blind as the one who will not see. Hogwash. Negative thinking. I chastised myself, shame on you. You know better. Why don't you say words that join Jesus at the door? Jesus said, "These words that you are using contain spiritual life." Do you believe in that, Norman? I embraced this truth in my own spirit and framed the truth with unspoken words.

Twice I had placed this verse before Melvyn, and both times Melvyn had shown no hearing for what God was telling him.

"Melvyn." Again I leaned toward him with a confidential tone in my voice. "God is facing you in this verse. I believe in my heart you know what He wants you to do." The air had the tenseness of a courtroom drama. I glanced down at the oaken flooring as I began to say, "as many as received Jesus … "

Then it happened. He tossed my Bible into my lap, and jumped to his feet. His face was livid with rage. I didn't know what to do. One thing was sure; I thought I was going to get punched. I didn't anticipate this reaction.

God's love for this man faced a crucial test. I laid my open Bible on the chair and stood up to face Him. His face said it all. Should I apologize? I can see the anger was at a boiling point. When our eyes met it was cataclysmic.

Before I could say a word his legs buckled from under him. He fell in a kneeling position on my chair. He buried his face into my Bible. We were alone and in the stunned silence I could hear him sobbing.

Immediately I fell to my knees beside him. I wrapped my arm around him. I tilted my head against his shoulder, and through his tears I could faintly hear, "He can … come in! He can come in! Whatever He wants. I'm tired of fighting. I'm tired of fighting. Now it's over."

He released the weight of his body. I could feel it onto my Bible. Jesus had been standing at the door of Melvyn's heart. Now he took up residence in his life! Melvyn had become a child of God.

"Thank you Father," I breathed a short prayer, "that Jesus has come into Melvyn's life tonight, Amen."

Slowly, we rose into our feet. I put my hands on his shoulders. With tears on our cheeks I looked into the face of new man. For the first time I saw him smile. Peace. Peace radiated from him. He destroyed his invisible prison wall to enter a land of faith in what God says.

He spoke with a new found boldness, "It is no longer my battle."

"I'm very happy to hear that." He was emotionally exhausted as he stood before me. I knew my time with him was over. He was too tired to get pointers on the living of the Christian life.

"Now you can get that breath of fresh air you talked about." I chuckled. I gave him a bear hug as he stepped out into the night. That was the last time I saw Melvyn, and I feel confident he went on in his new life. Feeling drained, I turn to put away the two chairs where the episode had played out. My open Bible lay on the chair and a small pool of tears lay over the verse he had read. I stood there a moment — teary eyed — reflecting on the scene I had been privileged to witness. For a long time after that I treasured that the page had a wrinkling on that twelfth verse. A great reminder of watching the Holy Spirit work.

The following morning, a phone call came into the seminary. It was Melvyn's mother. In a choked up voice she told the school secretary, "Please give the following message to the young man who spoke to my son last night. Melvyn came home beaming, 'Mom, sit down, and I've got something to tell you.' I held my breath. 'Mom, I don't know how to say it, but I became a Christian tonight.' I jumped out of my chair and couldn't stop hugging him. 'It's true, Mom.'" She went on, "There are a number of us who have been steadfastly praying for him. So you can see why we were so overjoyed. He had been living in petrifying fear of going to the veteran's hospital. But he was up early this morning. 'Mom, I'm checking in the hospital.'" She concluded, "If you can reach this young man, please let him know! And tell him thanks."

This true story brings us to the first secret of the life of faith: How can I know with certainty that I have been born again?

Saul: The Unusual Birth of a New Man

> *"The hero's journey is not taken by every man."*
> — *Joseph Campbell*

A small band of determined men set their faces towards the city of Damascus.

Their hatred surfaced in their fervor.

"A bunch of heretics! That's what we're after," cried their leader. "We chased 'em out of Jerusalem. But look! Now they're looking for converts in Damascus."

Their Mission: Snuff out these people who were followers of the dead Nazarene.

"We have to nip it in the bud. If we don't stamp 'em out we'll have Rome on our necks. We'll put 'em in chains, that's what we'll do, and then we'll bring them back to Jerusalem. We have the extradition papers from the Sanhedrin itself. They deserve to sit in jail. They could be stoned to death. That's what we did to their Stephen. No wonder. You should hear their poppycock. They say their dead leader is alive. You know He was crucified. They're crazy. They say He has been resurrected. Can you imagine that? They renounce Judaism. They're a bunch of fanatics. They have to be stamped out."

At the head of this police force of Judaism strode a twenty-four year old lawyer. He had the name of a king — Saul, a rising Pharisee. He was from influential family in Asia Minor, the city of Tarsus. His background: Jewish, Greek and Roman. He graduated from the world renowned college in Tarsus which was noted for Philosophy and Literature. He was a driven man, one who made the cause his personal fight.

Saul had appeared before the Sanhedrin in Jerusalem, the seventy-member ruling council, to get legal authorization to jail any members of this left-wing sect of troublemakers.

"Gentlemen!" he cried. "Look at my record. I am Pharisee, the son of Pharisee. Jerusalem has been my home, and I sat under his honor — Gamaliel. I condescended to the stoning death of one who got caught in their beliefs — a man named Stephen."

"Any dissension?" Asked the High Priest of council.

"None here. None here," echoed through the chamber. "Take a half a dozen students with you. I'll have my secretary fill out the extradition papers."

Saul's resumé said he had held the garments and personal effects of Stephen — the first Christian martyr — when he was stoned to death by his accusers *(Acts 7)*. He had heard Stephen say as he fell to his knees, "Lay not this sin to their charge."

"I'll never forget that hour," reflected Saul, "for I heard Stephen testify to his beliefs from our Scriptures. He said he saw the Son of Man standing at the right hand of the Father. Stephen's testimony had a lasting impact on my life."

Why was it personal? Here's why:

"I have sought to defend our ancient traditional beliefs," said Saul. "Already I have routed out of Jerusalem many of the radical followers of this preacher from Nazareth. Do you know what he said? He said he could destroy our temple in three days. Can you imagine that? It took a lifetime to build it. He taught that the kingdom of God was not in our temple in Jerusalem. He taught that the kingdom of God was inside a man in his heart."

"So," the high priest assured Saul, "you can bring to Jerusalem any man or woman who is a follower of this troublemaker. We commend you as a council for ferreting these fanatics."

Saul gave a sigh of relief. "I know we appraised, rooting out the bad guys will win me points with the council."

It was three days since the entourage had left Jerusalem. Now they were in the fertile plain of southern Syria. Donkeys, camels, carts and people scrambled on their way. Children wailed for their parents who hollered instructions. Saul was oblivious to the noise, the dust clouds, and the congestion as he thought of his strategy.

Without warning there was a flash of lightning.

"What was that!?" cried a startled man with Saul.

"Lightning!" shouted one.

A light brighter than a noonday sun flashed on the band from Jerusalem. Instantly they fell to the ground in a stupor. As they lay stunned, their leader heard a commanding voice. Saul propped himself on one elbow and listened. What's happening?

A voice out of a lightning thundered, "Saul! Saul!"

His heart pounded.

In his delirium he deciphered his name being spoken. Though blinded by the light he struggled to make sense of what he could hear. This time the voice thundered.

"Saul! Saul!" it rumbled through the hills.

He took hold of himself.

"Yes! Yes! I hear you." His voice trembled. Paralyzed by fear he heard the voice ask,

"Why are you persecuting me?"

Nothing like this had ever happened to him. "What can I say? Am I in a dream?"

In his bewilderment he asked the voice coming out of the lightning, "Who are you? Who are you?"

"I am Jesus! I am the one you are persecuting." Saul lay helpless as he tried to see. Now he grasped that his enemy's Leader was alive. This Nazarene was alive. "You can't win, Saul! Stop what you're doing!"

This charging man with his aides lay prostrate on the ground on the outskirts of Damascus.

They shivered with fear. "How did this happen? This wasn't part of our plan, and we're too scared to flee."

It broke upon Saul that he was confronted by the very One he had repudiated. He didn't say, "OK, I'll believe." He didn't say, "I'll join your band." His first words were words of obedience, so the blind man asked, "What do you want me to do?"

"Stand up!"

The men with him also stood speechless; though they had sight they saw no one. They heard the sound of the voice, but could not understand what was said.

Then Saul heard the voice say, "Go into Damascus. There you will be told what to do."

Saul opened his eyes but saw nothing. He blinked. "I'm blind."

He asked his men, "Are you blind also?"

"No. No," they answered. "We're not blind."

"Help me. I've been told to go into town."

So his friends took their leader by the hand and guided him into Damascus. They dropped him off at the house of Judas where Saul was in prayer in three days. He lived and relived the life-changing episode on the road. "I know He lives. He spoke to me. He knew my name." Remorse locked horns with joy. In those seventy-two hours he did not eat or drink fluids.

"Will I ever have my eyesight back?"

A believer by the name of Ananias lived in Damascus. While he was in prayer he heard, "Ananias! Ananias!"

Ananias jumped up.

The Lord spoke to Ananias, a believer in Damascus, "Ananias,

I have task for you."

"Here I am, Lord."

"Go to the Straight Street," directed the Lord, "ask at the house of Judas for a man of Tarsus. His name is Saul. He is praying there."

Saul also had a vision at this time.

"Saul!"

"Yes, Lord."

"I have spoken to Ananias. He's a believer."

"Yes."

"He is to come to the Straight Street. He knows Judas."

"Yes."

"Ananias will enter the house you're in, and he will lay his hands on you."

"Yes, I understand."

"You will be able to see again."

But Ananias rebelled at this news.

"This man has wrought havoc among the believers, Lord. He concurred with the stoning of Stephen. He was like a tornado with the followers in Jerusalem. We're scattering like chickens. Now he's here. He has delegated authority from the High Priest and the council in Jerusalem to put men and women in chains if they profess faith in your Name."

"Go!" replied the Lord. "Go! For this man is My chosen instrument. He shall bear witness to My name before the Gentiles, before kings, and yes, the descendants of Israel. He will suffer much for My name's sake, but I will make clear to him what he must endure."

Reluctantly Ananias entered the city of Damascus, and found the straight street. He was welcomed into the house of Judas and spoke to the blind man before him.

"Brother Saul, I understand the lord Jesus appeared to you a few days ago, as you journeyed along the road from Jerusalem. I am here to lay my hands on you that you may receive your sight and be filled with the person with the Holy Spirit."

Ananias laid his hands on Saul, and instantly he recovered his eyesight. Saul looked on his former enemies and with tears in his eyes he said, "You're Ananias! You're Judas!" He embraced his new-found kinsmen and was baptized. After a meal he found new strength. He remained with the disciples in Damascus for several days, but he preached immediately in the synagogue. His message was a testimonial: this Jesus is the Son of God.

Saul was a go-to man. He wanted everyone to hear the incredible story of what happened to him on the road to Damascus. He preached in the houses, in the street corners, and in enemy territory — the synagogue. And the more he preached, the greater the resistance grew. He argued. He compared and examined evidence that Jesus is the Christ, the Messiah. Confusion and dissension broke out among the Jews.

"This man's driving us crazy. He came here to jail the troublemakers. He heard God in a vision. Now he's the one of the crackpots. He insists this Nazarene carpenter is the Messiah Himself. He tramples over our traditions with his prophecy arguments."

With the passing of days and greater humiliation, the Jews secretly plotted to murder Saul.

"This man has to be stopped! People are listening to him. He will bring down our temple with his proselytizing. First off, we'll close all the gates to the city. Our guards will have him boxed in."

Saul's friends told him, "Your life is in danger."

"I'm not surprised," replied Saul. "I could see their hatred when they argued with me in the synagogue."

His friends continued. "The gates to the city are secured.

Guards are posted."

Barnabas spoke up. "We have one way out."

"And what is that?"

"We'll put him in a basket and lower him down to the wall. There are no guards there."

"Good idea." Some smiled with the scheme to save Saul.

When darkness had fully come they put Saul in a basket at the top of the wall. They carefully lowered him to the ground where he walked to safety. He took the familiar road to Jerusalem and tried to meet with the disciples who were in hiding there, but they did not trust him.

"Isn't this," they clamored, "the man who sought to kill us? He consented to the stoning of Stephen. Believers sit in prison because of him. He wants to infiltrate us as a spy. His word is less than dung."

"Wait! Wait! Wait!" Barnabas stepped in. "I hear what you're saying. What you say is true. He was an evil enemy, but the Lord spoke to him as he neared Damascus. He saw the light, and has witnessed with fervor about the messiah. You know my own personal testimony. I would never mislead you. So my plea is that you give him the embrace of the fellowship and recognize him as a part of our family." The believers embraced him, but it wasn't long before the Jews in Jerusalem agreed with the synagogue in Damascus.

INSIGHT

As you and I look back on the ministry of Paul we ask ourselves: Why was it necessary that Jesus reveal Himself to him on the road to Damascus? He was used by the Spirit to bring the Gospel to all the world. He championed the truth that salvation is by faith alone. He established the church: "The Mystery." "The body of Christ." "The new man." "The household of God." This includes all believers from the time of Christ to the present.

See Acts 9; Galatians 1 & 2; Ephesians 2.

Cindy at the Fairgrounds

Cindy knew about the special religious services at the fairgrounds. They were called "evangelistic meetings." Through the years it had not been her choice to go to things like this. She hadn't felt any particular need to do so. Now it seemed like the thing to do. Her friends were all leaning in that direction.

Her own religious world was defined by her church life. She identified with the organization. If one had asked her about the religious authority in her life, she would have thought for a moment. Then she would have said, it's my church. As she walked the hallway of life, there were Christian doors she had never opened — exciting rooms she had never entered. She was depriving herself of the knowledge which belonged to her rightly.

Years before, her dad had said something which had drawn the guidelines of her religious life. On religion he had a path-worn answer: "This is the way I was raised. My parents had me baptized when I was a week old. They took me to Sunday School. Confirmation lasted two years, and at fourteen I received my first communion. I was made a member of the church for life. That's the way my parents taught me. Since I was a child, that's the way I have believed"

Cindy's life had been the same — cast in the mold of her dad. "My view of God," she had told a friend, "is what I learned in confirmation." Lulled to sleep by complacency, she allowed strangers to do her spiritual thinking for her. She didn't know there was a land of treasure beyond her wildest dreams.

Her dad had also said it was offensive to talk of religious things outside of church. "Nothing but a bunch of opinions," he would fume, "No one knows what he's talking about." Religion to dad was a group experience, a time to socialize. It was not an individual encounter. Nothing was personal. It was a Sunday morning obligation. You felt good because you had done what you ought to do. It was all in the head.

The Lord's Prayer was essentially Cindy's prayer life. "Most of the time I am not even aware of what I am saying." And what would you say of your faith? "I suppose I express my faith when I say the Apostle's Creed in church." (One day she would look back and say, "I didn't know any better.") The knowing wasn't there. And if there wasn't any "knowing," how could she have certainty? Her ignorance wasn't a stranger. She had talked about the dark corner of my life. Unconsciously she knew it would someday be illuminated.

One day she heard the term "mind set." "Is that me? Do I have a mindset? "Often she found herself "unfriendly — a put-down manner," toward a new Christian insight. "Am I threatened?" She turned down a friend who asked her to go with her to a home Bible study. Her reason: it would confuse her. "I can't understand the theory of relativity, and I can't understand religion. Why try?"

Cindy's brother said about politics: "There are smarter people then I am who are Democrats. There are smarter people then I am who are Republicans. How can I say who is right?" Cindy used this logic in religion. There are people who are much smarter than I am — more knowledgeable — and they still disagree. So I guess the best place to be is where you stay away from arguments.

So she had a wary eye when it came to religious people. Those who brought their beliefs into the workaday world. The kind who wanted to talk church matters outside of church. How can they as lay people be so sure? The last thing in the world I want to be is a fanatic. Do you think I want to be one of those kooks who pass out tracts at the bus depot? Was that what God really wanted her to do?

So Cindy made a straw man of the religious world outside of her church life — an opponent of her own imagination. Her church was always right — "they," the opposition, were always wrong. (One day she would reminisce, "Like so many people I was running slipshod through life without taking the time to enter the riches of the Christian life.") She loathed hypocrisy — "I can't stand a phony." She stood behind the curtain of acceptability — not hiding — and when the light would come she would step out.

It was against this interesting backdrop that Cindy was to attend the Sunday afternoon meetings. She was leaving the protective custody of her environment. Everyone at church went along with the idea that it was the right thing to do. The pastor had said from the pulpit that meetings of this significance did not happen every year. He continued, "It could well be a once in a lifetime opportunity to hear this man speak." Was it any wonder that she was sold on the idea?

Last minute thoughts: What could she anticipate? I'll go along as a spectator. The ball's in his court. Could he answer the questions which never seem to surface? What have I got to lose? It will be entertaining. But then again, church in the morning, afternoon here, not much time to tend to unfinished weekend tasks.

She was surprised by the traffic going into the fair-grounds. Tie-ups everywhere. Neighborhood hawkers stood in the streets like demonstrators. Homemade signs said PARKING - $3.00. Cars darted into spaces in yard or alley. Cindy pulled into a yard where a child was shepherding cars on to the grass.

She joined the summer-dressed throngs on the sidewalk. They funneled themselves toward the grandstand looming ahead. A large woman carrying a black Bible commented on the beautiful weather. A harried man tried to get his children out of the street. After several futile attempts he joined them. The hurrying made Cindy wonder if they were late. Each in a hurry to get a seat.

Once in the stands she was caught up in the excitement. Anticipation moved through the crowd. The chattering was a great buzz. It could have been a baseball game. She did not know the peppy number the organ was playing. A grand choir of several hundred singers formed an amphitheatre behind the platform.

The bubbling song leader came on to the platform and led the crowd in "Oh How I Love Jesus." Cindy followed along from the paper program she had been given. The hymns were enjoyable. All was so grand. The ritual of the church service had been ripped away. Announcements were made, and the offering taken. The governor of the state arose from the line of dignitaries seated on stage. In a complimentary speech he introduced the evangelist. The crowd was quiet and hushed with a muffled cough here and there.

The speaker began by reading John 3:16.
> For God so loved the world,
> that He gave His only begotten Son,
> that whosoever believeth in Him
> should not perish,
> but have everlasting life.

It was a familiar verse to Cindy. One she had always loved. Someone had once said it was the Bible in miniature. She had never forgotten that. Ten minutes into his talk he told a story, a story that would change Cindy's life.

A certain lady had died and gone to heaven. She was met by God as she stood alone at the gate to eternity.

"I am delighted to welcome you here," he said, "We have had a Father-daughter relationship for such a long time."

"Thank you," she replied, "I have been looking forward to this meeting. It was one of my joys on earth to know I would be entering here someday."

Her confidence surprised Cindy. She had used the word "know." She repeated the phrase to herself, "It was one of my joys on earth to know I would be entering here someday." In her mind she elevated the word "know" on to a pedestal.

The guest at heaven's gate testified of her heart belief in the Person of the Lord Jesus Christ. It had been clear to her, as clear as polished glass, that there was no ticket to heaven for the one who was counting on his good works. She expressed her gratitude for his love in sending his Son to give her a new life.

As Cindy followed the story, inwardly she said her own amen to the testimony of the woman. Like the woman — she too — grasped that salvation was by faith and faith alone. If she had lived a good life, she still could not have earned her way into heaven. If works could secure one's entrance into heaven, why then was it necessary for his Son to die? It was of grace.

The Father drew attention to her "knowing," as the conversation resumed.

This Cindy wanted to hear. She listened intently.

Cindy sat upright, not missing a word. Rays of sunlight were breaking into a corner of her life. Can one really know for sure?

The woman before God asserted "From my first days as a child of God it was apparent to me that You will do what You say You will do."

"You will do what you say You will do." All were one syllable words in a profound statement, but were yet so simple. Even a five year old would grasp its meaning. A silent voice within Sylvia told her this was one of the high water marks of her life.

The evangelist elaborated. The guarantee to heaven is set in what God declares. He has pledged in John 3:16 that you and I have been given eternal life. It is an unbreakable contractual agreement in which the Father has granted the inalienable right to be counted a citizen of his heavenly domain. He cannot lie. He is bound by His word to carry out his promise. His Word is our title deed to eternal life.

The speaker went on. His Word alone sufficed for the woman at heaven's gate. It is not membership in a church. It is not because one has performed the right rituals. Nor, like I said before, because one thinks he has done the best he can.

Cindy continued to be enthralled by the new world of her discovery. She could know. Her Bible was like a legal document that assured her of her legal right to heaven. It was a high moment in her life. At such a moment a symphony could well have been playing. All was quiet. In the distance was the voice of the speaker.

The evangelist finished his message. He invited the audience to come forward to the platform.

"This is a moment in your life for a new beginning," he said emphatically. "Announce it to the world. Come forward. For some this will be an afternoon of first-found faith in the Person of the Lord Jesus Christ. Then there is the one who has left the fold. The backslider, the prodigal son. You want to come home. Come forward. How about you who want to serve? Take this opportunity to dedicate your life to Christ."

Cindy felt jubilant. The terse statement re-echoed in her ears, "You will do what you say you will do." She had never known this before. If she had found a gem of great price it would not have made her happier. The throne of her life had a new Sovereign. No longer would it be tradition or what man had to say. Who would rule in her life? Would it be the thoughts of men, or the declarations of God? She knew the answer immediately. Again she sensed a far off land. A land where she had just received a great inheritance.

The evangelist talked of a step of faith. "This is your time to cross a bridge. This is your time to turn a corner in your life. This is your time to enter a new land. Come forward."

Cindy's memory flashed back to the first time she saw the mountains. It was in the afternoon, like today. The mountains were far off. Low in the horizon. Barely perceptible. At first she thought they were clouds. No. They were not clouds. They were too distinct. They were the mountains. Her heart leaped. Here again was that same experience. She was seeing afar off, barely perceptible new horizons for her spiritual life. A new land. She tingled inside.

"In conclusion," the speaker stressed, "there are some of you who have been hiding out with the crowd. You have been deceiving yourself. You face God alone. It is one on one. Like the woman at heaven's gate, she was by herself. Others are excluded. This is done in the solitude of your own life."

Cindy stood up. She joined hundreds of others who were going to the platform. She squeezed her way toward the aisle.

"Excuse me. Excuse me." she whispered.

This was a celebration, a celebration to her new-found treasure. God will do what He says He will do. What lies ahead on this path I am now taking? I don't know. But I have to find out.

Cindy took her place at the foot of the platform. The size of the crowd surprised her. A lady introduced herself. She identified herself as a counselor.

The speaker spoke in an intimate way to all those who had come forward. He spoke of the new adventure they were embarking upon.

"Stick with the discovery you have found this day. Don't let Satan take it away from you."

Cindy's counselor filled out a card on her background. She assured Cindy would receive follow-up material.

"Do you have any questions?" she asked.

"No," replied Cindy quietly, "but I have found some wonderful answers this afternoon."

The crowd dispersed. Cindy retraced her steps to the car. In her preoccupation she was unmindful of the activity. She enjoyed a tranquility she had never known before. It was like an answer. An answer long sought. And, at last, found. New buoyancy gave spring to her step.

She sat in her car for close to half an hour. Content in her thoughts, she watched the shrinking crowd. She reflected, thinking of the new world she had just entered. Afternoon shadows lengthened. The streets were empty. Cindy started her car and drove homeward — a changed woman.

A Gift

Jesus left the house where He had spent the night and walked to the shore of the Sea of Galilee. He enjoyed the seaside with His disciples, but a noisy crowd soon gathered, and those in the back began to shout,

"We can't hear! We can't hear!"

Peter spoke up, "why don't you speak from my boat? Then more people will hear your message."

Jesus seated himself in the boat, and Peter took him sixty feet from shore.

"Sh! Sh!" cried some in the crowd as they strained to catch the words of this young preacher. Often He told stories so His listeners could picture in their minds the point He sought to get across. Today would be no different. The crowd grew silent in their anticipation as He projected His voice.

"This morning I want to tell you the story of a farmer who sows seeds on his land. He takes a fistful of seeds and scatters them with a swing of his arm."

All eyes were on Jesus as he formed a mental image of a farmer sowing seeds.

Jesus looked out on the crowd as He paused in His story. Again the audience grew quiet as they looked forward to what would happen next.

"Not all the seeds hit their mark," Jesus continued, "for some of the seeds fell on a heavily trodden footpath on the edge of the farmer's field."

Jesus took a break once more so His listeners could picture the errant seeds where pedestrians trod.

Jesus went on, "some of the seeds the farmers cast landed on shallow soil. It was only a half inch deep. Some of the seeds that flew out of his moving hand ended up in thorn bushes."

Jesus stopped to emphasize, not all of the seeds missed their mark, for some flew on fertile black soil.

Jesus spoke louder on his final point. "If you heard what I said, be sure to listen to the message."

Later, when He was alone with His disciples, one asked, "we don't get it."

"What is that?" enquired Jesus.

"You told a crowd by the seaside a story about a man sowing seeds on his farm."

"That's true."

"This is our point, if we can't make sense of this parable, how can the needy ones in the crowd grasp the meaning?"

Jesus studied the men who had been chosen to follow Him, and then said, listen,

> To you has been given spiritual insight, that through discernment you will understand for yourselves the secrets and mysteries of the kingdom of heaven.

See Matthew 3.

The Certainty of a New Birth

I find it impossible to live a life I do not have. I can live the life God gives, only by passing through the portals of the new birth. In other words, no one can be Christian in God's eye unless he has been born again.

When Jesus stated the necessity of the new birth, He provided childlike access to it so everyone could be sure of their birth.

But countless thousands are kept from the secret of the new birth. Why? They seek an answer outside of what God has to say about it. God's Word removes all uncertainty.

To be born again I must cross the threshold of faith. Faith itself comes from what I hear, and what I hear comes from what God says *(Romans 10:17)*.

You could well ask: "How can it be that God created with words? I don't understand. Are these the same words we use?" Yes they are the same words, but in the physical world in which we live they are simply used to communicate. In the spiritual realm God infuses his speech with creative power. This truth, God's Words, are filled with creative power, and will come to play an integral role in my search for the secrets of the life of faith.

How can I find God? (God is more anxious to find me than I am to find Him.) I need the witness of one who has found the way with certainty. Samuel, the great prophet who was a contemporary of David, reveals how he found God. He said "the Lord revealed Himself to me in Shiloh *by what He said." (Samuel 3:21)*

God took the initiative with Samuel as He does to you and me. God faced this question: "How can I show myself to Samuel?" To do this he constructed a bridge of Words. In that bridge, Samuel came face to face with God.

One asks, "That was Samuel the great prophet, or, That was in creation he used Words. How about today?" Time has not changed His secret of unveiling who He is. My eyes are opened to see God when His Words lodge themselves in my heart of faith.

Where can I find God? I had to find the answer to this before I went on to the second question. God said to Samuel, "Here I am! Open the eyes of your spirit, Samuel, and you'll see me." His eyes were opened as He read His Words, and a very happy God gave Samuel the sight to see Him.

I know where I can find God in what He says, so I go to the question: "How can I know Him?"

"I know," someone asserts, "that God does not speak audibly, so where can I find these Words that will enable me to know Him?" Good question. The answer: In the Bible.

Words are so many black specks on a white page. You may ask, "How can these black specks give me an intimate relationship with God Himself? Can you give an example? And it will have to be simple. I don't know much about the Bible."

John 3:16 serves as a litmus test: as a doorway to a new life.

> For God so loved the world, that He gave His only begotten Son, that whoever believes in Him should not perish, but have everlasting life.

These Words possess the same creative power as the Words in Genesis 1. They are supernatural Words filled with God's power to impart new spiritual life in my believing heart.

I see four things as I change the pronouns to make the verse personal.

First:
God tells me He loves me.
Second:
He proves this love by sending his Son to die for me.
Third:
He expects me to respond to this in kind faith in my heart.
Fourth:
God gives me new spiritual life when he sees my genuine faith.

I express my faith or I act on these words when I profess from my heart: "I know you love me."

How can I know God?

This question prompts another question.

Where Can I find God?

If I don't know where He can be found, how can I know Him? I cannot experience God in my life until I know where I can find Him.

Someone hollers, "You can find Him over here!"

I check it out only to find he's talking about his church membership.

Then I am waved down by a pedestrian who claims "I know the way. I'll find God in your behavior, and I'll earn my way to heaven."

There are many advice-givers out there who haven't done their homework, but I need a signpost that directs me to the correct way. Then I can shout with certainty, "I know for sure!"

I begin my travel with a simple conclusion: I live in a

physical world. I use my physical senses and faculties to construct my life in this domain.

God, on the other hand, lives in the spiritual realm. He doesn't use physical senses and faculties to achieve His ends. So, how does He function in the spiritual sphere? Good question. My journey takes me to the first chapter in the Bible.

Genesis 1 pictures God creating the world, so this is a good place to find out how God functions. Ten times in this chapter I read "and God said." For example, darkness prevailed, so God said, " Let there be light, and there was light." *(Genesis 1:3)* He created light with His words. He spoke light into existence. A trip through this creation chapter brings out that He created all things with His words. He manifested His creative power through what He said.

"I know Jesus died for me."
"I believe in my heart."
"I know I have been given a new spiritual life"
(eternal life).

Have I received the life God offers? Can I know with certainty I have received this new life?

I can know with certainty I have received new spiritual life when I meet the simple action set down in His Word — believe.

Isn't it too simple — just to believe? I find much more to faith than "mental acknowledgement."

With the mouth, states Paul the apostle *(Romans 10:11 Amplified)*, I declare openly and speak out freely my faith, so confirming my salvation. If I cannot speak out what I believe I have not been born again. God honors my words from the heart as He does His own Words. He hears my faith by the words I speak. I say what He says about my life. He hears me speak His Words — now my spirit has a voice.

What would life be like if there were no John 3:16? Oh, God would say, I have John 3:16 in mind, but I would rather not say it. If you and I had nothing to hear we would be doomed to a life of ignorance. In like manner, God wants to hear more than my thoughts, He wants to hear my voice.

I see three questions:
> Where can I find God?
> How can I know with certainty I have been born again?
> How can I see His presence in everything I do?

How can I find God? He reveals Himself by what He says. Secondly: How can I know with certainty I have been born again? I know I have a new life because He says so.

And, thirdly, in everything I do I find His will in what He says.

How can words in the Bible be alive? Do they really contain spiritual life? If they have spiritual life, how do they implant that life? From what source do they get such awesome power?

God's Words serve as spiritual seeds. Dormant spiritual life lies within each seed. My heart provides the spiritual soil. God's Words, like the Words used in the creation of the world, continue to possess supernatural power to create spiritual life. When the Holy Spirit plants these seeds into the soil of my believing heart, new spiritual life springs into being.

Where did the idea of the new birth come from in the first place? Jesus introduced the new birth in His talk with Nicodemus. He said no one could see the kingdom of God unless he had been born again.

Through the seed of Adam I have been born into sin with its penalty of death. Through the sacrificial death of the Lord Jesus Christ I can be given new life through God's grace.

Look at how telling this verse is:
> ... having been born again not of corruptible seed (going back to Adam) but of incorruptible seed, by the word of God, which lives forever *(1 Peter 1:23).*

My first birth found its life through the nature of Adam, but in the second birth my new life springs out of the creative power of what God speaks.

Jesus made this corroborating statement: The Holy Spirit gives life. Our flesh contributes nothing to it. The words I have been speaking to you contain spiritual life *(John 6:63).*

As the third Person of the Trinity, the Holy Spirit plays a key role in securing new life for the believer. He breaks through my blindness by opening my eyes to see what God has prepared for me. He interprets. He translates. Through His explanation He makes clear the revelation of God.

Paul saw the function of the Holy Spirit in the new birth when he said, I have not received the spirit of the world, but the Spirit from God, to the end I might understand the things God has freely given to me *(1 Corinthians. 2:12).*

Where can I find the things God has freely given to me?

Faith rests upon knowledge.

If I do not know something exists I cannot believe in it.

So the Holy Spirit takes my hand and leads me back to what God says in the Bible. Here I find the things God has freely given to me. His promises. Pledges. Guarantees. He cannot lie. He always does exactly what He says He'll do.

I need assurance. I need to know I have definitely been

born again. I enter through John 3:16. It provides knowledge. And when I embrace it in faith I live out its power. At this point the Holy Spirit bears witness with my spirit that I am a child of God.

The Holy Grail

Once upon a time a wise old man lived in a picturesque hut in the forest. Pine trees stabbed their way toward the sky as they formed a windbreak to the north of his garden. Today the resident of this cozy homestead worked the fertile soil. He glanced up from his raspberry patch to see a jaunty young man coming down the road.

"Howdy!" shouted the visitor, "I see you have a well."

"Sure," replied the host as he sized up the traveler, "help yourself. The dipper hangs on the pump handle."

"Some haven you have here," observed the traveler. He drank deeply from the refreshing well as a busy robin cocked his head in the garden in his search for a worm.

Neither man felt a need to speak. The dust-worn traveler reminded the older man of his own youth, when he looked for answers. Their reverie was interrupted by a yellow warbler in a lodgepole pine.

"I'm looking for something old," the young man broke the silence as he gestured with the ladle.

A puzzled smile crept over the other man's face. Something old, he mused. What did he mean "something old?" Is he looking for antiques?

"Yeah." Embarrassed by his confusion the visitor explained. "Yeah, it'd be like a cup … metal … decorative … like you'd find in churches … " Finding his way, he paused. "It would be an antique … like you'd find in museums … I know … A chalice. D'ya know what I mean?"

Insights

"Would that be ... say a cup for Communion?" inquired the older man.

"There you have it," clarified the youth "A communion cup, but in my case I'm looking for a special one, very old."

"Maybe they have it in the church in town," suggested the host. "It's an old church. Even the minister is old." The host chuckled at his humor.

Reverence crossed the face of the visitor as he spoke in a hushed voice, "I'm searching for the Grail ... the Holy Grail."

In deference to his visitor the host listened. He cupped his hand to his chin and gave respectful thought to the man's mission. "That's a tall order, the Grail itself."

The young man's eyes shined with pleasure as he spoke knowingly. "It is the cup Christ drank from at the Last Supper."

"Oh yes," he leaned against his hoe in thought. "I believe all the knights of King Arthur's round table gave their vow to search for the Grail."

"That's true. I see you know your history."

"Why did the knights do that?" queried the old man. A look of wonderment crossed his face. "Was it supposed to have magical power?"

"Right," agreed the young man with a sparkle in his eye. "The Grail will change the life of the one who finds it." Reverence crossed over the face of the one who as on a mission.

The older man leaned forward with interest.

"A changed life," he queried with a searching look.

"Yes," filled in the guest. "That's what I've been told. The one who finds the Grail will enter a new life. The Grail has the power to give new spiritual life."

After a pause the host replied, "No wonder the knights of the Round Table gave their life vow to search for the Holy Grail."

The Holy Grail

"You can appreciate," the young man went on, "why I have been on this quest. You might call it a 'pilgrimage,' it's what brought me here today. My shoes are worn thin, my coat's threadbare … but what the heck … " his voice trailed off in resignation "… I suppose my chances are one in a million." He appeared to be talking to himself about his dream.

The host did not counter the young man's discouragement. A gray squirrel scolded from a branch in the chestnut tree. His tail swished up and down in anger.

"That's Tommy," informed the elder. "He asks, who is the visitor?"

"This young man is my friend, Tommy." He talked to the squirrel with a laugh.

The time break with Tommy gave opportunity for their friendly exchange to move on. The old man led off.

"You spoke of what the Grail gives to the finder."

"Yes, it's what I've been told."

"A new life?" The older man took on the role of a mentor.

The young man concurred. Just think of that, a new life.

"I think I've found … " the host looked at the well for words, he wanted to say the right thing. " … I've found what we're talking about."

The young man studied the face of the older man with astonishment, "You've found the gift of the Grail? Ya' know, the new life …"

The older man slapped his knees with his hands and chuckled in embarrassment. He didn't know which way to go. He ventured forth. "Sir, ya' know what keeps us from God. You and I have to face that."

The young man studied the older man with renewed respect. I see a peace, he thought. Is it a restrained joy? Free. Free from entanglements. What is it?" The traveler saw in his host the same thing he had seen in his friend, Ken back home — a new life.

"Ken said," reiterated the guest, "that he had received the Lord into his life."

"Ken and I have something in common," smiled the host. "Maybe I can meet him some day. We'd have a lot to share with one another ... Like I said ... I don't like sermons but like you, I was on a mission when I was your age."

"How's that?" asked the young adventurer with keen interest.

"I too was looking for the Holy Grail." The older man smiled and shook his head in memory.

"You were? I find that interesting. You too were looking for a chalice when you were my age?"

"No. No. No. Not like you are. Not like the one you talk about, a cup. It was more like a spiritual Grail I was searching for."

"A spiritual Grail," quizzed the youth. "That's different."

Overhead a seagull lazily floated against the backdrop of a thin stratus cloud.

"It is different," filled in the host. "It's what the Grail represents, a new life. Oh! I suppose you could say I was searching for God, which is what the Grail pictures."

"Like me," agreed the young man.

"Like you, correct, but I was led to something else."

"What was that?" The guest showed great interest.

"In my quest to find God, I discovered God was searching for me."

"Interesting twist. I never saw it that way. How did he find you?"

"Through what he said. Ya' know, he does talk to us."

"Where would that be?" queried the seeker.

"The Bible. I found out in the Bible that God loved me and had a new life for me."

"Ya' know," interjected the smiling young man, "your words bring me to Ken."

"Ken? Oh, yes." The senior man expressed interest. "He's your friend back home. What does Ken say?"

"He refers to the Bible. Like you do."

"Like I said, I'm not much on sermons," mused the older man, "but what does Ken bring out?"

"First off," the youthful adventurer looked at a lodgepole pine for words, "I realize Ken has found his own spiritual Grail in the Bible message."

"How do you know that?" asked the host.

"He says he has invited the Lord into his life."

"When I invited him into my life" the host affirmed, "I knew I had the Life He gives. Ya' see, He never goes back on what He promises."

"Let me see if I get it straight. So you said what Ken says, you had a new Life. What d'ya mean?"

"It wasn't my doin', God did it. I picture Him knocking at the door to my heart. I opened the door. All I did was receive ... what He gave ... Life."

"I can't get over how you and Ken have so much in common. I always wanted what Ken had, but I didn't know how to get it."

"Tell me more about Ken."

"No worries ... seemed to know where he was going ... purposeful ... an inner joy. Like you have. He showed it. He did more than talk."

"Thank you for your compliment."

The traveler went on. "But ... my pilgrimage? What about that? Is this part of His leading?"

"Yes, I believe so," assured the host. "The Lord works in mysterious ways."

With a sigh the young man said, "You and Ken always see God

Insights

at work in your life."

"I think this awareness is the work of the Holy Spirit. I suppose," went on the guest, "you would say He directed my steps to this garden. Like you say, He's looking for me."

"No denying it," confirmed the host.

"It's so simple. It's all that simple," the guest mused to himself.

The older man waited in silence. He waited for the truth to sink in.

The young man looked toward the garden as he thought, "It's like someone giving you his word."

"Precisely. That's the same way I saw it," added the senior. "I don't think God is one to renege on his promise. He always carries out what He says He'll do. If He says you have a new life, then you do have a new life."

"I won't have to beat the bushes anymore. I can forget the Grail. My quest has come to an end. I'm ready to go back home."

"You're sure a decisive young man."

"I've done it."

"Go on."

"I've taken God at His Word. He said he'd come into my heart ... so I've opened the door. I know He has come in."

"Yes," a tear formed in the eye of the host, "it's as simple as that."

"Jesus has given me the new life I was searching for," testified the young man.

"You've done what I did when I was your age. You were looking for this." Unspeakable joy flooded the sunlit garden.

Ken will be blown out of his shoes when I tell him. "I've found the light?! Wow. He'll be one happy guy."

"Before we go in and have a bite to eat, let's take a fer' instance"

"OK, shoot"

"Fer' instance, Ken asks 'How are you sure Jesus came into your life?' What would you say?"

"I did it, man. I did it. I asked Him to come into my life."

"OK, OK," went on the host. "Let's call that the confirmation within yourself. 'Self testimony.' No one can question that."

"I get ya'. I know he'll be thrilled."

"I agree, also tell Ken you acted on what God says in the Bible," concluded the delighted host.

"No problem. God himself gives me my assurance 'cause I know He can't lie."

The two men stood up. Only hours ago they were strangers; now they were brothers in the Lord. The older man hugged the younger man in their newfound relationship. As they walked toward the hut, Tommy the squirrel chattered his approval of their new friend.

Insights

Some Questions About the New Birth

Why do I have to be born again?
The Bible pulls back the curtain.
I have to be born again to receive the eternal spiritual life God offers. I entered the physical world through birth by my mother. I enter the spiritual realm of God by the birth of the person of the Holy Spirit. I have to be born again because Jesus commanded it (John 3:3).

I believe in my heart on the Lord Jesus Christ, but I have never had a born again experience. Can I call myself a Christian?
You are a Christian because the Word of God says so. Everyone who believes that Jesus is the Christ, has been born of God. (1 John 5:1). What God says is your title deed to eternal life. A common error is seen here. You have been looking for a physical experience to corroborate what has already happened in your heart.

I have received Christ into my heart, but I act the same as I always did. Am I still a Christian?
Yes, you are a Christian. You became a believer through an act of faith, now you need to learn to live by faith. Faith comes, and comes, and comes (sense of original language) by the hearing of what God says in His Word.

Many say their "decision" was the doorway that led them into the Christian life. Isn't there more to believing than simply a "decision"?
If their "decision" contained faith, then it aligns itself with the Word of God. If one says he's a Christian because "he went forward," but has no faith, then it's an empty act.

How would you define faith?

Faith says I act. I pursue a course of action based on what God says in the Bible (Matthew 7:24).

I have no faith. I wish I had it. How do I get it?

Faith comes through what I hear and that hearing comes through what God says in His Word (Romans 10:17). Read John 3:16. Act on it. Speak your faith. Write it down.

I have read that many Christians live in an illusion. Do you agree?

Yes. Many people see themselves as Christians but what they believe is not in accord with what God says.

Here are some illusions:
> I know I'm a Christian because I have been baptized.
> My church membership makes me a Christian.
> I do good so I know I'm a Christian.

A friend of mine, says one reader, became a Christian when he saw a ball of fire go down a clothesline. Is that possible?

No. The ball of fire on a clothesline does not have the power to impart spiritual life. The Holy Spirit works through the Word alone to impart new Life.

One man said he saw God in Person. He stood one night at the foot of this man's bed. Should I try to see God like this man did?

No. God is a spiritual Being. He is invisible. You and I worship Him in our spirit (John 4:24).

Peter says (2 Peter 1:4) when you and I act on the promises in the Bible we actually share in the nature of God.

I am impressed by the spirituality of people who have all night prayer meetings. Are you also impressed?

No. Faith says I have already received that for which I prayed for the first time. If I need to ask a second time I reveal I did not have faith the first time I prayed. Receive. Let go. Then go home to bed rejoicing that God always does what He says He'll do.

My uncle says that once you become a Christian you're always a Christian. Is this true?

Yes. The Holy Spirit creates the new life in Christ. If one fears he can lose his salvation, he is looking at his behavior to verify his faith. If one renounces his Christian faith he was not born again in the first place because the new life is a work of God (Ephesians 2:8-10).

I have often wondered if angels are for real.

Yes. Angels are for real. They are a vast company of intelligent beings created by God (Colossians 1:16) and are frequently mentioned in the Bible. They are sent from heaven (which is their home) to minister to all who enjoy salvation (Hebrews 1:14). You could entertain an angel and not be aware of it (Hebrews 1:14).

They can take the form of a human being. They have the ability to fly. No Scripture is addressed to angels. I do not pray to angels (I pray to the Father). Fallen angels are in the employ of Satan. Demons (fallen angels) challenged Jesus. They are very curious about salvation (1 Peter 1:12). The word "angel" means messenger. Countless numbers were at Jesus' birth. Countless number were at His crucifixion. I will not become an angel when I die.

Interesting reading:

> Genesis 18 and 19
>
> Hebrews 1

A college girl writes: My college professor says he is an agnostic. What is that?

An agnostic is someone who doesn't believe in something (God) unless there is physical evidence for what he believes in.

She continues: What evidence do we have to prove the existence of God?

For one, the Bible declares the existence of God.

Another would be the countless millions who have been changed by believing in a God Who is alive.

One could also bring up the intellectual brilliance of the Gospel message.

She also asks: Why are intellectuals often against Christianity?

Paul the apostle says the natural man is limited by his physical nature. He does not have the spiritual faculties to receive the insights of the Spirit of God (1 Corinthians 2:14).

Does everyone have a spirit?

Yes. Everyone has a body, a mind (our soul), and a spirit. At death the believer's spirit goes home to the Lord (2 Corinthians 5:8).

Is there such a thing as "dead faith"?

No. The two cancel each other out.

Many people conclude their prayer with this phrase: " … if it be thy will."

This phrase says, I do not know Your will. If I do not know the will of God I cannot have faith. When I pray what He says in His Word, I pray according to his will (John 15:7).

I have often wondered what God looks like.

God created man in His own image (Genesis 1:28). God is a Person who looks like you and me.

Does eternal life start when I die?

No. Eternal life commences the moment I become a believer.

Jesus says a wise man builds his house on a rock. What does this mean?

He explains that when He says anyone who hears My Words and acts on them can be likened to a man who built his house on the foundation of rock (Matthew 7:24).

A friend dropped the term "Mystical Church." What did he mean?

The Mystical Church is a vast company of people, unstructured, who have been born again, and by their salvation are called out from the world to form the Body of Christ, over which He is the

Insights

Head (Ephesians 1:22,23). This includes all generations since the Church began.

The outward form of the Church is an assembly of people who meet in a building made up of a single generation, one locality, and may include saved and unsaved members.

I don't feel that I'm a bad person, yet the Bible calls me a sinner. How can I resolve my conundrum?

God says I have a nature — the Adamic nature — which is contrary to His nature. When I'm born again I'm given His new nature.

Let's Plow Deeper into Secret Number 1

The New Birth

I can know with certainty that I have the new life God gives.

All too many say to themselves, "I know I am a Christian but I have never been born again."

Some say, "I go to church every Sunday. Our minister preaches from the Bible, but being 'born again' is for those who are more emotional. I think we just "grow up" to become Christians."

"I don't get it," says another. "Why should I check the new birth? I'm contented where I'm at."

"You're always talking," complains another, "about eternal life. I'm knee-deep as it is, in the present."

Take a moment to look at it this way. If I am traveling through life without the vice grip certainty of my second birth, I am forfeiting (in other words, I have abandoned my right to) what the Lord Jesus Christ expects me to enjoy from day to day.

Call it self-disfranchisement. I deprive myself of the enablement — the rights — the privileges — the power — because I refuse to listen to a different point of view. The Bible draws a grand portrait of this new life, but it is impossible to live a life one does not possess.

Nicodemus came to Jesus late at night and said to Him, "I know with certainty you have come from God, for no one could do these miracles unless God be with him." This visitor was a Pharisee, a member of the Sanhedrin, an outstanding man of authority among the Jews.

"I have this to say," replied Jesus, "unless a person is born again he is not able to enter the kingdom of God."

"I am an old man," Nicodemus smiles in embarrassment, "how can I enter my mother and be born again?"

"No. No," assures Jesus, "your second birth would be by the spirit. That which is born of the flesh is flesh, but that which is born of the Spirit is spirit."

You and I live in a physical world, our faculties and senses construct our lives in this domain. God, on the other hand, dwells in the spirit realm. To function in this world God does not use the tools we use in the natural sphere.

God creates the worlds in Genesis 1. Notice how He works:
... And God said.
... And God said.
... And God said.

Ten times in this chapter you will discover how He functions. Darkness prevailed and God spoke, Let there be light, and there was light. He brought light into being by what he said. Mankind, the earth, the sea, vegetation, sun, moon, stars ... all brought into being with words.

You could well ask, "How can it be that He created with words? I don't understand. Are these the same words we use?" Our words have their home in the sphere in which we live, however, you and I can use His divine words to realize His creative power.

A godly lady by the name of Hannah gave birth to a boy. She named him Samuel, "heard of God," because God had answered her prayer for him. Moral darkness shrouded Israel at the time of Samuel's birth. Without God they turned to idolatry barbarous behavior. In this scene of rampant corruption, God looked for a man to lead Israel out of their night of horror.

Hannah placed Samuel in the temple as the boy-understudy to Eli the priest. One night when Samuel slept the Lord called.

"Samuel!"

He answered, "Here I am." He thought it was Eli so he ran to him. "You called me."

"No, Eli said. I did not call you, go back to sleep."

Again Samuel heard.

"Samuel!"

He ran to Eli to do his bidding, and Eli perceived the Lord was speaking to Samuel. At that time, the boy did not know the Lord or His presence.

"Go back to bed," said Eli, "and if you hear your name again, say, Here I am, Lord. What is your message?"

A third time the Lord came and stood.

"Samuel! Samuel!"

He answered with his new knowledge of the presence of the Lord. "Speak, Lord for your servant is listening." God predicted the judgment to fall on sinful Eli, his family, and Israel. After hearing God, Samuel slept till morning, and then opened the doors of the Lord's house, but was afraid to tell the news to Eli. Finally Samuel relented and informed Eli of what God had said.

God chose a six-year-old boy to bring His word of judgment on a nation in rebellion. Years later Samuel would write:
>The Lord revealed Himself to me in Shiloh by what He said.
>(Samuel 3:21)

He also wrote that He let none of His words fall to the ground.

Does God talk to you and me like He talked to Samuel? Yes. He spoke to Samuel in an audible voice because that was the only way he could communicate with him. He speaks to you and me through what has been written.

Words appear as so many black specks on a white page. I find it difficult, writes one reader, to understand how these specks make sense.

>For God so greatly loved you and me that He gave

67

Insights

> His only begotten Son to the end that those of us
> who believed in Him would have eternal life.

This is the question: Do these words contain the same creative power as the words of Genesis 1? The answer: Yes. Because God has spoken to them they are supernatural words. Just as He created light, here in John 3:16 He imparts new life.

The Word that God speaks not only contains life, but is also filled with divine power *(Hebrews 4:12)*. This verse also tells us it is the job of the Word to determine the genuineness of one's faith. The Word searches the deepest part of our being to analyze the purposes of our heart.

God's message in Christ is near you, not only is it in your heart, it is also on your lips.

> If you confess with your lips that Jesus is Lord and
> believe in your heart, you will be recognized by God
> as His child.
> ... with the mouth one confesses openly and speaks
> out freely his faith and confirms his salvation.
> *(Romans 10:8-10 ampl.)*

Jesus spoke to a tree. He spoke to the storm at sea. One time he spoke to a dead man (Lazarus). He confronted an enemy with words (Paul on the road to Damascus). He taught us to imitate the Father. I speak His promises to overcome the circumstances of my daily life.

He Who Believes in Me — *Has* — He Possesses

God, the Father, looks at the Christian and says to him:

I have given to you *life* in abundance. *(John 10:10)*
Everything you do will *prosper*. *(2 Psalm 1:3)*
You have a life *free* from worry. *(1 Peter 5:7)*
Fear has been removed from your life. *(2 Timothy 1:7)*
I will *manifest* myself to you. *(John 14:21)*
You *receive* what you ask for in prayer. *(John 16:24)*
I *work* powerfully in your life. *(Ephesians 3:20)*
I have given to you *all things* that pertain to life and godliness. *(2 Peter 1:3)*

God intended the Christian life to be a miraculous life, but Joe Christian says, "I cannot remember an answer to prayer. What is wrong?" Many Christians never see miracles in their lives because they only *hope*, they never *believe*.

>He who believes in me — *has* — he possesses. *(John 6:47)*
>
>Faith has *already received* what it believes for before it actually appears.
>
>Many confuse hope with believing —
>
>*Hope* walks in the shoes of expectation.
>
>*Faith* rejoices in the settled knowledge of possession.

Every circumstance in life is overturned to victory when faced with faith.

A telling test of faith reveals itself in this verse: "For we who

69

have believed *do* enter into (His) rest." *(Hebrews 4:3)* The rest says: "The work is finished."

All knowledge of God comes through what He says. Too many Christians stumble along "hoping for the best," failing to understand God has worked out the circumstance beforehand. This absence of faith shows that the Bible is missing from their lives.

> Twelve spies spied out the land from Kadesh Barnea, only two knew they already possessed it because God said so *(Numbers 13:30)*. Caleb & Joshua enjoyed victory beforehand.

> The Lord has delivered me out of the paw of the lion, and out of the paw of the bear, He will deliver me out of the hand of this Philistine. *(David speaking about Goliath, 1 Samuel 17:37)*. Goliath was defeated in David's spirit before he was slain on the field of battle.

> Jehoshaphat appointed singers unto the Lord, and praisers to rejoice in the beauty of His holiness, and they went out before the army, and to say, Praise the Lord, for His mercy endureth forever. *(2 Chronicles 20:21)*

Faith doesn't go to prayer begging and pleading. No, faith goes to prayer like Jehoshaphat went into battle, rejoicing in victory before it actually appeared. The miraculous took place in the heart before it happened on the field of battle.

No wonder Paul the apostle said, "If any man be in Christ he is a new creation, old things are passed away, all things are become new." *(2 Corinthians 5:17)* The old things — "I don't have the foggiest idea what's going to happen" — has passed away. The new things: God has done everything He's ever going to do about this circumstance. My responsibility lies in finding what He has said about it. The entrance of His Word not only gives light, it also imparts faith. He who believes in me — *has* — he possesses.

The Father Testifies to the Validity of My New Birth

An Oath by the Father

Ted and Earl, life-long friends, met one day to compare notes in their friendship. After some family talk, they agreed they had observed much blindness on the subject of the new birth.

"I think a lot of folks," noted Ted, "base their Christian conviction on an illusion."

"How's that?"

"Well, they lack the Biblical facts," Earl went on, "we need a reliable authority to stand behind what you and I believe."

The two talked at length about man-made roads to Christianity. Some say: "I became a Christian the day I was baptized. I joined a church, so I know I'm going to heaven." "I do the best I can," defines another; "you earn your way to heaven by being a good person."

So we have a cacophony of voices in the land. Satan loves it. If he can get people to believe they are Christians by their baptism or their church membership, or their behavior, then we win the battle for souls. Satan's aim is to misrepresent the easy to understand way of the new birth as sketched for you and me in the Bible.

Ted thought many people were unacquainted with the Bible so they reach out to a fictitious authority invented by false information.

"You know what the Word says," agreed Earl, "you shall know

Insights

the truth for yourselves, and the truth shall set you free."

They agreed to meet at a later date in Minnehaha Park.

Earl's parting shot: "I'm going to bone up on the new birth subject."

At the appointed time the two men met at a picnic table in the park.

Their discussion took them to the third chapter of the Gospel of John. Jesus lays down the dictum that for a person to be a Christian he has to be born again.

"Does that simply mean," injects Ted, "that a person turns a corner in his life?"

"Some see it as that;" Earl went on, "but stop for a moment and look at the word 'birth.' Birth, as a word, demands the impartation of life. For example, entrance into the human family came through physical birth."

"So, what you're saying," filled in Ted, "is this; one becomes a member of the spiritual family of Christ by spiritual birth."

"At this juncture," cited Earl, "many look for an experience to validate their new birth. I like the brevity of the verse that says that all who believe that Jesus is the Christ have been born of God." *(1 John 5:1)*

On another table in the park two bluejays hunted for scraps of food. They complained about these two instructors.

"Look at the word 'believe,'" mentioned Earl. "Everything rests on its shoulders, but what does it mean? For example: if I 'agree' that Jesus is the Christ, am I born again?"

Ted jumped in, "No. Agreement does not say one believes. Agreement speaks of mental assent. That's in the head. Genuine faith reaches deep down in my spirit."

"We have to be careful here," warned Earl, "after all, this impartation of spiritual life is the work of the Holy Spirit."

"Yeah!" joined in Ted, "it is the question of the Who is the life-giver." *(John 3:36)*

"He creates with the power of spirit-filled Words." Earl went on, "I don't need to fight to prove that I am a Christian, the Father has testified (in an oath, see Hebrews six) to the validity that I have this new life."

"I hear a lot of certainty."

"That's what the Father wants us to have. I like that word — 'certainty.' The dictionary says it is a firm and settled belief in the truth of something."

"We're talking about the new birth." Earl looked at an old oak, in search of words. "My Bible," he weighed his words, "gives me the certainty of my spiritual birth."

"I have a little secret."

"What's that?" enquired Ted.

"I add my name to a verse."

"Give me an example."

"Well, take the new birth."

"Right."

I say, "Earl, you must be born again."

"I see. Like, 'Ted, I will never leave you.'"

"It makes it more personal."

The bluejays directed their screeching at a squirrel on their table. The two men laughed at their entertainment.

"In our quest for certainty in the new birth," Ted read a verse from his New Testament, "the Holy Spirit, in person, constantly bears joint-testimony with my human spirit that I am a child of God."

"Where was that?"

"Romans chapter eight, verse sixteen."

"It clamps on to the new birth."

"You can't dispute the Person of the Holy Spirit," laughed Ted, "it's like He stands before the tribunal of the godhead."

Insights

"You can embrace the fact," added Earl; "my new birth has divine confirmation."

Their conversation turned a corner. "Ya' know, Ted mused, in that song 'Amazing Grace,' we sing, 'That saved a wretch like me'?"

"I hear where you're going … Do I have to feel I'm such a bad person to become a Christian?"

"Much is said about repentance."

"I know."

"So, how do you account for that when someone says, I think I'm a good person?"

"Let us look," ventured Ted, "at a person who is not a Christian. What does his résumé say? He has a fallen nature from Adam. He denies the existence of God. As a non-believer he rejects the love of the Lord Jesus Christ. As far as he's concerned, the Bible is just another book. His life is ordered by his natural endowments. He scoffs at the truth of living by faith. Though he sees himself as a 'good' person, God sees him as a sinner."

Earl climbed on board, "I can see where he shuts God out of his life."

"We can also see," Ted resumed his insight, "where repentance is necessary."

"I notice you said he has no faith. I'm sure he believes himself. He has faith in his marriage."

Ted chuckled. "You're right. He does have faith, but not the kind of faith God is looking for."

"I concur, but if he wanted the faith that would be pleasing to God, how could he get it?"

"I'm sure there are many who would like an answer to that question. The apostle Paul answered this question. Faith comes from what you and I hear, and the message we hear is the (good news) Words about the Lord Jesus Christ."

The Father Testifies to the Validity of My New Birth

Earl stood up to stretch his muscles. He winged his hands overhead. Then he responded. "What you're saying is that we get faith from words?"

"I'm not much on illustrations," admitted Ted, "but you and I know when we drink a bottle of water it becomes a part of our body. In like manner, when you and I drink in the Words concerning the Lord Jesus Christ, they become a part of our spirit."

"Words are containers, like you say about the bottle of water."

"That's true. You can see it in creation. God said, let there be light, and there was light."

"I get it. Light was like a bottle of light, when He spoke it, then the light was manifested."

"What about the words you and I use," asked Ted, "are they like God's Words?"

"Are they also containers? Yes. They can be Spirit, filled when we say what God says," and then Ted read:

You and I have not received the spirit of the world, but the Spirit which is of God that we might come to know the things which God has lavished on us in grace, which things we put into words, not human words, but in words taught by the Holy Spirit, fitly joining together spirit-revealed truths with Spirit-taught words (1 Corinthians 2:12-13).

"I like the phrases, 'Spirit-revealed truths,'" Ted said with insight.

"Ya' know what that's referring to?"

"Of course, that would be the Words in the Bible."

"So, when I say what the Bible says about the circumstances in my life, I am utilizing supernatural Words."

"As we wrap up our time together," Ted said, "I would like a parting insight on knowing for certain one has been born again."

"That's where we started," observed Earl.

"Ya' know, when God gave a promise to Abraham, He nailed it down with an oath. He gave him promise based on His personal integrity."

"That's true. You and I have this new life — the certainty of it — with the settled knowledge that the Father has sworn — has personally given His Word to carry it out."

Secret Number 2

GOD ALWAYS DOES WHAT HE SAYS HE WILL DO

Jesus explained at the beginning of His ministry (in Mathew 4:4). "Man shall not live by bread alone, but by every Word which proceeds out of the mouth of God." Our bodies live through the sustenance of food, but our spirit (the heart) receives life from what God speaks in the Bible.

In another place *(John 6:63)* Jesus says the essence or fundamental nature of what He speaks is not only spiritual, but also contains spiritual life itself.

As we learned in Secret Number 1, "I have been born again, not of a natural seed, but by the Word of God." *(Peter 1:23)*

The certainty I enjoyed in the first secret comes from God's faithfulness to always do what He says He will do.

The Wellspring of Faith

Faith is a gift to the one who exercises it.

Paul the apostle made clear that faith comes from what I hear and what I hear comes from the Word of God *(Romans 10:17)*. You can see this in Secret Number 1: Life eternal sprang out of what God said in John 3:16. This verse contained the seed of eternal life, and the Holy Spirit sowed that seed in the soil of my believing heart.

Faith came out of what I heard, and what I heard came out of the knowledge of John 3:16. I could never have believed if I had never heard the message of this verse.

I have to remind myself I cannot have faith in something I do not know exists. In other words, faith finds life on the food of knowledge. God knows I cannot have faith in the unknown, so He has lavished on you and me a storehouse of promises.

One says, I know a little about the Bible, but I do have faith. I suppose I could say, "I have faith in my faith. Is that ok?" No, faith in faith is empty faith. Nothing has been believed. How can anything be received?

God lives by faith. He sees the potential for me to live as He does. I live like He does when I act on what he says. I can know what He says after I have gone through the passageway of knowledge.

Where can I find faith?

Secret Number 1 imparted the new life in John 3:16. Can I now say I am a person of faith? For the first time in my life I put

The Wellspring of Faith

into action the spiritual law. I took a course of action on what God said. The apostle said I go from faith to faith, so I move on to employ these mechanics of faith where required. In order to do this, I will have to know the promises given for the particular living of the Christian life.

Jesus likened God's Words to seeds in the parable of the sower *(John 3:16)* as a seed containing eternal life. God has planted this seed of Life in my believing heart. It is created after its kind. Other verses have different seeds essential to my new Life.

To enjoy these other promises — or seeds — I have to find them. I discover the first seed or promise I need is an antidote to worry. I'm caught up in needless worry. To make matters worse someone tells me that worry is a sin. I worry more. A few days later someone tells me that worry kills more people than any other sickness. My worry increases. Then I learn that worry amounts to meditation on my fears. I'm confused. Where's my new found Christianity?

I say to myself, "if a verse from Bible contains the power to impart eternal life (and it does), then a verse from the Bible certainly has the power to throw out chronic worry from my life." My first obstacle in my new life — overcoming worry. I seek the mind of God the Father. I go back. When I needed new life I found it in a verse. Why not apply the same mechanics that worked in John 3:16?

I look for God's thoughts on my worry. Where can I find the seed that provides healing from my worry? I find it in 1 Peter 5:7:

>Throw all your worries on Him,
>Because He affectionately and
>Watchfully cares about you.

Jesus speaks to my worry:
>"Norman, you can throw all your
>Worries on me because I love you with

A personal and tender affection. You
Know I watch over you all the time."

How can this verse change my life?

Father, you revealed the seed for a new Life in John 3:16, now you offer me the seed that releases me from the shackles of chronic worry. Norman, He informs me, you worry because you are ignorant of my love. Yes, I confess, I am ignorant, and I make a decision as I did in John 3:16, to receive this seed of 1 Peter 5:7.

What do I have to do for this verse to live in my life?

He carried all my worries up on the cross. I embrace that truth the moment I catch myself worrying. "You took that torment up on the cross, but now you live out a new life in me."

In the word "addiction" I see "diction" — "to say." In my addiction to worry I spoke my worries. I said what was on my heart. I needed to be changed in my heart. Now I put into words,

"I know you love me with tender affection."

"You personally watch over every detail of my life."

"I know my worries have been taken up on the cross."

"I know the seed of 1 Peter 5:7 lives in my life."

The book of Numbers reveals the tragic story of the Children of Israel. The year: 1490 B. C. They had crossed the Red Sea with the miraculous parting of the water. Now they were poised on the outskirts of the land of Canaan.

"I have given you this land," God assures them.

One man from each of the twelve tribes was chosen to make up a search party.

"Men," said Moses, "you will spy out the land that God has given to us. Bring back a report of the discoveries you find." After forty days they returned from their mission. Ten of the twelve reported a picture filled with terror:

"We saw giants who come from giants. We were in our own sight as grasshoppers, and so we were in theirs."

At this depraved news the people wailed: "We have nowhere to go! Why did we ever leave Egypt?"

"Hold on! Hold on!" cried Moses. "We didn't hear from two of the spies!" The last two scouts tore their clothing in frustration.

"Listen! Listen! Listen!" shouted Joshua and Caleb, "God has given us this land! Let us take it at once!"

At this shout of faith the rebellious mob picked rocks to stone Joshua and Caleb.

"Kill 'em! Kill 'em!"

Into this scene of macabre violence the Lord appeared in the tabernacle. Even though Moses interceded for the people, God sentenced them to die in the desert.

Centuries later Jesus said, " ... if you have faith as a seed ... you would say ... " *(Matthew 17:20)*. Joshua and Caleb had faith as a seed for they said, "God has given us this land. Let us go up at once and take it!" God brought these two men into the land of Canaan forty years later.

God condemned the Children of Israel to forty years in the desert because they failed to act on what He said.

"No, I don't think you can do that." This is what they shouted by their needs. When I do not take someone at his word, it is tantamount to calling him a liar. The Israelites called God a liar. This denies His very existence.

I want the kind of faith that says "God lives!" Where can I find it? I know I am not born with this kind of faith. In other words, I do not come by faith naturally. The Bible says faith is a gift, yet I have to make a choice to believe.

Someone says, You can make faith a skill. Why not? Like knowledge, I learn faith. I search for faith. Faith involves two people: one the Guarantor, the other the recipient.

I can have genuine faith in one area of my life, yet have no faith in another area of my life. How can that be? In the area where I have no faith I am ignorant of what God has done in that sphere.

I can see where faith comes from in Secret Number 1. Life eternal sprang out of what God said in John 3:16. This verse contained the seed of eternal life, and the Holy Spirit sowed that seed in the soil of my believing heart. Faith came out of what I heard, and what I heard came out of the knowledge of John 3:16. If I had never heard the message of John 3:16, how could I have believed?

I have to remind myself I cannot have faith in something I do not know exists. Faith lives in the substance of knowledge. God knows I cannot have faith in the unknown, so He has provided dormant seeds. These promises provide the food for faith to live.

Someone says, "I know little about the Bible. How can I have faith when I don't know what He says?" (See the 31 Professions of Faith at the end of Part I.)

Jesus understood that faith rested on what God said. He began His ministry in the desert after He had been led there by the Holy Spirit. He went without food for forty days and forty nights. Satan appears on the scene at his vulnerable moment to test whether or not He was God. So Satan challenged Him.

> "If you are God's Son, command these stones to be turned to bread."

Satan was sure Jesus would fail this test of divinity, for he had struck at His point of weakness. It could have been a small matter for Jesus to turn the stones to bread, but He countered Satan with a quotation from Deuteronomy (Chapter 3).

> "It stands written, man shall not live by bread alone, but by every Word that comes from the mouth of God."

Though defeated in his initial attack in the desert, Satan persisted in his onslaught. Each time Jesus rebuked him with what God said. After a third assault Satan departed and the angels ministered to Jesus.

Satan's war with God's Words started in the Garden of Eden. God had said:
> You shall not eat of the tree in the middle of the garden. If you do you will die.

Satan undermined what God said with subtlety:
> Did God really say that? Certainly you will not die.

His conspiracy in his battle has been to destroy the credibility of God's Words. He knows God wields His Life and power through what He says. Through His Word comes faith for salvation and the living of the Christian life.

With the new birth God has opened up to the believer a realm of spiritual living where limitless possibilities dwell. I need someone to stand behind what I believe in. My faith cannot find air to breath in empty space. No faith life exists in a void or the unknown. Faith says I need a Guarantor, one who secures that for which I believe. So my faith shouts for joy when God stands as the Guarantor. He gives me a Written Guarantee (the Bible), a binding pledge that He will carry out in My life exactly what He has said He'll do.

Look at two startling truths:
> All things are possible to him who believes *(Mark 9:23)*.
>
> My life in eternity depends upon my faith.

What do these say to me?
> First or all, my life can have unlimited possibilities.
>
> And, secondly, life and death hang in the balance on the preciseness of my faith.

Knowing that faith possesses staggering implications, I have to ask myself, do I exercise the kind of faith God expects me to practice?

Biblical or the God-kind of faith says I pursue a course of action on what I know. If I know nothing, I have nothing to act on. A simple equation demonstrates this truth:

Faith + Nothing = Nothing

"Wait a minute," says one man, "the very definition of the word 'faith' means to believe in the unknown."

If I am blind as to the outcome of my expectation, I am not practicing faith, I have nothing but hope. If I trust in the unknown, I have to move from hope to faith. How do I do that?

Authentic faith acts on something God has guaranteed. In other words, what God says provides the knowledge to give faith substance.

Look at the prophet Samuel at the age of thirty:
> And the Lord appeared again in Shiloh: For the Lord revealed Himself to Samuel in Shiloh by the Word of the Lord *(1 Samuel 3:21)*.

If you could hear God's prayer for you today, he wouldn't pray for you differently than what He says in the Bible.

Genesis 2 pictures for you and me the origin of life. It declares that "God breathed into man the breath of life and man became a living soul." The apostle Paul uses this picture to explain how the Bible came into being. God breathed into the Scriptures the breath of life so these Words give (you and me) God's will in thought, purpose, and action *(2 Timothy 3:16 amplified)*.

King David wrote in the Psalms: you have magnified Your Word above your own name *(Psalms 138:2)*. You and I have to ask: why is His Word all important? The answer: His word reveals who He is. If no revelation existed, there would be no God.

God breathed life into man. He also breathed spiritual life into what He wrote. He does this through the life-giving power of what He speaks.

Being born again, not of corruptible (Physical) seed, but of incor-

ruptible seed, by the word of God, which lives and abides forever. (1 Peter 2:23)

You can read in the fourth chapter of the New Testament Book of Hebrews that the Words God speaks (in the Bible) are alive. This verse, the twelfth, goes on to say these Words are not only alive, but that they are filled with divine power.

The obvious question raises its hand: How can that be? How can small black figures on a printed page be alive and filled with divine power? This I know, as long as the words stick to the paper they are nothing more than Words. These black specks in the Bible are seeds — dormant seeds, but when you and I embrace the truth the verse reveals, they move from the printed page into our lives. The words in the Bible cross the bridge of faith to enter our lives.

As the believer goes from one act of faith to another act of faith, he is forever causing these dormant seeds to be germinated. The Father has lavished upon us this Written Agreement of things He will do. Isaiah writes *(Isaiah 46:11)* about what God says: I have spoken it, I will also bring it to pass; I have purposed it, I will also do it.

My Words are Soldiers

My words are soldiers who pass in review
They march so the crowd can see
The place from which these words grew
a secret room within me

My words are soldiers who play to the crowd
The drum major marches with glee
He struts like he's on a cloud
He's the one who lives within me

My words are soldiers who boldly decree
His promise for every need
These soldiers set my spirit free
With words that intercede

My words are soldiers who sing of love
a love that comes at great cost
a love that moved the Father above
To give His Son for the lost

My words are soldiers who voyage
Sailing stormy seas of the heart
Maps are speech from Heaven's page
His ports the promises I chart

My words are soldiers in the know
my spirit listens to what they say
Words that beget as they go
Shaping each passing day

My words are soldiers who bravely fight
For every room they find in my heart

My Words are Soldiers

Fear and worry are caught by sight
They were doomed from the very start
My words are soldiers — seasoned men
Who know where the power lies
Secrets of life they open
For the Lord Himself satisfies

The Power of the Scriptures

Jesus was led by the Holy Spirit into a wild and unsettled terrain the day after His baptism *(Luke 4:1-13)*. At thirty years of age He had laid down His carpenter's tools and commenced the work God sent Him to do. As He communed with the Father in prayer and meditation He fasted. For forty days and forty nights He ate no food. In His famished state He was carefully watched by crafty Satan who knew this was the moment to launch his attack.

"In light of the fact," sneered Satan, "that you are the Son of God, and you are God by nature, I would like to see some evidence for that. Prove to me your power."

"If I can abort His ministry," thought the devil to himself, "I can destroy His ministry of redemption to mankind."

In His weakened state of hunger Jesus comprehended what was at stake, the redemption of imprisoned mankind.

"I know he can't think straight, so I'll make it simple," conspired the contemptuous devil. As he glanced about he spotted the rocks in this barren region, so he turned to Jesus, "It's simple. See these rocks? If you are who you claim to be, the Son of God, give me a demonstration of your power. Turn these rocks into bread. Then you'll have something to eat."

Jesus looked back in His mind to Moses and the feeding of the children of Israel with manna. God reminded Him of another wilderness starvation. The children of Israel rebelled against God and He banned them to the wilderness for forty years. He fed them with manna that they might recognize and personally know that man does not live by bread alone, but by every Word that comes out of the mouth of the Lord.

Jesus declared to Satan, "it has been written that man shall not live by bread alone, but on the power of every Word that comes out of the mouth of God." *(Deuteronomy 8:3)*

"I have food," Jesus informs Satan, "that has sustained me through the days of my fast." If Jesus had turned the rocks into bread He would have been using God's Words for Satan's purpose. Just as physical food is changed into bodily life, so what God speaks is converted into spiritual life.

So, Satan has been thwarted in this first test to dethrone the Son of Man, but he regroups to scheme up a new plan of battle. This time he takes Him to a place set aside for worship and service — the Temple itself. They stood together on the pinnacle, high above Jerusalem.

"Aha!" Leers Satan, "this time I'll outsmart Him. He thinks He's the only one who knows God's Words. I have a surprise for Him — I'll use God's Words myself."

Satan goes on.

"Since you are the Son of God, and since you have the nature of God, I want you to jump off this spire, for it has been written in God's Words that the angels will take care of you, and they will hold you up in their hands, lest you strike your foot against a stone." *(Psalm 91:11,12)*

"Now I have Him!" Satan said maliciously. "He'll have to commit suicide. He didn't know I know the Scriptures."

Jesus stopped him dead in his tracks. "On the other hand," He declared, "God has said you shall not put the Lord your God to an all-out test." *(Deuteronomy 6:16)* He understood Satan wanted to kill Him early in His ministry, so as He looked down from the pinnacle Satan violated the will of God by asking Him for an all-out test.

"I quoted the Scriptures," boasts Satan, "for my own benefit. I don't believe that Scripture business. I know He would have been killed if He had jumped off that spire."

In the third and final test Satan takes Jesus to the top of a mountain. "I'll tell you," snarls Satan, "what I'll do. Look at all the kingdoms lying below us. As the God of this world I will give you these kingdoms. Here's the condition: you have to prostrate yourself before me. That's all. You can own all this by simply making me your lord."

Jesus understood this man standing before Him. He was incapable of telling the truth. His nature was to misrepresent — to lie. He is the antithesis of the Father Who always keeps His Word.

Jesus looks at His enemy.

"Get behind me, Satan!" Again He uses the power of God's Word, "you shall worship the Lord your God, and Him only shall you serve." *(Deuteronomy 6:13)*

On these Words Satan said, "I've had enough! I'm getting out of here," and sped away from Jesus. Three testings and three times Jesus used the Word of God to counter Satan. As Satan fled the angels came and ministered to the victorious Jesus.

Satan's deception with God's Words started in the Garden of Eden. God made this emphatic:

"You shall not eat of the tree in the middle of the garden. If you do, you will die."

Satan undermined what God said with subtlety and deception:

"Did God really say that? Certainly you will not die."

His conspiracy in this battle was to destroy the credibility of what God said. He knows God wields His life and power through the Words He speaks *(Hebrews 4:12)*.

Today is no different. Satan still asks, "Did God really say that? His work site is small, only a few inches by a few inches — the mind of man. He says, if I can get a man to believe he has something, when he has nothing, then I've got him."

Paul tells us as believers to be wary of Satan's arrow in Ephesians 6:11-18: "Put on God's armor in your fight with Satan, for we wrestle against the spiritual forces of darkness."

Jesus Faces Satan

We know Satan is a person. Once he was next to God in power, but through rebellion he was thrown out of heaven. He has a kingdom, and fallen angels are his subjects. In the Garden of Eden he deceived our first parents with the entrapment: Did God really say that? He usurped the power given to man, thus gaining allegiance of the human race, and positioned himself as the God of this world *(2 Corinthians 4:4)*. At the cross Jesus removed Satan's power over those who are believers. He clearly understands that the Bible is the Word of God. The Lord's ministry opened and closed with a triple declaration of the Word of God *(Mathew 4:4, 6 and 7,* and *John 17:8, 14 and 17)*.

Built on Rock

In the Sermon on the Mount Jesus relates the story of two men building two different houses. The first man has this to say:

"I'm going to dig deep. I don't know. I may go down six feet. I have to hit rock. That will be the support for my foundation."

"No. No." says the second man. "That's too much trouble. I'm going down five feet. The sand will give me plenty of support."

So the houses are built. One rests on rock, the other rests on sand. Everything goes fine for the first year, but a day comes in early summer when storms move over the land. The wind blew. Rain fell in sheets. Storms battered the houses the two men had built. To the dismay of the builder, the house on the sand toppled to the ground. The storm passed to the east. People came out to see the aftermath. The house built on the rock foundation stood as bravely as the day she was built.

The two houses picture the lives of two men, so Jesus poses this question: "Which one of these men shall enter the kingdom of heaven?" There are those who talk a big show. They say:

>Lord. Lord. We have prophesied in your name.

Or they will boast:

>Do you know what we did? We cast out demons in your name.

We can brag:

>It is true. We have wrought miracles in your name.

Jesus responds to this empty pretense:

>From a public square I will disavow you.
>I never knew you!
>Get out of my way!

(You are trying to enter the kingdom of heaven with your works).

"Listen carefully," says Jesus, "now I will let you in on the secret: Who shall enter the kingdom of heaven?"

"It's simple. It's like the man who built his house on a rock foundation. When the storms of life came, he stood unmoved. How did he do it? Both he and the man who built his house on sand had heard the word of God. Here's the difference. The man who built his house on rock took action on what God said. The man who will enter the kingdom of heaven is the one who has experienced for himself the life changing power of what I say." *(Matthew 7:21-27)*

I Bummed a Ride on Como Avenue

"How far ya goin'?" he asked, as he flung open the door of his '41 Chev four-door.

"To South Minneapolis," I cried gratefully, "if yer goin' that far." I scrambled in to the passenger seat.

The sun bathed the street with eye-squinting brilliance this spring afternoon. I thought I had talked myself into the idea of walking home. It'll take over an hour. You could use the time for study. So I opted for a lift.

"Ya got some books," said the man who responded to my thumb, "goin' to the U?"

Como Avenue looked abandoned. "Nice of you to pick me up. No. I'm in the school on the hill. Couple blocks back. A seminary. Luther Seminary."

"So yer into theology. Like it?"

"We do a lot of study on how to run a church. Church history, stuff like that. Languages. Greek and Hebrew. I wouldn't call myself a theologian, with the little I know."

"How far ya 'long?" queried the smiling man behind the wheel. I liked him instinctively. My age, round thirty. Smooth shaven. A twinkle in his eye, and a voice that said, "I'm lookin' for the funny side." His car was as manicured as he was.

"Second year. One to go. Three year course, obviously." My face flushed in embarrassment. Too much talk centered on me. I glanced off to the south to see massive clouds of steam arising from the Waldorf paper mills.

"So in 1951 you'll be ordained a Lutheran minister. Am I

right?"

"Yer right." I replied weakly. I felt vulnerable. I've got to do something. I know, I'll put him on the stage. He can have the spotlight for a while.

"How 'bout you," I said, trying to sound peppy, "I would guess yer a salesman." Immediately he enjoyed my speculation. His laugh filled the car. I smiled along with him.

"Why's that," he forced out while still laughing.

"Yer ease round people. Yer interest in people. Ya strike me as a man who is not bothered by a lot of things."

"Well, thank you," he acknowledged in a high voice. Now I could see a slight pink glow cross over his features. I glanced at the huge marshaling area under our overpass on Raymond. "Funny you should say that."

"How come?"

"Well," he paused to concentrate on a driver from a side street. Other drivers did not upset him. Was this his maturity? Perhaps his temperament. Could be consideration for others. "I manage a superette," he continued.

"I wasn't far off," I said with confidence in my insightfulness. "I can see you in that role."

He talked about the challenges of being a manager of a superette. Picking good help. Stocking the correct merchandise. I felt my shoulders relax as he shared his life with me.

"Did ya grow into this," I sought to know, "like it's in the family, that kinda thing?"

"No, no," again he laughed easily. "My dad makes cabinets, kitchen cabinets. Works with his hands, ya might say."

I didn't interrupt him. He quickly grasped that I was interested in his story. I waited for him to go on.

"I took business in college. At the U. Always wanted to own my own business. Ever since I was a kid, I guess."

"I identify with you," I inserted.

"Had you dreamed about ownin' yer own business some time?"

"Only in passin'. I come from a family of entrepreneurs myself. Our home filled itself with talk on different ways to make money. Sometimes it got pretty hilarious." I replied.

"How was that?" he enquired.

"Oh, like the winter Dad got carried away talking about a turkey farm out on an island."

My new found friend laughed hysterically.

"Forgive me for laughing," he apologized, "I wasn't laughing at your dad, I got a kick out of the way you said it."

"Yer goal is a going grocery store," I surmised as our laughing subsided.

"Takes capital," he said with a dreamer's look in his eye.

"Ya know," I reflected, "any success you can point to started with a dream. There are always those with a wet blanket. Ya know what I mean?"

"I suppose," he deduced, "those are the ones who say we should play it close to the vest. Why take chances? Right?"

We sat in a holding pattern for the stop light at University Avenue. "Keyes Restaurant," said the sign on a building. He didn't wait for me to answer.

"Faith hits Fear," he said laughingly, "on the side of the head, and sends him reeling."

I easily picked up the sense that one was not taking a chance when he followed through his dreams with faith.

"Every once in a while," he continued, "I have to take myself by the nap of the neck and say, 'What are ya scared of? Why don't ya simply accept what God pledges in His Word, as true?' I live by faith, ya see. Everything I do, I act by faith. Any decision, or challenge, yes, any dream, passes through the filter of faith. I'm sure you know all about that."

"No, I don't know all about that. Yer the first person I have ever, and I mean ever, come across who speaks straight forward about his faith. 'N that's including ministers I have known." I paused. Town and Country golf course came into view on our left. My candid friend remained silent. "I confess I'm supposed to be a professional. I put that 'professional' in quotes. Yer the courageous one, I have never told anyone I live by faith."

"Do you? Please excuse my audacity." He laughed off his embarrassment.

Who has the guts to ask a seminarian if he lives by faith? You wouldn't ask a doctor if he knows anything about medicine. I knew the question was couched in love. He had a bare knuckle kind of faith. A fist-swinging faith that survives brawlings in the market place of life. Unadulterated. Unaffected. Authentic. I immediately knew it sprang out of God's Word, the Bible, the only source or fountainhead for genuine faith.

"Sure, I live by faith," I answered, "but it's more private, concealed. Like I've heard someone say, 'closet faith'."

He waited at the red light at Marshall Avenue. Off to the right I could see the Lake Street bridge. "We were talking about opening a business," he wanted to go on, "and the financing needed. A verse in the Bible" (See! I told you his kind of faith would come out of the Bible) "guarantees that God is able to accomplish far above what you and I can ask or think." He chuckled, "And certainly this would include my dream of owning a supermarket."

"Yer not expectin' somethin' out of the blue?" I said, not hiding my incredulity, " ... like ten thousand dollars plopping into yer lap, or some guy walkin' up to you and saying, 'God told me to give you this ten thousand dollars'."

He listened to what I said. A few seconds passed. I could almost see the cog wheels turning in his head.

Insights

"If I did that, I'm afraid I'd be walkin' by sight, rather than countin' on what God says."

"You refer to yer Bible," I observed.

"Sure," he countered, "where else would faith come from?"

"I don't follow." I smiled lightly.

"Take light," he gestured with his free hand, "where does it come from?"

"Simple." I answered. "From the sun, of course."

"This follows then, just as the sun gives light, the Bible gives faith."

His logic reminded me of a story. I said, "A small boy stands at the top of the cellar stairs. In the darkness below stands his father with outstretched arms. 'Jump,' says the father, 'and I'll catch you.' But the boy says, 'Daddy, I can't see you!' A preacher I know says the blind leap of the boy pictures faith."

"If we say God has to make something, we're wrong. God has *already* made and kept ready what you and I believe for. You can check the Word on that."

"So what's yer comment on the illustration?" I asked.

"If God has already made what you and I believe for, then He has already caught us!" He explained.

"No leap is involved at all," was my conclusion.

"What you and I have to grasp is that what we believe for has already been made. That's grace. Makes believin' easier."

"I get the point," I assured him.

"Forty-Third Avenue," said the sign on the corner.

"Here's where I get out."

He pulled over to be curb and stopped. I jumped out. He extended an uplifted palm through the open door.

"Todd _____." I didn't catch his last name. Our hand-shake was like the coupling of freight cars. I gave him my name.

Still holding my hand he said with a big smile, "Norm, this has been great. The best to you in your studies." He released his grip, and I slammed the door.

"Thank you, Todd," I hollered through the door glass. He pulled away from the curb and joined the traffic flowing west on Lake Street. I watched his car until it disappeared out of sight.

Someone Has To Stand Behind It

> *A certification is usually a statement in writing, especially one that carries one's signature. A certified check carries the guarantee of a bank that the signature is genuine and that there are sufficient funds on deposit to meet it. The bank guarantees payment. The certainty the believer can enjoy in God's Word is that the Father will always fulfill the promise the believer acts on.*

"If you have a bushel basket of this money you'd still be broke." The young woman speaker on the platform laughed with the crowd. "How could that be? More money that you could carry," she paused to emphasize, "and you'd have nothing, just scraps of paper. There must be some solution to this mystery, and there is."

The speaker walked back and forth to give time for her introduction to sink in.

Sylvia had been looking forward to these meetings. They had been billed as an Advanced Seminar on Faith, Saturday morning, 10 a.m. nondenominational. In the Auditorium. Everyone welcome. Her she sat with her Bible, a notebook, pen in hand, and the air of expectancy. Where is she going with this bushel of money? Her mind switched back to the speaker who had laid her Bible down on the lecture and continued.

1919, that's the year were looking at. Germany. World War I has just ended. The dollar bill, or currency, was called Mark. Deutsche Mark. German money. Like I said, you could have a bushel of it and be penniless. It was worthless.

Someone Has To Stand Behind It

Paper Marks valued at ten thousand were passed around as souvenirs. I can hear you ask, how can that be? And here's the answer: They had no backing. The German government had collapsed. No one would warrant their value. No gold. No silver stood behind them.

The lady on the platform brought back memories to Sylvia. I remember when I thought the word faith meant blind acceptance. One man had said, "That's what's wrong with religion, it can't prove anything, it makes a lot of claims with nothing to back it up." She knew he was wrong when he said Christians still believe the world is flat.

"Many times in His ministry," the speaker broke into Sylvia's reminiscing, "Jesus was asked, 'where do you get your backing? Who stands behind you?' Nicodemus brought this to our attention when he said, 'No man can do what you do unless God is with him.' When Jesus addressed the secret of His power He spoke about the One who stood behind Him. One day a paralyzed man was brought to Him, and He said, 'I forgive you of your sins.' 'No. No. No. You can't say that,' accused some Jews, 'only God can forgive sins.' Jesus said, 'for you to know I have divine authority to forgive sin, I pronounce this man healed.' I hear Jesus declaring, 'Yes, I am God as is proven by what I did.' And I see in those who carried this man to the Lord, Yes, you have the power to heal."

It broke on Sylvia that her faith required a promise to make it live, but she had to laugh at herself. Only a few minutes ago she was ready to go back home and work in the garden. "If all she can talk about is worthless German money, I'm out," she thought. "Now I like the road she's taking: faith requires a Personal guarantee or it's worthless." She thought about the friends who had brought the paralyzed man to Jesus. Their faith said to Jesus, "we know You can heal our friend." Their confidence

Insights

rested in things they had seen Him do. Sylvia wandered through the rooms of her mind; she stumbled on the word "Camelot"… that one brief shining moment. She had enjoyed so many of these breakthroughs in her Christian life. She was intrigued by their surprise and their joy. "How come I never saw that before? I'd like to run out on the street and do cartwheels. An epiphany. Can I share this with someone?" Then it came to her; this is the way the Holy Spirit works.

That's it, it's in the Word. "Though you have not seen Him, yet you love Him; and though you do not see Him, you have believed in Him; and now you exult with heavenly joy." *(1 Peter 1:17)* Sylvia felt like jumping up. With raised hands I shout "Hallelujah!" People would say, "What's wrong with the lady? Has she gone bonkers?" Oh well, Maybe they can see it in my face.

The speaker snapped her out of reverie. Put this phrase in your notes: "If money has no backing it's worthless." Sylvia wrote it down word for word. And you could add, faith without a backing is also worthless.

Someone raised their hand: "What about faith in faith? Is that OK?"

The speaker answered: "Faith in my own faith is empty faith. It says, I'm the one who backs what I believe. Living faith requires the backing of the Father."

Another hand went up, "How can someone warrant or back what I believe?"

The speaker met this head-on. "The guarantee, or warrant, as you called it, comes from the Person of Christ Himself." The lady on the platform raised the Bible high above her head. "Jesus spoke the Words of John 3:16, and if you are to die and appear before the Father in heaven, He would ask, 'How do you gain entrance?' You would hold up your Bible like this and say, 'Jesus gave me eternal life in John 3:16.' The Father would reply, 'enter

Someone Has To Stand Behind It

in, my child, I do not lie.'"

A hand was raised and the lady pointed to him. "I appreciate that spiritual insight, but I am aware of Satan's deceptions. How does he misconstrue this truth that faith needs a backing?"

"Good question." The speaker walked back and forth before she spoke. "Some say, 'I'm a Christian because I had a road to Damascus experience.' It's true that a person can experience joy on becoming a believer but one needs more than an experience."

"Earlier you and I looked at the worthless German money. The problem was that no one stood behind it. I can have faith that I own my house because it is recorded in the county records. If I shout, I have faith. Let me ask, faith in what? Are you putting faith in an experience?"

"Detroit stands behind your car. Just as the Christian life begins with a warranty, John 3:16, so the believer's faith backed by the warranty of His word."

"Have you ever heard this?" The speaker laughed as she said. "We'll have to go by faith on this one because we can't find any facts to support it. In other words," she continued, "faith to this misguided individual is blind acceptance."

Before she could continue a tall man in the audience stood up and said, "Blind acceptance appears to be the counterfeit of Christian faith." Then he sat down.

"Precisely," replied the speaker. "Genuine faith rests on the rock foundation of a promise. What about this. If I have faith in my faith, I have to ask: What is believed? Where's the faith? Is there a promise? Where's the backing? Is anything guaranteed? No. No promise. No backing. Nothing guaranteed. So faith in my faith is dead faith. It's worthless."

"Have you ever heard this? 'If it be thy will. Time will tell. And it'll work out.' These phrases picture empty faith for the circumstances of life. No one stands behind any of these phrases."

Insights

The lady next to Sylvia stood up and asked about prayer.

The speaker smiled with delight. "The other day I talked with a lady who had been a believer for a number of years. She told me this truth had revolutionized her prayer life. She went on to say that she had found more answers to prayer in ten minutes than she had in the previous ten years. How's that possible? Simple. She explained how she had been through a period of grieving. Then she found Isaiah 53:4 which promised that the Lord had personally carried away her sorrow. Her prayer went like this:"

"'Father, I understand from Your Word that the Lord Jesus Christ has carried away my sorrow. I know You always do what you say you will do, so I consider this matter done. I thank You in His name.'"

"Before she could get up and go on her way her prayer had been answered. This is how. She personally appropriated the love of Christ found in Isaiah 53."

The lady on the platform chuckled. "That's some word I used: appropriate. A jaw breaker. I'm sure you know the meaning: To make one's own. Here she made His gift of comfort her own. She appropriated His love. She provides all of us a model on how to appropriate His workmanship in our daily life."

The speaker finished her talk with a review of her theme: genuine faith is backed by the Word of the Lord Himself. Several from the audience went on stage to chat with the speaker but Sylvia packed up her little office. A verse came to her mind. "My people are cut off and destroyed for lack of knowledge." *(Hosea 4:6)* She smiled to herself. It was a joy to learn. "I can't believe," Sylvia muttered to herself, "any further than I have knowledge. I guess I could say, The more I know, the more I can believe." She checked her chair to make sure she didn't leave anything, and followed her route out the auditorium. She was greeted by a spring morning of warmth and sunshine.

The Day the People Cried

"We want to hear what God says! We're tired of idols!" shouted the people. Nehemiah, chapter eight, tells the story.

"Tell us what Moses said!" cried all in the crowd in the broad place.

"What about the Red Sea?" cried one woman, "or Abraham?"

"We've forgotten God! We've forgotten He fed us with manna in the wilderness."

Another reminded them of the idolatry in the molten calf they worshipped.

"Murderous tyrants killed our prophets!" Shouted one man.

Israel had fallen into the pit of sin, and the man in the streets rebelled against the idolatry.

"We're sick of sin," they shouted

"What about our Scriptures?"

"Read to us what Moses wrote."

Thanksgiving came: The Feast of the Tabernacles. The seventh month, the fifteenth day. People streamed in from all over the country to overflow the grand plaza.

They called on their priest.

"Ezra! Ezra!" A chant rose up from the throng.

"Read to us."

"Read to us about our heroes."

Expectancy ran high through the throng.

Carpenters had built an elevated wooden pulpit so the crowd could see the reader. A hush fell as Ezra climbed the stairs. He

The Day the People Cried

looked over the excited crowd and understood the moment — a time for repentance. A tear ran down his cheek.

When he opened the Scriptures all the people jumped to their feet. All eyes were riveted on Ezra.

"Bless the Lord!" With that invocation he ignited the chord of worship.

"Amen! Amen!" shouted the eager crowd with uplifted arms.

"Lord," prayed Ezra, "You made a covenant with Abraham."

"You are the One Who divided the Red Sea."

"You led us in the wilderness with a cloud by day, and a pillar of fire by night."

"You spoke to us on Mount Sinai."

The word came as spiritual nourishment. When the people heard the Scriptures they cried. Contrition engulfed them as they heard the word of the Lord.

Ezra raised his arm. "Please. Please. No crying. This is not a day to mourn. Do not be sad. Let the joy of our Lord be your joy."

In this story from Nehemiah we see the power of what God speaks. Not only do God's Words live, but as the writer in the Book of Hebrews makes clear *(Hebrews 4:12)*, they are filled with His divine power.

"I don't get it," says one reader. "I always saw the Bible as just another book on the shelf. How can words be alive?"

Paul the apostle addressed this concern. "Every Scripture," he says, "has been God-breathed." *(2 Timothy 3:16)* Someone could ask, "'God-breathed,' what does that mean?" We make our way back to the second chapter of the book of Genesis. There we read, in verse seven, "The Lord God formed man from the dust of the ground and breathed into man the breath of life and man became a living being. Just as He breathed the breath of life into man, He has breathed spiritual life into what He speaks."

One could ask, "How can words in the Bible have life if they were spoken thousands of years ago?" I have been told that ancient seeds found in the pyramids still sprouted when they were planted. Jesus refers to His Words as seeds. Soil, water and sunshine cause the seeds to sprout in the physical realm. What causes God's Words to spring to life? Faith. When you and I pursue a course of action on what He says, we make alive these little black marks on a page of white.

You and I can see the seed of a new life when we read John 3:16. As long as that seed remains inactive on paper it continues to be like dormant seed, alive, but not activated. When you and I pursue a course of action on this promise of a new life, the Person of the Holy Spirit activates the life in the verse in our lives.

The servant boy of the Roman soldier was critically ill, so he said to Jesus, "All you have to do is speak the word and my servant will be healed." Jesus spoke the Word and the child was healed immediately *(Matthew 8)*.

His Word can be likened to an X-ray machine; it reached into our innermost being. The Word springs to life in our spirit. It lives in our lives when you and I pursue a course of action found in the Seed.

After All, It Belongs to You

> *Faith — not my doing something —
> I simply receive what
> God has already done.*

After the miraculous crossing of the Red Sea, 600,000 Israelites prepared to enter the land God had promised to them. Twelve chosen men scouted and explored the land for forty days.

When they returned, ten of the spies wailed, "There's no way we can take that land, the inhabitants are giants!" Joshua and Caleb quieted the mutinous mob before Moses, and called out, "Let us go up at once and possess the land God has given to us."

"Here we are" screamed the people, "stranded in the desert with our wives and children; all of us will be killed. Why did we leave Egypt?" They never saw the land God had given to them. They refused to believe God could do what He said He would do, so that generation perished in the desert for forty years.

The rabble-rousers reiterated the words of the ten unbelievers, but Joshua and Caleb repeated what God said about taking the land.

> Fear cannot exist where God's love lives. Love throws fear out-of-doors, and expels every trace of terror, because fear brings the sense of impending doom.

Joshua and Caleb embraced God's love, and His love threw the fear of the giants out-of-doors. James admonishes the believer "not to lie against the truth" *(James 3:14)*. When the ten led the mob in rebellion they lied against the truth, they failed to act from God's declaration. Courageous faith for Joshua and Caleb rose out of the verse itself, for they grasped this simple fact, *what He had pledged He wanted them to have.*

God says, "I swore in My wrath, They shall not enter My rest (the land); even though the promise had been in place from the beginning of time." But the Israelites did not profit from the message they heard, because it was not coupled with faith.

"I defy the ranks of Israel this day; give me a man that we may fight to the death!" In a booming voice Goliath shouted his defiance of Saul's army. This embarrassing scene had been going on for almost six weeks. That's right. Every evening and morning for forty days Goliath had taunted the army of the living God!

"Why have you come out," he wanted to know, "to draw up for battle? Am not I a Philistine, and are you not servants of Saul? Choose a man for yourselves, and let him come down to face me. If he is able to fight with me and kill me, then we will be your servants; but if I prevail against him and kill him, then you shall be our servants and serve us."

Who was this brazen champion of the Philistine army? What did he have going for him that he could openly shame an entire army? He stood a few inches under ten feet in height, and he wore a body armor of mail that weighed 180 pounds. Helmet, shoulder pads, and shin guards were made of bronze. His metal spear head weighed a surprising 21 pounds. This ponderous giant could have tipped the scale at 700 pounds. A carefully picked warrior went before him as his shield bearer. Goliath was a man in the pantheon of Philistine heroes.

Saul screamed in his humiliation, "Isn't there a man who can kill this infidel?!"

He searched the faces of his men. No one made eye contact. "I don't want to die. You fight him. It's suicide." Their grumbling

After All, It Belongs to You

> *Faith — not my doing something —
> I simply receive what
> God has already done.*

After the miraculous crossing of the Red Sea, 600,000 Israelites prepared to enter the land God had promised to them. Twelve chosen men scouted and explored the land for forty days.

When they returned, ten of the spies wailed, "There's no way we can take that land, the inhabitants are giants!" Joshua and Caleb quieted the mutinous mob before Moses, and called out, "Let us go up at once and possess the land God has given to us."

"Here we are" screamed the people, "stranded in the desert with our wives and children; all of us will be killed. Why did we leave Egypt?" They never saw the land God had given to them. They refused to believe God could do what He said He would do, so that generation perished in the desert for forty years.

The rabble-rousers reiterated the words of the ten unbelievers, but Joshua and Caleb repeated what God said about taking the land.

> Fear cannot exist where God's love lives. Love throws fear out-of-doors, and expels every trace of terror, because fear brings the sense of impending doom.

Joshua and Caleb embraced God's love, and His love threw the fear of the giants out-of-doors. James admonishes the believer "not to lie against the truth" *(James 3:14)*. When the ten led the mob in rebellion they lied against the truth, they failed to act from God's declaration. Courageous faith for Joshua and Caleb rose out of the verse itself, for they grasped this simple fact, *what He had pledged He wanted them to have.*

God says, "I swore in My wrath, They shall not enter My rest (the land); even though the promise had been in place from the beginning of time." But the Israelites did not profit from the message they heard, because it was not coupled with faith.

"I defy the ranks of Israel this day; give me a man that we may fight to the death!" In a booming voice Goliath shouted his defiance of Saul's army. This embarrassing scene had been going on for almost six weeks. That's right. Every evening and morning for forty days Goliath had taunted the army of the living God!

"Why have you come out," he wanted to know, "to draw up for battle? Am not I a Philistine, and are you not servants of Saul? Choose a man for yourselves, and let him come down to face me. If he is able to fight with me and kill me, then we will be your servants; but if I prevail against him and kill him, then you shall be our servants and serve us."

Who was this brazen champion of the Philistine army? What did he have going for him that he could openly shame an entire army? He stood a few inches under ten feet in height, and he wore a body armor of mail that weighed 180 pounds. Helmet, shoulder pads, and shin guards were made of bronze. His metal spear head weighed a surprising 21 pounds. This ponderous giant could have tipped the scale at 700 pounds. A carefully picked warrior went before him as his shield bearer. Goliath was a man in the pantheon of Philistine heroes.

Saul screamed in his humiliation, "Isn't there a man who can kill this infidel?!"

He searched the faces of his men. No one made eye contact. "I don't want to die. You fight him. It's suicide." Their grumbling rose to a howl, but the giant's scornful guffaw drowned out their shameful wail. Every Israelite saw himself slaughtered, but the more they moaned the greater became their fear.

Three brothers soldiered for Saul, and their kid brother, a shepherd boy, brought them food from home. Only seventeen, David came on the pitiful scene to hear Goliath throw out his challenge. David enquired about the giant as he watched the terror stricken Israelites flee the field of battle.

"Who is this man who defies the army of the living God?" asked David, horrified at what he watched.

When Saul learned that David wanted to fight the giant, he called for him.

David's certainty surfaced as he addressed Saul, "As a shepherd in the Lord I have slain the lion and the bear, and the Lord has given this infidel into my hands." David, with Saul's blessing, walked to the no-man's land of battle with five smooth stones he had chosen from the brook.

When Goliath spied David's shepherd staff he roared with delight, "Have you sent a kid with a stick to fight me? Keep comin', Boy, I'll feed your carcass to the ravens!" With his shield bearer going before him he lumbered toward the speedy David.

Positive of the outcome of the fight, David positioned himself before Goliath, "My Lord has given you into my hands!"

With that he whirled his sling shot till it hummed and released the stone. With the speed of a bullet the stone went into the giant's forehead and he fell forward dead.

"Hurrah! Hurrah!" shouted the soldiers of Saul as they burst out of their hiding places. They pursued the fleeing Philistine army as they enjoyed the worship of their newfound hero. What did David know that the soldiers did not know? He knew the secret of possession. He possessed what he believed. He spoke about his victory before it happened in his life. If he had not spoken about the victory beforehand — "My Lord has given you into my hands" — he would not have been living by faith, and he would not have defeated Goliath. David's profession establishes his possession. God saw David victorious over Goliath before the encounter took place. David's faith shouted, "I see as God sees!"

There are those who will say, "This secret poses a problem for me. I find it hard to believe I possess His promise before it actually appears in my life. "

If these same people examined their faith, they would be surprised to find they have "in place" in their lives, things which are yet future. For example, life after death. They see life after death as a present possession.

Jesus taught that the one who believes *has* — possesses now — eternal life (which includes life after death). If I say I will live after I die, I possess *now* something that has not happened in my life. In other words, I see as God *sees*. I embrace in my heart what God wants me to have in His word.

David believed, and immediately he realized the fruits of his faith. *He acted on what God said* (an excellent definition of faith), and proved his faith with action. Sometimes the gears of faith turn slowly. In my heart I know I have received the promise, but it may not come overnight. Months, even years, may go by before I see the manifestation of my faith.

Smith Wigglesworth tells the revealing story of a woman healed in one of his meetings. Even though the visible growth on her neck remained after she had been healed, she continued to testify that God had healed her of this condition. A year passed without any evidence of healing. Her appearance denied her words, but in her heart she claimed ownership of that for which she believed.

"God says," she avowed, "He has healed me, and I simply take Him at His word." She refused to find substantiation for her faith in physical evidence. Another year went by and she looked the same. People put their hand over their mouth to hide their derision. Others, entrenched in their foolishness, scoffed openly when she bore witness to God's honest. "I know He cannot lie. Jesus doesn't have to come back in person. what He says is as good as though He were actually here." Majestically she walked the corridors of the heroes of faith, of whom it says ... the world was not worthy. But the cries of those who walk by sight drummed in her ears, "You haven't been healed. Can't you see that? Look in the mirror. If you had faith, we would all be able to see it."

Two long years had passed, but she never staggered in her confidence that her Lord saw her as healed. After another scornful meeting she found herself alone at home. "Father, I have everything I need to know I have been healed, but some are stumbling because they look at me rather than You. I ask You to make evident what You have already done so my detractors might know You keep your word." She slept peacefully.

She awakened the next morning, and glanced into the mirror. She wasn't surprised. The growth was gone. As far as she was concerned it had never been there since the day she was healed. Her experience helped many learn the enriching lesson of genuine faith. This episode was a long time ago. Today we would know she should have seen a doctor before the tumor took her life. That decision would not have compromised her faith, or been less wonderful, for she would have acted in agreement with His will.

She could have joined the crowd: "I give up! OK, you guys are right! What God says is not true. He hasn't healed me." Her faith enjoyed a life of its own, because her faith took the place of the healing, till the healing showed itself. She passed the test of trial because she had "squatter's rights" to the promise.

Walt Jensen: A Life in the Dark

*I cannot become what God sees me to be,
by remaining what I am.*

Ray Bosley lived on skid row, a fifty-three year old derelict. He slept at the mission under Casper Street Bridge. Kelley's dumpster served as his preferred cafeteria.

I can get better food there, he bragged with a laugh, than I get at the Mission soup kitchen.

Unneeded deprivation ruled the life of this man who people called a bum. How could they know the hidden story? Even muggers passed him by. Why rob him? He hasn't got a dime to his name.

Ray Bosley never knew, nor did anyone else know, he possessed immense wealth. He alone survived a wealthy aunt in Pittsburg, but he had disappeared from her life long ago. Ray had forgotten her in his blurry yesterdays, and when she died no paper trail connected him in a far away city to her estate.

Why should a millionaire live in the harsh reality of squalor? Why would one subsist in scarcity? Simple, no one had told him she had willed her large estate to him. He had no knowledge of what had been given to him. What he didn't know deprived him of what he should have had. If he had heard one sentence, just one sentence, it would have changed his life. Like Ray, your aunt in Pennsylvania has died and left you everything. No one knew, so he lived in the darkness of ignorance. At fifty-nine Ray died. The mission buried him in a Potter's field in a pauper's grave. He left nothing.

I shared with you the story of Ray Bosley because it reminded me of another man. He, too, forfeited great wealth — not intentionally. He too didn't know his riches existed. This story becomes more tragic than Ray's, because it reaches beyond our daily bread, as I think of this second man I have to suppress a wave of grief, so much of the blame comes back to his own doorstep. Whoops! I'm getting ahead of myself. I have to go back and begin the story on a spring morning. My wife and I planned a trip to the Salvation Army.

She hollers down the stairs, "when we can go to the Salvation Army?"

"What's up?" I shouted back to her from my workshop.

"I have some clothes and things to drop off."

"How about Friday after lunch?"

"Fine and dandy," she agreed, "that'll give me time to get it together."

When Friday came, boxes overflowed the trunk of the car, and the surplus spilled over into the back seat. Star, our Shetland sheep dog, panted and fussed over the delay. She sat between us as I flipped on the ignition. We knew we would come home with a tale to tell. We always did, but I didn't suspect I was to meet a tragic man through the lens of what he left out of his life.

Joggers and walkers dotted the west shore as we cruised past Lake Calhoun.

"Must be low humidity," observed Glorian, "downtown looks so close."

"It does, doesn't it?" Star yapped at dogs through her open window.

"Not too many here," Glorian mentioned as we drove past the newly-opened Farmer's Market. Too early for grown produce.

I steered into the warehouse district west of downtown Minneapolis. "Donations," said the red sign at the sprawling Salvation Army complex. Two big guys tossed our boxes on to rolling carts.

"Thank you!" They waved as I backed out.

"Our pleasure!" I threw back.

"Shall we poke around in the store for a bit?" Glorian gestured toward the front entrance.

"Good idea." I like to look around in the used books.

I dropped her off at the store entrance and parked the car in the lot across the street. After cracking the windows for Star I told her we'd be right back. Her bark said, Don't be gone too long.

Dusty, stagnant air greeted me as I walked into the store. I threaded my way through the racks of used clothing as I headed for the book section in the far northwest corner of the store. Three or four preoccupied people browsed in the book aisles. A huge fan from yesteryear made slapping sounds as it worked valiantly to suck the sluggish air out of the store.

Two dozen discarded Bibles lay on the top of a shelf marked "Religion." I studied my way through them. *Maybe I can find a special translation. A Moffett. Or Goodspeed.* Some were the New Testament alone. Most were the entire Bible. All were cheaply made. Nothing in leather. *No keepers here. Whoops! Wait a minute. What's this?*

At first glance I took it for an antique. It had some years under its belt. Reverently, I removed the old Bible from the pile. I turned it over slowly in my hands. A sense of awe swept over me. *Hallowed ground.* I thought of all those who had been martyred for their devotion to this Book. The lives it had changed. *If you could only talk,* I muttered to myself, *what a story you'd tell.* I felt like an intruder. *Maybe the Book will expose the former proprietor.*

"Old girl," I said to the Book, "you've lain abandoned on a

sun-drenched shelf for a long time." In my wonder I found myself talking to this Book. Did that lady over there hear me? She glanced at me. "Who cares at a moment like this?" I continued, "your black imitation leather curls upward. I have to admit your fold-over edges look like brown mummified muslin. You haven't forgotten your sovereignty. Gold leaf reflections touched by burnished red shines from the patina edges of your pages."

I squeezed my way out of books and met Glorian at the checkout counter.

"I see you found an old Bible," she observed.

"Yeah. I think I'll do some excavating."

"Look what I've found." She gestured toward the counter. I looked over the butter dish and sugar bowl she showed me.

"Ya' know," as I studied them, "these were made in England."

"English China, how about that," she smiled. "That's some find."

The clerk behind the counter said, "Fifty cents for the Bible."

Star greeted us with a yap and a wagging tail. I've been waiting for you guys. We cut along the west shore of Lake of the Isles and crossed over Lake Street. I reflected on the many used Bibles I had come across through the years. Usually they were inexpensive like the one I had just bought. They seldom showed use. That didn't surprise me.

After lunch I sat down to eagerly study my find. I have to admit I felt like a snoop. Inside was a black protective page. I thumbed past that to the title page. Yep! A name had been therein the top right hand corner, but it had been carefully scissored out. Someone had said to the buyer of this Book, you don't need to know who owned this Bible. It's none of your business. Why not? Did I see some embarrassment?

So, whoever had given this Book to the Salvation Army had chosen to hide the identity of the owner. Have you ever said, if this or that could talk, what story it would tell? I thought that about this old Bible. If it could talk, what a revealing tale it would spin. No, it didn't have a voice but it did have clues, tell-tale signs about its owner, I pictured myself as a sleuth out of Scotland Yard. At that moment of playing detective this sadness slammed against me: This Book which could have given new life to its owner had never been opened! The person had no use for it. He chose to live in spiritual darkness.

King James translation. Both Testaments. Dictionary. Concordance. Maps. Colossians exposed a brilliant blue attached ribbon, page keeper, rotted off at the spine by the ultraviolet rays of the Sun. A pressed flower, thrown into the Book, popped the Book open to Romans eight, the very heart of the New Testament. A funeral? A wedding? I left the fragile flower undisturbed with its hidden memories. As I cradled this Book in my hands I thought of the prophet Samuel. Samuel says *(1 Samuel 3:21)* "the Lord revealed Himself to Samuel through the Word of the Lord."

Faded pencil writing on the back of the title page said:
Prov. Det. (Cons. Obj)
163 Depot Brigade,
Camp Dodge
Iowa

This inscription broke open his world to me. I repeat, "have you ever said to yourself, someone should write a story of my life," or maybe you have said, "I would like to take a trip on a magic time-carpet." So why don't we let Walt tell his story. Oh, who's "Walt"?

That's the name I've given to the owner of this Bible. "Walt Jensen." He can tell us the story of his life. He can take us on the imaginary trip:

"My name is Walt Jensen and I'll share with you the story of my life. I was born in South Minneapolis in 1898. I dropped out of South High School in the ninth grade. At fourteen years of age

I studied confirmation to become a member of our Church. That was in 1912. The Great War broke out in Europe a few years later and I didn't relish the prospect of having anything to do with it. I didn't want to die. In 1917, I was just a nineteen year old kid, my draft number came up. It wasn't long before the government had me at Fort Snelling. You'll find this interesting. The Bible you hold in your hands was given to me by the army. As a matter of fact, each doughboy got one.

I was assigned to the First Infantry Division as a combat soldier. That night I did not sleep. I pictured myself dying in the trenches of France. In the morning I walked straight to the adjutant's office. I told him I did not want to be killed, nor did I want to kill someone else.

"Well, son," he replied, "do you want this complaint to land up in the courts? You know you could be court martialled."

With all of his bullying I remained steadfast that I would not go into combat. He called me a coward and swore at me. In the end of our talk he finally said, "Son, you're going to live with this for the rest of your life, and you will always regret this shameful decision you made." He did ask me if I was a deeply religious man. I told him not necessarily. I simply didn't believe in war.

He waived my assignment and listed me as a conscientious objector. That's what "Cons. Obj." means in my Bible. As I look back on it now I can see the adjutant knew I would never survive combat. My distraught state was apparent to him. So he reassigned me to the quartermaster corps in Camp Dodge, Iowa. That was a day's journey, from South Minneapolis to central Iowa. Weekend passes enabled me to get home to Minneapolis.

You'll recall the Great War ended on November 11, 1918. All of us were sure this would be the war to end all wars. My dream was to be out of the service by Christmas. That's all we talked about, and I made it. Hurrah! I'll never forget that day. It was a Saturday, December 14, 1918. My buddies and I boarded the train for Minneapolis. We sang and laughed all the way. Relief engulfed us. We had survived the war.

At dinnertime we arrived at the Milwaukee depot in downtown Minneapolis. In our jubilation we agreed to have a reunion, but that's the last we ever saw of each other. I jumped on a streetcar to get to my parent's home in the south part of town.

Sunday, December 15, 1918. How can I forget it? I even remember the weather as a sunny winter day. Christmas filled the air this first Sunday home after the Service. Mom and Dad were as proud as could be as I wore my uniform to Church with them. I felt like a celebrity. Everyone gushed over me and made me feel important. After all, it was here I had been baptized as an infant. Here I had been confirmed and as a teenager I had belonged to the youth groups. My membership gave me the badge of being a Christian.

I had to stand up as Pastor Johansson welcomed me home. I blushed in my embarrassment. He preached a sermon on "Reaping the Peace." You can see, I can still remember the title. No one carried a Bible. No need to. It was mentioned in passing. You'll find the following story very revealing."

I picture an evening in Walt's life when Walt and his wife waited for a young attorney to stop by. He had asked them to check over legal papers on their home. He arrived on time and they expedited their legal work. Walt's wife offered the visitor coffee. He said, that'd be nice, and they settled back for a get-acquainted visit.

After some chit-chat about the weather the quest brought up the subject of ownership.

If a lawyer from the city asked you, "are you sure you own your own home?"

You would reply, "yes."

And then he would ask, "what evidence can you show me as a proof of your ownership?"

You have to establish the truth of your ownership with a legal document, and that paper is called a title deed. When you show this to the city lawyer it gives evidence to everyone that you are the legal owner to this property.

The visitor noticed a Bible on the bookshelf. "I see you have a Bible." Walt and his wife looked at the unused book lying on the shelf in the sun.

"Ya'," asserted Walt, "they gave me that when I went to the army. Everybody got a Bible."

"I don't know if you ever thought of it this way, but the Bible is a title deed," cited the young man.

At this point Walt's wife brought a warm-up of coffee and the small talk took off on caffeine and chocolate.

With determination the guest reminded them, "I was saying that the Bible is a little deed."

"Oh, that's right, you were," said Walt's wife with an air of apology.

"Here's what I'm saying. Why do I you have a Bible title deed? Well, let's say I were to die and go to heaven."

"Now God asks me, 'what right do you have to heaven?'"

I reply, "I have a Title Deed to heaven."

And God would ask, "what's that?"

"Your Word. You would say In Your Word it says that whoever believes in your Son has the title to heaven."

Walt thought to himself: "I was baptized as a baby, I was raised in the way of my church, I do the best I can. I figure this goes a long way. After all, I proved my religion when I was a conscientious objector during the war."

"My proof or evidence," asserted the young man, "is that I have met the requirements of His Words — the Bible — and then I have everlasting life."

Walt bristled. "This kind of talk," Walt thought with resentment, "belongs in a church on Sundays, not in friendly conversation."

"Does any of this make sense?" Enquired the young man who appeared to have the gift of evangelism.

Walt and his wife said nothing, so the young attorney stood up. As he took the handle of the door Walt stammered in measured words, "Religious talk causes nothing but trouble, that's why I've kept my mouth shut."

As the young attorney sat behind the wheel of his car, he relived his visit with Walt and his wife. He pictured a sign hanging above Walt's life: CLOSED. Not open for business. No innovations. No breakthroughs. No exploration. No revelations. He felt like crying. Such is the cruelty of indoctrination. When I forfeit the right to think of myself, I have lost all, for I am allowing someone else to do thinking for me.

As you and I study the life of Walt Jensen I think of some of the milestones he encountered along the way. How did he cope with trying times? His unused Bible says, "He didn't turn to Me. I slept on the shelf."

As I reflected on Walt Jensen I was reminded of another man — the man of Psalm One. His delight is in the Word of God. He shall be like a tree firmly planted by the big the rivers of water (the Word). He will prosper in all his ways.

When the storm clouds buffeted Walt's life he perceived them as brash intruders. Now what? One right after the other. Intruders, that's what they are. Through the swamp, and now, a mountain looms up before me.

Walt could have reversed all his thinking if he had embraced the lesson of the first chapter of the book of James. Here's what it has to say: "when trouble comes your way, a time when you feel like throwing in the towel, don't grumble and moan — shout Hallelujah!" Wow! What a reversal! "Don't run away from diversity," writes James, "give it a big bear hug." How can I do that? Simple. This testing has a purpose. And what is that? It will show to the world that you have real faith, not counterfeit faith. New doors will open because your faith speaks about the faithfulness of God.

When Walt returned home from army service, he faced the play-out of his philosophy of life. He placed his Bible on a shelf with the tragic thought, there's nothing in there for me, and he slammed that door shut for the rest of his life. Walt crossed many bridges in the days of his life. After his army service, he found a job. He courted a young lady and they married. The forgotten Bible watched in silence as children shouted in play. Insightful truths on death and grief went unnoticed as Walt experienced the death of his parents. The Great Depression hit him in the most demanding days of his life, and he suffered a breakdown in his own personal health.

When the young attorney drove away from Walt's house he asked himself this question: "Was I too brash with Walt?"

The answer to his question is answered by Walt's statement at the close of his life: "Only one person in my entire life took an interest in my soul. He was a young attorney."

You and I began this story in New York with Ray Bosley, and then we met Walt Jensen. Both men possessed great wealth but they never knew it. Both men were heirs — Ray was the only heir to his aunt's wealth — and Walt could have been an heir to the promise found in Christ. Neither man acted on their riches. Through ignorance they forfeited — what a tragic word — what belonged to them.

The word "Testament" means a covenant between God and man, in which God lavishes on man His majestic guarantee.

Walt's Bible could have been a life-diary of fulfilled promises. This in turn would have become a testament to his friends and loved ones, but what he didn't know deprived him and his loved ones of what they should have had.

Letter from Ted

In this letter from Ted I learn that the promises are like the land.

Hi Norm,

Enjoyed your letter on facing problems with joy. I recall the translation you used was Kenneth Wuest's New Testament from the original language (which was Greek).

Count it a matter for pure joy when you are surrounded by trials. You can prove your faith is genuine by how you react. That's why these tests came your way in the first place. (James 1:2,3)

The first question that came my way was, where do these "problems" come from. I found the answer in the simple realization that they often come from life itself (so I can't blame God).

I wanted the verse to be entrenched in my spirit, so I cast about looking for a way to do that, and I came up with idea of not only saying it out loud, but of also writing down my faith. I wrote that I was trusting God for His joy.

You'll find this interesting. My title deed shows I have ownership to my car. The same goes for my house. I have a deed that shows I own my property. This simple understanding of "ownership" applies to a promise in God's Word. When I believe the Father for joy in the above verse (which is what He promises). I take ownership of what He guarantees — joy. I take up a squatter's rights to joy.

This truth comes to the surface in Romans 4:16 when Paul says, "... I inherit the property of a promise when I believe in my heart." I got this out of the Amplified translation. In other words, each promise is like a piece of land, and you and I can gain title to it by genuine faith. This knowledge of ownership comes from the spiritual law that you and I have been declared "heirs." Here's an example of that ownership. Take John 3:16. The thing which is promised is eternal life. The land to be owned in that verse — because I am an heir — is eternal life. As I believe for that promise I gain "ownership" for eternal life.

The county verifies I own my property, and the state recognizes my ownership of my car. God stands behind or guarantees my ownership of what He pledges in His Word.

If you talked to a professor in psychology at the university he would say: "Studies have shown that to meet your trials with a positive attitude is the healthy way to do it." He would emphasize, "People live longer if they know the secrets of coping with worry." However, not everyone agrees with us. When Satan hears that I am claiming ownership of the land in a promise, he becomes madder than a hornet. He realizes this is saying, "God is alive and He always carries out what He says He'll do."

I am sure you'll recall that faith is said to be a substance *(Hebrew 11:1)*. Some use the word "deed," a title deed. This confirms what I found. The promise is simply "land to be claimed" because I am an heir.

Someone says "I own land in Montana."

I reply, "I own land, too."

He wants to know where my land is located.

"In the Word of God," I reply.

"I don't understand," he counters.

"Easy," I tell him, "the promises in the Bible are lands that I own when I believe in the heart."

"That's a new twist," he laughs, "I never heard that before."

Norm, you and I have much to be thankful for. You'll recall 2 Corinthians 5:14 from the King James translation: " … the love of Christ constrains us … "

In his expanded translation from the original language, Kenneth Wuest enlarges on that verse:

> *For the love which Christ has for me presses on me from all sides, holding me to one end and prohibiting me from considering any other, wrapping itself around me in tenderness.*

When you and I mine "the land" of what He speaks (in the Bible) we buy up His tender love.

With love,

Ted

Proof

God, the Father faced tough choices in eternity past. First, He said I have created mankind. I love him with greatness of love, but he has a fallen nature. As such, he denies my existence. My love for man moves me to reach across the chasm — to build a bridge — to fellowship with man. He understood He would have to sacrifice His Son to reach across this gulf. He would give eternal life to all who believed His message.

The Father sought a family through which His Son would come. The litmus test would be faith. The man I select must believe that through his lineage the Christ will come. He selected Abraham because he had believed God for a son. He had proven his faith in the birth of Isaac.

We pick up the story in Genesis the twenty-second chapter. This is the blessing the Father lavished on Abraham when He promised:

In this blessing I will truly bless you. I will multiply your family line from out of your son Isaac. Like the stars of heaven, so will I multiply your seed, Yes, in number, they shall be like the sand by the seashore, so shall they multiply.

And in your Seed shall all the nations of the earth be blessed. I do this because you listened to what I said. You obeyed what I promised.

The "Seed" that will bring the "good news" to all the nations of the world is the Person of the Lord Jesus Christ.

But back to Abraham. As the story unfolds, Abraham will be given the opportunity to prove the authenticity of his faith by his actions.

Take your son, your only son, one you love so greatly, and journey to the land of Moriah. So Abraham arose while it was yet dark and saddled his donkey. Isaac and two young servants also readied themselves for the journey. On the third day of travel, Abraham saw their destination in the distance.

Wait here, Abraham addressed the two young men. Take care of the donkey and Isaac and I will set off for that hill in the distance. We'll return shortly.

In this test conceived by God, they took with them the firewood, a knife, and the fire. Isaac became curious as they approached the place of sacrifice. Father, he said, we have the firewood, the knife, and the fire, but we have no lamb for the burnt offering.

My son, Abraham replied with a tear in his eye, our heavenly Father will provide Himself a lamb for the burnt offering. They built an altar in the designated place and laid the wood in order. Abraham bound Isaac and laid him on the altar of wood, but as Abraham reached for the knife to slay his only son, an angel from heaven called to him.

"Abraham! Abraham! Do not lay your hand on your son. Do nothing. You have passed the test of your faith in your willingness to sacrifice your son." Abraham breathed a deep sigh of relief as he glanced about. He spied a ram caught in the thicket and took him as a burnt offering instead of his son.

Abraham aptly called the place Jehovah Jireh, translated; This is the place the Lord will provide. Another translation says, In this mountain the Lord will be seen.

Christ, in the Person of an angel, spoke to Abraham about the high and holy blessings which had been lavished upon him. In a nutshell: Out of your lineage shall come the Christ. So we read the commitment:

On the basis of my person of who I am, I swear I will carry out my promise to your descendants.

God can't swear on the authority of some superior object because He alone stands as the highest.

I swear, says the Father to Abraham, to carry out my promise to Abraham on the authority of which I am — God himself.

He could have spoken the promise by itself and that would have been sufficient, but He adds the oath to give Abraham confirmed certainty. The promise explains to you and me what the pledge contains. In the oath, the Father adds commitment. So Abraham sees the promise as an absolute truth that cannot be altered with God's certain word of fulfillment.

This chapter in Genesis (22), about God's test with Abraham, played out 2000 years ago. In it, you and I can see the Father's love, the prediction of Christ's death and resurrection, and worldwide redemption for mankind.

Now we jump ahead to the New Testament book of Hebrews. In chapter six the writer reminds the fledgling church of God's promise to Abraham. He asks them to lift their eyes to better things. Listen closely, he says, focus on what is on God's heart for you.

You have been caring for one another. That's fine. Fellowship. Housing. Food. Counsel. Money. Great! You have done a good job. Honestly, I have to commend you for your staunch dedication in facing up to these pressing needs.

I want you to take this same industry you have shown toward one another and redirect it to better things. Better things? You ask. Yes, better things. I am firmly convinced of things which accompany salvation. (In the parable of the sower, the Lord taught us that the good ground is he who hears the Word, understands it, and reaps as much as a hundred fold).

You and I pick up the story from here and ask: what are the "better things" the writer requests? Jesus closed His ministry with this command, "Go into the entire world and preach the gospel." We know seeds produce after their own kind. Believers produce more believers. The Lord also said it succinctly, "There are those who say it is four months to harvest time. No, lift up your eyes and look at the fields. They are already white for harvesting. "

A Letter

Hi Ted,

A note on a verse we talked about last week. David prays in the one hundred forty-first Psalm and verse three:

> Set a guard, O lord
> Before my mouth;
> Keep watch at the door
> Of my lips.

Words. Speech. What I say. David talks about what I communicate when I open my mouth. My words reveal who I am. If I speak worry and fear that's what is riding the horses of my heart. I have no authority over what's going to happen so I tell everybody about it. I bring into today the problems of tomorrow.

James writes much about the awesome consequence of the tongue in the third chapter of his New Testament book. He concludes that speech is like a tiny spark that ignites a devastating forest fire. He also likens our words to a small rudder that generates the power to alter the course of a grand ship. So you and I come down to "control." How can I get control of that tiny spark of fire? How can I control that rudder?

Look again at that verse from Psalms. David does not say "I" have set a guard at my mouth. He does not say "I" keep watch at the door of my lips. He looks to the strength of the Lord to provide the enablement. The Psalmist knows that the control of what he speaks is an action of faith. Only by the Spirit can he shout, "The Lord works in my life." He sows a seed in his own life, and in the lives of those who listen to him.

Ya' know, if I choose to speak fear and worry I cancel out my faith. That's true. My speech reveals my heart. You can see I have brushed aside what the Lord says, and I interpret my circumstances from a human point of view. At this time of fear you would hear me say, There's no way out of this mess.

Jesus was walking along the shore of the Sea of Galilee when the Scribes and Pharisees from Jerusalem caught up with Him. They had a bone to pick with the young Teacher. They wanted to know why His disciples failed to observe the ceremonial washings of the Law. "What we eat," replied Jesus, "is not what corrupts our spirit. What we say springs from the inner person, from the heart, and this is what can bring corruption." *(Matthew 15)*

Negative statements can repudiate the Word, so if I refuse to utter negative words they have no life. Words unspoken die unborn.

In touch,
Norm

The Hidden Treasure of Faith

A Word To The Wise

Biblical faith receives its life and power from what God says in the Bible. If I know what God says about the particular circumstance of my life, I have taken the first step towards the faith that will get the job done. On the other hand, if I am blind and ignorant as to what God has in mind about my need, it is impossible for me to exercise faith. I can put this truth in the form of a question: "How can I take a course of action on something I do not know exists?"

Someone says, "What you are saying is this, for faith to be alive it has to know something."

Precisely. As an example, look at the pain of loneliness. If I know nothing of what God thinks, how can I act on what He says? What does God have in mind concerning my loneliness?

In the last part of the fifth verse in Hebrews thirteen Jesus says, "I will never leave you." I am not alone. I have One who never leaves me or forsakes me.

"I want you to know," says the Father, "you have not been abandoned. Wherever you are, whatever you do, I am your constant companion."

I find faith in this verse. I find life in it because it changes my life. I see power in the verse because I now see my situation from God's point of view.

Secret Number 3

I NOW KNOW THE HOLY SPIRIT LIVES IN ME SO I CAN EXPERIENCE FOR MYSELF WHAT GOD PROMISES ME IN THE BIBLE.

"I have received the Spirit Who is from God that I might know (enjoy) the promises the Father has freely given to me in His Word." *(1 Corinthians 2:12)*

You and I do not need to be spiritual beggars. Take prayer for an example. One could ask God to hear his prayer. That's not necessary. He has made clear in His Word that He does hear our prayers. *(John 15:7)* Or, one asks the Father for His presence during hardship. Again, not necessary. He has gone on record that He will never leave us or forsake us. *(Hebrews 13:5)* Everything we need to enable our new life is found in the Bible. When I say what the Father says about the circumstances in my life I am giving Him the glory, and I realize the resolution of my concern.

He has given you and me His living Words to use in our daily life. In the stories that follow we see different ways in which the Holy Spirit works.

A Mirror

> *God's promises are given to you and
> me for one reason: to be activated.*

Peter writes *(2 Peter 3:15, 16)* to all those "who have like precious faith" that brother Paul talks about things which are not easily understood. All of us would agree with Peter that there are spiritual truths which are not "easily understood."

Paul writes to the Christians at Corinth *(2 Corinthians 2 and 3)* that he sees three people in the world. The natural man, the casual Christian and the spiritual believer. The natural man has nothing to do with God — he lives out his life with his senses and faculties. The casual Christian has received the new life in Christ, but chooses to ignore the prompting of the Holy Spirit. The spiritual man lives under the enduement of the Person of the Holy Spirit.

Paul says *(Romans 10:17)* that faith comes ... and comes ... and comes (original language) by the hearing of the Word. Life-changing truths may not be captured overnight. Read and re-read. Only then will you enjoy the experience of a "revelation."

"The word of God is like a mirror."

So writes the brother of our Lord, James, to twelve tribes scattered throughout the world. *(James 1:21–26)*. I know you enjoy, he writes, this new life because His word has been planted and rooted in your hearts. Continue to welcome His word, he pleads, so you can keep on growing from day to day. You and I know it is easy to lose our grasp on what is valuable. We get so busy in side-

A Mirror

street details that we lose our way.

So, what am I getting at? In the first place you and I know we have received this gracious new life by what He spoke. This should establish for you and me the significance of what the Lord says. It stands written. In light of this you and I can enjoy regular breakthroughs into His power.

"Reify" says I can see as a concrete thing that which is invisible. So I ask myself, how can I reify what the Bible says? In other words, how can I make concrete a spiritual truth? Let's start out with the book of Ephesians. Here's a tip: you'll find two majestic prayers in Ephesians *(Ephesians 1:16–23; 3:14–21)*.

Let's put the magnifying glass on the word "faith." Your faith, my faith talks about invisible things as though they can be seen. I can hear one reader say, I don't know about that. What about Heaven? Eternal life? Faith reifies. It sees as a concrete thing that which is invisible. Knowing this, I want it to walk in the shoe leather of daily living. Let's go back to Ephesians.

Paul prays this for the faithful Christians at Ephesus *(Ephesians 1:17)*.

> Might the Lord give to you a spirit of wisdom and revelation in the personal knowledge of Him.

How can I make that spiritual truth a reality in my life? I am excited to see it move from a mystery to something I personally experience.

According to James my problem lies in forgetting the admonition of the Holy Spirit. I think of what Job said ... decree a thing, and it shall be established for you; and God's light shall shine on your ways *(Job 22:28)*. I can decree a truth by speaking it.

Faith has a voice. My spirit has a voice. Since the beginning of my Christian life I have talked about unseen things as though they are visible. I say the Lord Jesus Christ lives, and with my spirit I can see Him. With my spirit I picture Ephesians 1:17 in my life.

> Father, you have lavished on me, in Your love, a spirit of wisdom and revelation in an intimate knowledge of the Person of the Lord Jesus Christ.

When you and I pray this prayer, our spirit decrees it as a fact in our lives. Faith sees it as an accomplished fact. These two great prayers in Ephesians were Paul's faith for the believers in Ephesus. You and I can pray these prayers for ourselves and for others. They serve as a prayer model.

Catch of Fish

Sunshine burned off the lingering morning mist on the north shore of the Sea of Galilee. Doctor Luke called this the Lake of Gennesaret from the place by the lake. Sleepy towns along the lake began to stir as they shook off the chill night air. Commercial fishermen dragged their boats up to the shore after a night on the lake.

"Grab the other end of the net," shouted Andrew to his brother Peter. "Hook it to the rack for me." Peter set down his pail of bait and hoisted the heavy net to the drying rack.

"How was your luck?" Peter hollered over to his partners, James and John.

"Same as yours," shouted James. "We'll try again tonight."

"Beep. Beep." The circling seagulls seemed to ask, "Have you got any fish parts? We're hungry!"

Peter glanced up at the squawking birds. "I suppose you've gotta eat." With that he threw his leftover bait in the water. Gulls scrambled over one another to gobble up a bit of breakfast.

Zebedee, the patriarch of this fishing business, was the father of James and John. His white beard and hair contrasted with the red gnarled hands of an experienced fisherman. He was the favorite target of Peter's banter.

"You know, Zeb," Peter would laugh, "the fish caught on to your tricks years ago."

Zeb always had a comeback. "You can't catch 'em with your hands, Pete."

"I don't know about an old coot like you, Zeb," chided Andrew, "but I'm ready for bed."

It was a busy beach with boats anchoring after a fruitless night on the lake. James paused from his tug-of-war with the nets to glance to the east. Mount Herman silhouetted itself against the rising sun. "Do I detect a halo?" he asked himself. "It isn't all bad," he mused as he looked at the empty boats. "Look at the beauty of a new day." A warm smile crept across his face.

Peter interrupted James' reflections, "Ya know, it's been a year."

"A year?" James broke away from his study of Mount Herman.

"Since we were with the Master."

"That's right. It is a year. I can't believe it. Time flies. I guess that's what being does. But I'll never forget that wedding."

"There musta been a thousand people there." That's when He changed the water into wine."

"Don't forget His baptism," Peter reminded James. "The baptizer was a funny guy. He dressed in goat skins like Elijah of old."

"I understand he lived on locusts and honey."

Andrew reminded the talkers that Jesus had healed a nobleman's son over in Capernaum.

"The whole family became believers," mentioned John.

Up and down. Up and down. Their boats would rise and settle with the waves — a rhythm of their own. The water splashed the boat as it rocked up and down.

"There are so many," John looked toward the plain of Gennesaret.

"You're not talking about fish," blurted Peter as he laughed.

"No, No. I'm talking about people," smiled John as he smiled at Peter. "Think of those the Master touches; the blind, the deaf, the hungry."

Catch of Fish

As the tired fishermen ended their night of work, Jesus visits them at their place of work. He is engulfed by a large crowd who want to hear His message of returning to God.

He knew these men as family and may very well have stayed in their homes prior to this incident.

Andrew glanced northward toward the plain of Gennesaret. Waves of people came as an unending stream, and the one they followed was their good friend, Jesus. All eyes focused on Him who carried Himself like a leader.

He greeted the tired fisherman as the pressing crowd sought to push Him into the sea. An older woman called for healing as her children bring her on a litter.

"Can you put your boat back in the water?"

"I don't know what He's doing," thought Peter, "but that's ok with me."

"Sure, Lord, no problem," blushed Peter, and he slid the boat into the water.

"Now what?" asked James, who read authority in the face of Jesus.

"I'm going to use the boat for a pulpit," Jesus informed His friends. "Take me out a few yards, then more people can hear me."

After He had seated Himself He began to preach to the crowd on the shore.

"Repent," He proclaimed, "for the kingdom of heaven is at hand." John observed that the people on shore listened attentively for they were eager to hear the word of God.

Murmuring and shouting disappeared as they strained to hear the voice of the young Man. The beep-beep of the sea gulls accompanied the voice of the Speaker. No one listened more closely than His fishermen friends, and they sensed He was here for them. Their minds pondered over the epic year behind them: His

Insights

baptism, the wedding in Cana, the fulfillment of prophecy and the healing of the sick.

Jesus finished His message and He turned to Peter. "Pull up the anchor. Go out into deeper water for a catch of fish."

A quizzical look moved across Peter's face. "This won't work," he said to himself. "You don't catch fish in the daytime, and we've fished all night. Caught nothing. Someone has to say something."

"Master," Peter stammered, "we have fished all night.... even to exhaustion ... we've caught nothing ... not even a single fish."

Peter paused in his spokesman role to study the face of Jesus. In resignation he looked at the bottom of the bobbing boat. He found no satisfaction there. Reluctantly, he blurted out,

"All right, if you say so."

With Peter's acquiescence Jesus looked out to the sea. After a studied moment, He turned to Andrew who sat at the helm.

"Take the boat out to the deep water."

INSIGHT

Peter could have refused the command to go out into deeper water for another try. After all, it didn't make sense, but the Words of Jesus overruled his judgments.

"Here's the spot," Jesus pointed. "Now you can let down your nets."

As the nets were lowered into the deeper water, James and John looked at each other and the shore.

"It isn't every day," laughed John, "that you see Peter do as he was told."

The crowds on the shore asked what was going on.

"Is He crossing the sea?"

"When will He come back in?"

"Are they going to fish?"

In this trying moment of expectancy, Jesus turned Peter and Andrew, "Now you can take up the nets."

The two fishermen hoisted up their nets as they had done during the night hours, but this time it was different.

"I can't believe it," shouted Andrew. "Our net is breaking."

"We are sinking," blurted Peter. "We need help!"

"John, James bring your boat." Peter waved frantically to his partners in shore who scrambled into their boat.

Zebidee hollered "Go! Go!" to his sons as he shooed them out. Soon both boats were swamped with fish. So argument and terror took hold of Peter and the others and he fell on his knees before Jesus.

"I am only a man, a sinner. Master, how can you have anything to do with me?"

After they had run their boats on shore under the scrutiny of the crowds, John said, "We've never seen anything like it, truly this has to be an act of God."

INSIGHT

All looked on Jesus with awe for no man could dispute that this was a supernatural incident. These men knew that the Man before them was the long-awaited Messiah. Jesus knew what was in the heart of man, and He selected these men to reach out to mankind with the gospel.

Jesus read their eyes. He also read their hearts. A year had passed since He first met with these men. They weren't ready then, now they were.

"I know you were afraid. You have nothing to fear, "consoled Jesus. "You will no longer catch fish. From now on you shall enjoy the miracle of catching men."

A Tree

"I can't get over it," ventured James, "how the Master does it. This lady touched the hem of His garment and she was healed. She said she had been sick for twelve years, but when she touched His clothes she spoke of her healing."

"She also said she had seen many doctors," admitted Doctor Luke. "All they did was take her money, what little she had."

Monday morning, very early, Jesus walks with his disciples towards Jerusalem.

"You recall," Peter spoke to John about the servant boy of the centurion, the Roman soldier.

"Right, I'll never forget it."

"He healed that boy when he was at death's door. And the Centurion said to the Lord, all you have to do is say it, and my servant will be healed."

"And the man with the withered hand up in Capernaum."

"Who can forget it," interrupted James,

"He stretched out his arms and his hand had been healed."

"Amazing," said another.

"But here's the question. This is the question of the day. Why can't we do what He does?"

"Yeah," broke in Philip, "we've been with Him for two years and we're still spectators." Each one had a different view.

"He teaches us through parables."

"He has told us all along that we needed more faith."

"Maybe love is the answer."

"I get tired," Peter blurted out, "of your bickering."

"No," Andrew countered his brother, "we're not bickering, we're searching."

Peter laughed. "Now you can claim to be students, but I've been listening to you since we left Bethany. I'll ask Him."

"Rehearse it with me," cut in Matthew, "what will you say?"

"That's easy, faith is the key, so, how can we get more faith?"

"Okay go ahead," Matthew encouraged.

Peter quickened his pace to place himself next to Jesus.

"Master," Peter enquired.

"Master, all of us want to do more. The men feel we haven't done all we could be doing."

Jesus answered, "That's commendable."

"As you can see," Peter walked slowly as he worded his question, "we don't have the kind of faith You have. I think we could do more if we had more faith."

Jesus listened in patience as they hiked. "So you're talking about faith."

Jesus led Peter to his questions.

"Here's what all of us want to know. How can we have more faith?"

"Good question," praised Jesus. As they continued their trek little was said.

Thomas took a position next to Peter. "What'd he say? What'd he say?"

"He didn't say anything. Only, that's a good question."

Again Jesus spoke: "Peter, I haven't had any breakfast. I'm hungry."

"Can you wait till we get the town?" answered Peter.

"Look," Jesus pointed, "there's a fig tree. Why not check it out?"

The tree had leaves so it should have fruit, but Jesus found no fruit on the tree. His disciples watched Him carefully as He

Insights

stepped back and appraised the tree. Then He said to the tree, "No one shall ever eat fruit from you again."

"Did you hear that?" Thaddeus laughed nervously under his breath. "Did you hear that?" He turned to Andrew, "that's got to be about the goofiest thing I've ever heard, talking to a tree." He threw an embarrassed side-glance at the Master, but Jesus remained meditative as they neared Jerusalem.

"What about Peter's question? How can I have more faith?" John asked. "No, He hasn't answered it yet," answered Peter. "After all, He's talking about a tree without fruit."

Simon continued, "I feel faith in my bones. I feel something inside. I'm sure He'll answer my question when He feels we're ready."

Twenty-four hours later they passed the fig tree again. The leaves had withered.

"Master," Peter was astonished, "look, the fig tree you spoke to has died."

The entourage had stopped in the roadway. Now He was ready to answer Peter's question. Jesus observed the tree, then with measured words He declared, "You should have the kind of faith God has."

At this point one has to ask, "What kind of faith does God have?"

Early Monday morning Jesus looks for breakfast. He asks the fig tree if it has fruit, but it replies it has none. He tells the tree, you'll never bear fruit again. With these words, He kills the tree.

Jesus turned to His disciples, "You have asked for greater faith. Here's the answer: God uses words. You use words. Use words filled with faith. Speak to the problem as I did to the tree."

The disciples mulled over His answer: Use words. Words ... filled with faith. James turned to his brother, "Do you get it, John?"

"It appears so simple," answered John. "Let me ask the Master to explain it."

"Can you enlarge on that? What do You mean when You tell us to speak to the problem?" John asked the Master.

"By the way of illustration, John, let us say a mountain is in your way."

"Right. I understand."

"God would speak to the mountain. He would order the mountain to do something. Pick yourself up and throw yourself into the sea. But this is pivotal. God has no doubt in His heart, but He believes what He speaks comes to pass."

"What about prayer?" asked John.

"When you pray," answered Jesus, "no matter what it is, believe you have received it, and what you prayed for will be yours."

INSIGHT

What can we learn?

Your words, my words are more powerful than mountains, more powerful than the circumstances of our daily lives. Jesus admonishes us to check our prayer life. Whatever it is when you've prayed for it, believe you have received it. Even though it is not manifest your words of faith shout, "I have received it"! If you and I do this, we shall have whatever we speak (Mark 11:22-24).

Priscilla of Samaria

In the fourth chapter of the Gospel of John, you and I find Jesus and His disciples in the heathen land of Samaria. To reach the town of Sychar with the "good news," He employs a woman who has made some mistakes in her life — Priscilla. This event is a gold mine with majestic Christian truths. Priscilla abandons her water-pot to hurry to town to share with them a love she has never seen before. And the town which has held this lady in contempt takes her hand as she leads them to her Savior.

You'll thrill to the careful way Jesus leads Priscilla to salvation and how her testimony leads to a revival. No longer can her worship be found in a mountain. Now she worships in her spirit. And the sustenance for her spirit can be found in what God speaks.

A great crowd pressed along the road from Sychar to the well to hear the Man who had the Living Water. Priscilla had found life in His Words and in her new-found love, she wanted to share this life with her kin. Jesus had sent His disciples to Sychar to buy meat, and He watched Priscilla scurry into Sychar with the news of a new life.

Sometimes, she is called the woman of Sychar. Others have called her the Samaritan woman. I call this woman by the well, Priscilla. To give her personage we'll give her the name of Priscilla. She had a common look. When Jesus looked at Samaria and Sychar in particular He could say, "you people worship the unknown." He said to Himself, "I wanted to give to the people of Samaria someone to believe in. I need an evangelist. These heathens need to know there is a living God." For this anointed task he chose Priscilla, an unlikely selection.

Nathaniel had to remind Jesus, "Samaria is not for us, I know you want to get Galilee, but why do we have to cross Samaria? Can't we go around?"

Jesus nodded that He listened to what Nathaniel had to say. The Master knew John the Baptist was preaching in Aenon, so He did not want to disrupt John's ministry by choosing that route. He also knew the Pharisees sought to drive a wedge between the two groups of disciples. "I want to select a route," thought Jesus, "that discourages the propaganda of the Pharisees."

He would keep His disciples separate from John's by crossing Samaria — the accursed land.

"Our ancient tradition," said Matthew, "is to never set foot on this heathen soil. Everyone will cry, Heretics! Heretics!"

Jesus smiled at Matthew's dramatics.

Matthew went on, "What about the Samaritans? They'll see us as rebels. So don't talk to them. In that way we'll slip through to Galilee without any trouble. We're foreigners to them so the quicker we make our way out of here, the better it'll be."

Jesus seated Himself by Jacob's well. This had once been the land of Jacob, and he passed it on to his son Joseph. Tired and thirsty at the noon hour, Jesus had no pail to draw water. His mind wandered back to His talk with Nicodemus. He reflected on the Pharisees and their subterfuge to create dissension between Him and John the Baptist. He thought of His twelve disciples who had gone into Sychar to find food. He enjoyed this quiet time when He could lean back and enjoy companionship with the Father.

He looked across the fields to see a lonely figure walking His way. The person appeared to shimmer in the noon time sun. When the person came into focus it turned out to be a woman. On her shoulder was a water jug.

Insights

"Aha," thought Jesus, "now's my chance to get a drink."

The woman set her jug down about ten feet from Jesus. She made no eye contact with the Lord and she said nothing to Him.

"I don't talk to Jews," she concluded in her mind. "They look down on us. They see us as heathens. I'm taking on a big risk, being alone and all, but I can take care of myself. He doesn't look like someone who would hurt me. I have to keep my mouth shut. Then I won't get into any trouble." As she stood with head bowed, looking at the ground she asked herself, "why don't I leave? I don't have to be here. I shouldn't have walked into this situation." She was at the point of leaving when she heard Him speak. "What did He say? I didn't make it out." Then she heard Him say, "You have the bucket. I would like a drink."

Priscilla continued looking at the ground. "I can't believe it. A Jew, and He's talking to me. Is he tearing down the wall? A Jewish man talking to a Samaritan woman — unheard of. Little did I know what I was getting into when I left town. Should I look at Him? Should I answer Him? After all, there was something in His voice that said He would not hurt me. I'll ask Him." She raised her sight to look into eyes of the Lord. He had a deeply personal look.

"Sir," she asked, "how is it that you being a Jew would speak to a Samaritan?"

Priscilla paused. "Not only are you speaking to a Samaritan, but a woman, a Samaritan woman. Don't you know your people have nothing to do with us?"

Priscilla was proud of herself, given the circumstances, she had been forthright. "After all, I have a right to speak my mind, if it's the truth."

Jesus seemed to read her mind as He said, "First of all, you're unaware of the gift God has for you. You do not know who you're talking to. If you had known God's gift and who I am, then you would have asked me for a drink and I would have given you living water."

Priscilla tried to arrange His words in her mind. "He's talking about the gift God has for me. He also tells me I don't know who I'm talking to. And, if I had known these things, then I would have asked Him for a drink of living water."

She answered Him, "You don't even have a bucket. You have no way to get the water out. You know as well as I do that the well is deep. It makes no sense to me that you can provide living water."

"He did talk about who He was," pondered Priscilla, "and He talked about the gift God has for me. What did He mean? I might as well ask Him."

"Sir," spoke up Priscilla, "can you tell me where You get Your living water? You prompt me to ask many questions about what You are saying. For example, our ancestor Jacob, now he was a great man. By what You are saying, are You superior to him? He used this well himself a long time ago. His sons and his cattle all drank from this spring."

Jesus answered, "If you drink of this spring your thirst will not be fulfilled. You will have to come again and again to satisfy your thirst."

"What you are saying is true. However," Jesus went on, "the drink of the water I give becomes a spring of water in the person himself. It flows constantly on into external life. His thirst is satisfied forever."

Priscilla believed what Jesus offered. "Sir, she said, give me this water you have talked about. Then my thirst will be satisfied. I won't have to come to Jacob's well all the time."

"What I want you to do," prompted Jesus, "is to get your husband and come back here."

Priscilla replied, "I have no husband."

"You have answered truthfully," recognized Jesus, "when you admitted you have no husband. Actually, you have had five husbands and the man you are now living with is not your husband."

Priscilla queried to herself, "How did He know I was not married? How did He know I had been married five times? How did He know I am now living with a man I'm not married to?" It had broken on Priscilla that Jesus was not an ordinary man.

"As I have carefully listened," she noted, "I am coming to the understanding that you are a prophet. Our forefathers worshipped here on this mountain, but your people say Jerusalem is the worship center." She thought He might ask her to worship at Jerusalem, but He quickly informed her. He was not talking about a physical place of worship but a spiritual indwelling.

He moved the conversation to what takes place in the heart of a person in the spirit.

Priscilla couldn't believe it. "What's going on? Here I am, talking to a foreigner, talking about things people never talk about. He says our worship should come from inside us. Forget about our mountain. He even set aside Jerusalem as the center for worship. I have always been candid. Maybe that's why I've had such a rocky life. But when I come to face to face with the truth, I don't back off. And I know He speaks the truth."

Her reflections were interrupted by His question, "What do you worship?"

After a pause, Priscilla responded, "I don't know what I worship."

"You face the truth, your worship is empty. Your worship is an end in itself. True worship requires knowledge of the truth. My people know who they worship, so salvation comes out of us. The time is coming when true worshippers shall look to God the Father from the spirit — from the heart. These are the ones — those who believe in the heart — that the Father looks for."

"You see," Jesus continued, "God is a spirit, so you and I worship in this realm. You can understand why I said this mountain or Jerusalem is not the place of worship."

Priscilla looked off to the hills with a faraway look. "I know without doubt the Messiah is coming with the promise of redemption. He is called the Christ, for He has been anointed by God. He will tell us all things for He will be our Savior." She showed knowledge far beyond her station in life.

Jesus looked at her with a look she had not seen before — a look filled with love.

"I am He," Jesus revealed.

At that she received the Living Water. Through her physical birth she had entered the human family. Now, through three life giving Words, she was born a second time — into family of Christ. Peter wrote about the life-giving properties of what Jesus declared when He said, "You have been born a second time through what God speaks." *(1 Peter 1:23)*

"Wait'll the people in town hear this," mused Priscilla. "I know He's the Messiah because He told me all about myself. Only a divine being could do this. I know He's the anointed One, the person of Christ Himself." On a street corner in Sychar — the most unlikely of all candidates — Priscilla became the first person to bring the gospel to the Gentile nations.

"You all know me," about she stammered, "but you don't know the One I've met today."

"Where did you meet this person?" cried a woman in the crowd.

"At the well. At Jacob's well."

"Is He still there?" inquired a young man.

"Yes ... yes ... I just came from there."

Insights

Meanwhile, at the well the disciples had returned from Sychar with food, and they kept begging Jesus to eat.

"Did He eat while we were in town?" asked Peter.

"I don't think so," another replied.

"Then He must be very hungry."

In the midst of this speculation Jesus spoke up, "I have food that you are unaware of."

The disciples chatted among themselves as to who had given Him food. In this confusion Jesus brought enlightenment. "My food is to do the will of Him who sent Me and to see that His work is finished. Some of you," Jesus went on, "are looking to the fall of the year and harvest time. But look, lift up your eyes. Look closely at the fields. The harvest is now. One sows, another reaps. I send you to reap. You will reap where another has sowed."

As Jesus encouraged His men in the mission before them, He looked up.

He saw Priscilla coming toward Him.

"I see you have returned."

"Yes, I told the people of Sychar that I had met you. They know you are the Messiah Who was coming. I told them you knew all about me. Only the Christ could do that."

Jesus told the assembled crowd from Sychar that it was necessary, that He move on to Cana of Galilee.

"Please. Please," they pleaded. "Stay with us. We want what Priscilla has. We know what you say is true and we have been looking forward for this all our lives."

Jesus glanced at the excited face of Priscilla. "You have the Words," she pleaded, "and that can bring life eternal to my people. I know you have the Living Water that you told me you gave."

The disciples were surprised. "We'll go to Cana but for now we will stay there two days as Jesus teaches the people of Samaria about a new life."

Children are the Products of Words

Children are the product of words, not only of the words spoken *to* them, but also of the words spoken *by* them. Words are windows — peer through them and the true inner child steps on stage.

A child's words are ambassadors of his thoughts. One man said, "Be careful of your thoughts, they may become words at any moment."

As a child perceives of himself — so he speaks — so he becomes. *Change his words and you change his life.*

Many think a child learns only from without — from "incoming messages." Not so. He also learns from within — from "outgoing messages." Words he is "taught" form him, but words he speaks return to the inner child to reshape and change his perception.

When the inner person decrees, "I don't have friends," the child will go friendless. He perceives of himself as friendless, and he is friendless. Change this child's speech to, "I am nice to other children, and I have friends." He seeds the inner child, and it won't be long before the garden of his spirit changes his outer life.

"You shall have whatever you say."

> " ... whoever shall say to this mountain, 'You be removed, and you be thrown into the sea; and shall not doubt in his heart, but believes that those things which he says shall come to pass; *he shall have whatever he says.*" (Mark 11:23)

These words spoken by Jesus tell the awesome power He placed on words.

A child's words locate him. Courageous words unveil a brave spirit. Fear-filled words assert, "Something bad is going to happen to me."

Words imprison one, or words set one free. No wonder Solomon taught, "You are snared (taken captive) by the words of your mouth ... " *(Proverbs 6:2a).* But the prophet Joel calls out that our words need not imprison us, " ... let the weak say, I am strong" *(Joel 3:10).*

Words set the parameters of the child's life — take down these barriers and you and the child will be surprised at the new horizons that appear. The child sets up the detour sign, "I am no good at arithmetic." You can bet your boots he will do all he can to dodge math classes when he gets to junior high. Remove this barrier by teaching him right words.

The child's words translate into deeds. What the child says reveals his strengths or his weaknesses. Through his speech the child prepares for failure — he readies himself for defeat.

The solution is to spend time — at home and in school — changing wrong language for right language. Through the knowledge of what he says the child will better understand who he is. And when we as teachers and parents "see" the child behind the child through his words, then we can respond to his "cry" for help.

What I Say

Words are like windows. At any given time the words I speak unveil my relationship with God.

> I say to you (Jesus speaking), every word which you speak which has no legitimate work (words which nullify one's faith), you will have to give account of in the day of judgment. For by your words you shall be justified, and by your words you shall be condemned *(Matthew 12:36, 37 literal from Wuest's*

trans.).

When my heart embraces God's word, and my own words become one with the conviction of my heart, then and there I become mighty for God.

What I say and my inner spirit influence one another. Not only does my spirit express itself in my speech, but my spirit always responds to everything I have to say.

Faith — an exercise of my spirit — can be measured by what I say. When my speech mirrors what God says about a matter, faith listens to that and grows thereby. My *faith cannot rise above what I say,* for what I say are the display windows to my faith.

My usefulness is also measured by what I say, for sooner or later I become what I say. Tomorrows are the outpourings of today's faith, for faith or doubt proclaim themselves with words. What I profess I possess. Many Christians possess little because they profess little. When I change my speech I change my life. Words of fear and doubt keep faith in check. I can never be a conqueror unless I speak the words of a conqueror:

> In all of these things I am more than a conqueror through Him who loved me *(Romans 8:37, literal).*

God-honoring words are the property of the Holy Spirit and are given to the believer. Read what Paul the apostle says on this:

> I have not received the spirit that belongs to the world, but I have received the (Holy) Spirit who is from God in order that I might come to know the gifts God has bestowed upon me in grace which things I also *put into words,* not in words taught by human wisdom, but in words *taught by the (Holy) Spirit, fitly joining together Spirit-revealed truths with Spirit-taught words.* (1 Corinthians 2:12,13, Personal, literal of Wuest)

I say God's thoughts when I say God's words. Nothing in life compares with the majesty of being one with God's word; nothing gives Satan more pleasure than to see Christians using Satanic words. He will do everything in his power to keep the Christian from professing what God says on the matter.

Say this with me: I confess His Lordship. I embrace His Word, His power, His presence, His victory (and you can go on and on from here). I refuse to give glory to Satan for his work — despair, defeat, doubt, problems, sickness and depression. *My profession overcomes every problem!*

What I Say

It is the design of God and His expectation that the believer live in another state of being other than the natural man. He lives in the law of faith. The law of faith says that I enjoy the Christian life as "the great confession." My "confession" is that I possess a thing (in my spirit) before I actually have it in hand (visibly). The greatest things that have ever happened to me have happened in the realm of the spirit.

Confession preceded the new birth in my life. Confession preceded eternal life in my life. Confession precedes healing; healing comes after I confess *(Isaiah 53:4,5)*. "Confession" unveils my spirit's perception, and not, in this sense, an admission of sin.

Mark 11:23 says, For verily I say unto you, That whoever shall SAY to this mountain, Be removed, and be cast into the sea; and shall not doubt in his heart, but shall believe that those things which he SAYS shall come to pass; he shall have whatever he SAYS.

Just as Jesus spoke to a mountain, to a tree, to the sea, or to the dead, I must understand I speak to the problem by name: "Problem, I'm talking to you. I take authority over you in the name of the Lord Jesus Christ. Out! Get! You are no longer around because I have ordered you off my property."

My mouth must do its' work. God's Word automatically decrees authority, now it is up to me to act accordingly. It is true that my speech windows the inner man, what God has said unveils who he is. Homologeo, the Greek word for confession, means "to say the same thing." In other words, I say about any situation exactly what God says — this is confession.

A confession may be positive, neutral, or negative. The last two are of Satan. "I don't know what I'm going to do about this," is a neutral confession that ignores the "words" of God. This is why the natural mind is said to be an enemy of God *(Romans 8:7)*. A negative or neutral confession destroys faith, for the inner man *hears* what the mouth is saying. Listen to my speech and you will locate me, you will be able to set the parameters of my life, and you will know whether or not my speech challenges you to faith.

God has a language (the Bible), and Satan has a language. Satan's language is doubt, fear, hatred, cursing, sickness and defeat. A confession that is plumbed with God's word will put you over every single time. All is lost from the beginning with a confession agreeing with Satan.

What I confess with my lips I possess in my life!

I Say About Myself What God Says

"If an earth-shaking insight was as close to me as my nose, I wouldn't see it," said one man with a chuckle.

Let's put that statement a little differently: If this earth-shaking insight was as close to me as my mouth, would I see it?

Once upon a time, this story begins as all good stories do, there was a young man heading in the wrong direction. The right direction was as close to him as his mouth. Did he know it? No.

The year: 629 B. C.

The young man: Jeremiah.

God unveils to him: "You are my prophet."

You may find this surprising, but Jeremiah's words took him in the wrong direction. Look at his answer:

"Ah, Lord God! behold, I cannot speak: for I am a child."

Many believe that speech simply mirrors the true inner person, but God takes a different approach: when I change his words, his heart will follow.

God rebukes him sharply, "Do not say you are a child!"

(When God spoke to Jeremiah *[Jeremiah 1:5]*, He spoke to him exactly as He speaks to you and me today, through what He has written. Jeremiah says, "Your words were found, and I did eat them; and Your word was to me the joy and rejoicing of my heart: for I am called by Your name, O Lord God of hosts." *[Jeremiah 15:16]*)

Jeremiah's earth-shaking insight was as close to him as his mouth. God almost shouts, "You are saying the wrong words! We'll never get anything done with you saying you are a child. Your life will never rise above the words of your mouth. If I can get you to change your words, it will cause you to change your life. You will have to exchange your human words for my words. Begin to say what I say."

As Jeremiah meditated on the newly found book of the law *(2 Chronicles 34:14)*, he said, "Then the Lord put forth his hand, and touched my mouth. And the Lord said to me, 'Behold, I have put my words in your mouth.'" *(Jeremiah 1:9)*

When I begin to say what God says I have a break-through into the earth-shaking insight Jeremiah experienced. Follow this closely: Christ said that all power in heaven and in earth was given to him *(Matthew 28:18)*. God's words go on to explain that as a Christian, I have God's nature, I am an heir; and a joint-heir with Christ *(Romans 8:17)*. "Power" can also be translated "authority."

Seeing I have been given God's nature, and I inherit what belongs to the Lord Jesus Christ, then it follows that the authority given to Christ has also been given to me. I only say about myself what God says when I say, "In the Lord Jesus Christ I have been given authority over every situation and circumstance of my life."

Mary

The town of Nazareth didn't get much respect. One man asked, Can anything good come out of Nazareth? Most of the Jews lived a three day walk to the south, in the land of Judah. Nazareth was a mish-mash of cultures and peoples, a squalid village with a handful of holding-on Jews. Among them was a maiden named Mary.

A double knock brought Mary to the door.

"Rabbi Joas, won't you come in?" He bowed in reply.

With a drink in hand he laid back with a mischievous smile.

"I have news for my Princess." It was his pet name for a girl he loved as a daughter. Mary waited with her hands folded in her apron. She knew he wanted to savor the moment.

"A traveler stopped at the synagogue this morning and inquired about you."

"Who would want to see me?"

"I have no idea, my dear." He could see that his Princess was nervous. "He has an aristocratic bearing. Maybe he's a nobleman. He doesn't fit in with the riff-raff we have here."

"He gave you no clue as to why he was here?"

"None whatsoever. He would like to meet with you in my office."

Mary learned little more in their two-block walk to the synagogue. Apprehension crept in like the coolness of the morning. Does the Rabbi think I'm too scared? Tough-willed, she pictured her forefather Abraham. What a man! He left no room for fear. When God said something, as far as he was concerned, that was the end of the matter.

Sacred memories crowded Mary's mind as she crossed the threshold of the synagogue. "I'll introduce you and leave."

"I'll be fine," Mary assured him.

After introductions Mary sized up the traveler. Could he be here about her impending wedding? What about a business franchise? A strong masculine laugh stopped the thoughts scurrying about her mind.

"Here we stand!" Again he laughed at his thoughtlessness. "Please be seated." He gestured with open palm toward a chair.

"So you are Mary." She could see he knew much more than his simple repetition implied.

"Yes."

"You're planning marriage?"

"That's right."

"You and Joseph are descendants of David?"

"True. That goes back a long time." Mary played along with the small talk. It gave them a chance to set up a rapport. "David lived over a thousand years ago."

"Now that we're acquainted we should cross a bridge."

"You know who I am," countered Mary, "but you haven't told me who you are."

"You're forthright. That's good. Now for the bridge I mentioned." His paused signaled an announcement. "First of all … " He weighed his words. He stood up and walked to a window. "First of all … " he turned and locked eyes with Mary. " … I'm not a human being."

Mary sprang to her feet. "You … you are not a human being?!" Her mouth was open. She covered her face with her hands to hide from this moment. Am I with some nut? Should I run? Her mind skipped back and forth. After all, he has garnered my respect. His voice brought her back to the Rabbi's study.

Mary

"I am an archangel whose task is to bring good news. My name is Gabriel, and God has sent me to talk with you."

Mary's eyes were riveted on the man before her. "This doesn't add up. If God wants to talk to someone, why not talk to the Rabbi, or to someone special? Why me?"

"Rejoice, Mary, God has specifically chosen you, and He will provide you with the needed enduement. As you know, God loves every person very much."

"All of us know that."

"This love has moved Him to offer everyone redemption from sin and reconciliation to Him.

"To do this He would have to come to earth."

Mary wondered if she was in a dream. Minutes ago I was doing my laundry. Now this man talks about what God has on His mind. "I believe you speak the truth so I don't need a sign of some kind to validate it. I have waited with everyone else for the promised messiah." Mary pondered her words. Am I too quick to say what I think? I feel like a spectator to all of this.

"I still don't see my role?"

"I'm coming to that. I told you I had bridges for you to cross. You believed me, now you come to the second bridge."

"Go on."

"Here's a good question for you, Mary: How is God going to enter the world?"

"I'm sure He has that figured out."

"Well … " Gabriel raised his brow in speculation, "He could appear just like I have…as a man. Or, He might choose to present Himself as a teenager. Or He could say, I wish to be seen as a wise old man."

"I find this speculation interesting."

"Mary," again Gabriel walked to the window, "He's not coming here as any of those." He turned to face Mary. "He will make

His appearance as a baby."

"As a baby!"

"Yes, as a baby, and this is where you come into the picture." Mary stood up. "Me ... ?"

"That's true. You. God would take up residence in you by the Holy Spirit, and God would be born as a baby."

Mary's knees buckled. She staggered back into her chair. The blood drained from her face. With her hands over the back of her head she buried her face in her lap. Through her weeping Gabriel heard the simple request, "Can I go home?"

"Rabbi ... Rabbi," Gabriel called out, "would you please take Mary home?" Head lowered, supported by her bewildered Rabbi Joas, Mary stumbled home.

Mary sat motionless as the noon hour passed. Of all the women in the world, why me? Just think, the one who created all of this will reveal Himself through me! I'm not married. What will Joseph say? What about my friends and relatives? It boils down to this: do I say what people say about my life, or do I say what God says about my life? Shame or no shame I know I want to say what God says about my life.

A soft knock on the door ended Mary's preoccupation.

"How ya doin', Princess?" Rabbi Joas entered. "Did you get any lunch?"

"I wasn't hungry, Rabbi." Mary thought of the Rabbi's courage. How he stood up against the rabble of Nazareth.

"The gentleman's back in my office. Be sure to let me know if I can help in any way."

Bravely she sat in the Rabbi's office. Many women would have said, "Your words are so preposterous that they have to be a lie. Ha, Ha. Why would God come to earth as a baby? Utter nonsense! God has shown us who He is through His prophets. Gabriel, you're an ordinary man. You're trying to rip these people off."

"I knew you would be back." His voice exposed the joy that was in his heart. "I'm sure you have some questions."

"Please tell me again how I would have this baby?"

"You would receive the seed of God through the work of the Holy Spirit. Because of sin you would not conceive the child through the seed of man. He shall be known as the Son of God. You shall name Him Jesus. He will be great, and He will be called the Son of the Most High."

"If I have a baby while I am engaged to Joseph, he could rightfully have me put to death! It's written in our laws."

"You're right. That's true." Moment slipped by. "I'll have a man to man talk with Joseph." Assured Gabriel, "he'll come around to see things from God's point of view."

"You have a big job ahead of you," cautioned Mary, "even his mother says he can be pretty bullheaded."

"God works majestically." Gabriel sees an opportunity to strengthen Mary's faith. "Look at your cousin Elisabeth."

"She comes from the line of Aaron, a priestly family." Mary had become chatty with Gabriel.

"She, too, has conceived as a middle aged woman."

"Wonderful news!" cried out a surprised Mary. "Contentious acquaintances would kid her about being 'sterile' or call her 'the barren one'. In her long wait she reminds me of Sarah, the wife of Abraham."

"You should visit Elisabeth," suggested Gabriel.

"Good idea! We'll share with one another that we embrace the Words you have brought. I'll tell her I know it will happen in my life exactly as God said it would!"

Prayer

The apostle Paul encourages you and me to take the sword the Spirit wields, which is the Word of God, and pray on every occasion by means of the Spirit. *(Ephesians 6:17 and 18)*

Two truths: The Sword which the Holy Spirit uses in prayer is the Word of God — the Bible, and he who prays should do so through the Person of the Holy Spirit.

One could ask, "How do I pray the Bible?" And, secondly, "How do I know I pray through the Person of the Holy Spirit?"

To answer these questions we'll use a simple illustration. Your friend Ted has landed in the hospital with a medical need, and you feel led to pray for him. You say to yourself, "I recall the words of the apostle Paul. First, I want to pray what God says in His Word. And, second, I want the surety that I pray through the Person of the Holy Spirit."

You know from Ted's testimony that he is a believer, so you feel you are working with the harmony of the Holy Spirit. You also understand from Ted's personality that he could feel abandoned. This feeling, that of being forsaken, is what you pray for.

You know the need in your friend — a sense of helplessness — so this is the need your prayer meets. "And I am told," you say to yourself, "I am to pray what God says in His Word." After you look at several verses you came across Hebrews 13:5. This says, "I will not, I will not, I will not leave you." That's it. Perfect. Just what Ted needs. A sense of the constant presence of the Lord Jesus Christ in his life. So you have resolved the first of two considerations — the need to use the Sword of the Spirit, the

Word of God.

Now, for the second encouragement, Paul says I should pray in the Holy Spirit. You ask yourself, "How can I pray this verse for Ted and know I am praying in the Person of the Holy Spirit?" Jesus said His words are spiritual words *(John 6:63),* so when you pray your verse for Ted you are praying in the Person of the Holy Spirit. So you have used the Sword of the Spirit in your use of the Bible, and you have prayed in the Holy Spirit by using the Spirit filled Words of the Bible.

So your prayer should go like this: "Father, I enter your presence with your Word in my hands. You know more than I do that Ted can feel alone, so I come with the knowledge that Jesus will not, will not, will not leave him, and he will be given an awareness of His constant presence. Thank you, Father that you always do what you say you will do *(Isaiah 46:11).* Amen."

You have used the Sword of the Spirit in this prayer when you prayed Hebrews 13:5 for Ted. But you counter, "Was I praying in the Holy Spirit?" And the answer to that is, "Yes, you were praying in the Spirit when you used His Words. You prayed over Ted what the Father had already said." You rise up from that brief prayer with the certainty Ted received what the Father has guaranteed.

One reader says, "I have problems with the phrase 'praying in the spirit'."

"How is that?" I ask.

"I guess I always associated it with something weird. Something mysterious, an out-of-the-world experience."

In response to this labored view, I suggest we look at 1 Corinthians 3 where we understand that the carnal Christian seeks to verify spiritual truth with his physical senses.

You ask, "As I prayed for Ted I used the verse in the Bible. I understand I prayed in the Spirit, but where does faith come into

Insights

play?" The verse in the Bible provides the answer. Hebrews 13:5 is impregnated with God's faithfulness or faith. Not only does the verse possess the presence of the Holy Spirit, but it also has the substance of the unfailing presence of the Lord Jesus Christ. You receive your faith for Ted from this verse.

You tell me you have found out that Ted has an inflamed appendix, and he is scheduled for surgery. You want to add healing to your first request. In other words, just as there was a verse for the unfailing presence of Christ, is there such a verse for healing?

Yes, there are verses for healing that you can embrace for Ted.
> By His wounds you have been healed *(1 Peter 2:2)*.
> He Himself carried away our infirmities and diseases *(Matthew 8:17)*.

Your prayer based on these verses would go like this: "Father, again I come with Ted. Your Word tells me that through the wounds of the Lord Jesus Christ Ted has received healing. I understand Jesus has carried away his sickness. You always do what You say You will do. I pray in thankfulness in the name of the Lord Jesus Christ. Amen."

You have prayed what God says about Ted's impending surgery, but you ask this question: "How often do I pray this prayer?" Seeing you have prayed the prayer once, there is no need to pray the prayer again. If you pray the prayer a second time you say that the first prayer was not heard. In other words, you failed to receive the faithfulness the two verses gave. If you pray the prayer a second time you also say that it is through your 'works' you will receive grace — you have not set aside the substance of faith.

At this point you ask, "You used two verses for healing. How did you find them?" You go on, "In the dozens of subjects I could pray, how do I find the verse that will answer my request?"

The happiest way to discover the verse is through reading the Bible. A friend may be helpful. If you have a key word for the request, such as you do in 'sickness,' you can look up your subject in a concordance.

Have the kind of faith God has. "For speak the truth in Him. I say that whoever says to this mountain, uproot yourself and throw yourself into the sea, who has no doubt in his heart, but believes that what He speaks shall come to pass, he shall have whatever he speaks." As a result I have this to add. "Whatever you desire when you pray, believe you have received them. And you shall have them." *(Mark 11:21-24)*

Jesus encourages you and me in the verses above to practice the kind of faith God practices. He goes on to explain the kind of faith God used. Moving a Mountain: God believes in taking on the unbelievable. Notice: the mountain (not you and I) moves itself, and this is accomplished by the faith filled words of the believer.

In the last part of the quotation Jesus turns to the subject of prayer. Believe you have already received what you have prayed for and you shall have your requests. When you and I pray the Word, we have the guarantee of the Holy Spirit that we have already been given what we requested. So as we rise up from prayer we are filled with thankfulness and praise.

Now this question comes up: Did you receive in your spirit what you prayed for?

"I have to wait and see."

"Of course, I have to wait and see," answer one reader.

"In other words," I reply, "you want to verify the validity of your prayer with your physical senses. You did not pray in the Spirit so the words of your prayer fell lifeless to the ground."

Let's go back to the earlier picture of your friend Ted in the hospital. The first thing you prayed for was that Ted would enjoy the presence of the Lord Jesus Christ. You'll receive. We based this request on Hebrews 13:5. From our study in Mark 11 above you

Insights

can say, "I know I have received that for which I prayed," or, "I know Ted enjoys the awareness of the presence of the Lord."

"And you prayed for Ted's healing ," so you say. "In Your word, Father, You assure me You heal, and I have brought this assurance for Ted. I have received healing on Ted's behalf. I understand from the teaching of Jesus, that I order the mountain to throw itself into the sea. So, in kind, I order the sickness in Ted's life to leave his body. In my spirit I see this as being done by the Person of the Holy Spirit."

And God said, "Let there be light and there was light" *(Genesis 1:3)*. God created with Words. Nothing was done until He spoke. Not only has He created words, but He has impregnated His Words with divine power. When you and I look at the Father's faith we always come away with His Words. So we return to Mark 11:22, where Jesus commands, "Practice the God-kind of faith." So what kind of faith is that? Words. I say what He says about my need.

As you read these insights into effectual prayer I ask you to be patient with yourself. I remember with daylight clarity that I did not learn these truths overnight. At first I saw Biblical prayer like a distant city, but with studied travel I found myself in the city.

To whom will He teach knowledge?

And, to whom will He make to understand the message? Those who are babies, just weaned from the milk and taken from the breasts.

"But the Word of the Lord was unto them precept upon precept, precept upon precept, line upon line, line upon line, here a little, and there a little." *(Isaiah 20:9,13)*

After his conversion, Paul the apostle spent three years in Arabia. He studied every detail of the life of Christ. He later writes that faith came by hearing…and hearing…and hearing (literal from original Greek language) the word about Christ *(Romans*

10:17). Paul spoke from experience. He understood a physical seed or a spiritual seed takes time to develop.

Centurion

I called her "the pioneer lady." She wore long dresses and walked with the stride of one going someplace. As neighbors we would meet on walks and chat in passing. Her approach was utterly single minded, coupled with a robust common sense.

Her candidness prompted me one day to ask, "When you look at the word faith; what does it mean to you?"

"You know, Norman," she did not hesitate in her childlike openness, "there's a story in the Bible about a Roman soldier. He had a servant boy who was very sick, and he asked Jesus to heal him."

"I remember the story."

"This is where faith comes in," she went on. "The soldier told Jesus all he had to do was say 'you are healed' and the boy would be healed. That soldier had faith."

I found Melanie's answer insightful. I knew she had not invented her answer on her own, but it prompted me to look again at the story in the Bible. Who was this unusual soldier? To create a living person we'll call him Augustus.

Augustus was a captain in the Roman army, a career soldier, prominent in Capernaum and wealthy. He built the synagogue with his own money. When he walked down the street in his distinctive uniform, he conveyed an unmistakable aura of power that inspired not only respect, but awe and obedience. I am sure his troops monitored the surging throng that followed Jesus.

You could ask, "Where did Augustus learn about the power of words?" He answers this himself: "I know something about word commands. I live with them every day. For example: I say to a soldier, 'Go,' and he goes at once. Or, I might say to another soldier, 'Come,' and he comes at once. Or I might say to a servant, 'Do this,' and immediately he does it. My words are always converted into action." Soldiers and servants jumped to obey him because of his authority, but when it came to sickness and death he stood helpless and he knew it.

His servant boy, whom he loved as a son, had unexpectedly become seriously ill so that he was paralyzed and near death.

"What am I going to do?" muttered the captain as he glanced at the inert boy. "My own army doctors tell me he'll be dead in a matter of hours."

"I know this sounds ridiculous, Sir," his lieutenant spoke up. "There is a healer, a Jewish man; he's an itinerant preacher, huge crowds. He's been healing people."

"Good. Bring some Jewish elders in, I'll see if they can talk to this man."

"My servant boy is near death," spoke the captain to the Jewish elders. "My staff has told me of a Jewish man who heals people. Can you persuade Him to come and heal my servant?"

"Captain, we'll talk to Him, but we can't give you much hope. We have no say over this Man called Jesus."

"Do something. Do anything. He is my last hope."

As expected, the Jewish elders found Jesus busy with the crowds.

"We beg of you," interrupted one elder, "that you do this for a special man. He built our synagogue. He loves our nation. He's a good man, a compassionate man."

"Did the Jewish elders speak to him?" Augustus was running out of time.

"I'm sure they did for the crowds are moving this way."

"I've changed my mind, Lieutenant. I'm going to scrap my

plan."

"You're *what?*" exclaimed the surprised lieutenant.

"I feel ashamed of myself. I'm not worthy of His care, Lieutenant. Take some men and go and tell Him that."

"I know. I know. Who am I to him? I am not worthy for Him to enter my home. Why should He allow me to stand in his presence? You could think of me as vacillating, Lieutenant, but I must speak from the heart."

"Yes, Sir. I'll tell him what you said."

"Oh! One more thing. I know this sounds crazy but tell Him this. From what I have heard, all He has to do is give the command and Jason will be healed."

"I don't get it. Would you repeat that, Sir?"

"If He simply says, 'be healed,' Jason will be healed."

"Yes, Sir, I'll tell him exactly what you said." Augustus could have asked Jesus to pray for the boy. He could have asked Jesus to send a disciple to pray for him.

"I have an idea," suggested one of Jewish leaders. "Our community could administer last rites for the lad."

In Jesus' encampment, a short distance away, a different story played out.

"This soldier surprises me, on the message brought by the lieutenant. Your captain sees the boy healed by my simple command. Great faith. Yes. Great faith. And, just think. He's a stranger. He's a Roman. I look at my own nation — Israel. No. I have not found in all Israel such great faith."

The lieutenant returned from his mission to see Jesus. Augustus met him at the door.

"He's completely healed! Completely healed," shouted Augustus in joy. "Look at him: Jason's running with his friends as though he had never been sick."

"Tell me about the preacher. Can Jason visit him?" He whirled to face the lieutenant.

"Crowds engulf him. I don't know. I'm bewildered. What happened here?" admitted the lieutenant.

"He healed by simple command, Augustus. This I know you had told me this. What He spoke had supernatural power."

"Amazing."

"In my heart I know that, and I had to tell him that."

Already Prepared

There is no need to ask for something that has already been given to you. You simply thank Him.

"God is not a chef! A lot of people think He is. They think their order goes to the divine kitchen. Then God whips it up. He hustles about the kitchen making it up. 'Comin' right up!' He hollers. No. No. No. That's not the way it is." The speaker laughed.

He went on. "Some of us think that God owns a factory outside of town. Here, orders are made up by angel workers. When you and I pray, the machines start humming. There, God fashions an answer to our prayer. Like I've already said, this is not the way God works."

The speaker on the platform was in his twenties. His dress was casual. Sylvia had read about these meetings in the newspaper. "Free seminar on faith. Thursday through Saturday. Non-denominational. At the auditorium. All welcome."

"The point I'm making is this," the speaker went on, "Everything, and I mean everything, for the Christian life has already been made. Not only has it already been made, but it stands ready and waiting for you and me to use. The Bible makes this 20/20 clear in many passages."

With Bible and pad in hand Sylvia had chosen to attend this Saturday morning meeting. She had no inkling of the far-reaching consequence of the moment. However, she had learned that

Already Prepared

Camelot moments do happen in the Christian life. Her friend, Peg, had called them "experiences of the heart." I think I have an open mind, Sylvia confided, so these thoughts went tippy-toe through her mind. Who knows, maybe this morning will be like an open window — a time when my whole world looks differently. A Camelot spot.

She jotted down — "Everything for Christian life has already been made." A whispered "hmm" passed over her lips. She reflected on the power in her own Christian Life. If the truth were spoken she would have to admit she did not enjoy success in her own prayer life, but the speaker says the answer to my prayer has already been made. I don't get it.

The young man interrupted Sylvia's reflections, "God has a Storehouse. This is true. It's like a giant Warehouse." Some in the crowd chuckled. "In this Storehouse or Warehouse He has everything needed for the Christian life. The answer for loneliness. Grief. Healing. Wisdom. Knowledge. You name it. It is already made and ready to be shipped out. Does it sound too simple? Faith is simple. All you have to know is the law of faith."

Fifteen months had gone by since "D-day." She smiled warmly to herself. She called her Fairgrounds experience "D-day." Here's what had happened. She had dropped in to the chapel at the Fairgrounds. A woman greeted her, and they chatted.

Her recollection was broken, "You and I have learn to use the Warehouse."

Vividly she recalled the woman at the Fair. It wasn't so much of her features, it was what she said: "The Father always does what He says He will do," I'll never forget that as long as I live. It was written in big print on her mind. "The Father will always do what He says He will do." So indelible, it was like yesterday. A Camelot moment.

"What do I mean, God has a Storehouse?" He let the question

sink in. "Let me say this: it is a place of abundance and wealth. You could even call it the Treasury of God."

Sylvia returned to her reverie.

The Father always does what He says He will do. She had seen His Word in a new light. She was lifted out of the swamps of doubt. It's amazing, she mused, ten little Words can throw open the window of my life. She had told Peg, "My eyesight has been changed."

"How's that?" asked Peg.

Sylvia answered. "When I read His Word about His presence in my Life, I see this as something that's real, something factual."

The speaker was quiet. Sylvia waited. He cast about his mind how to make this pivotal point clear.

Sylvia guessed to herself as to where he was going. He is going to tell us the Storehouse or Treasury of God is the Bible. In the past fifteen months she had become a confirmed student of the Bible. She preferred to call it "the Word of God." It has been a Camelot time, she liked to say.

Sylvia was right. "As many of you have guessed, God's Storehouse is the Bible." admitted the speaker. We chuckled. "Call it what you will, a Treasury. A Warehouse. Whatever makes sense. So let's turn to this Treasury. *(John 3:16)*. What does God guarantee?"

"Life! Life eternal!" The crowd shouted answers. They were wide awake.

"That's right. Life eternal and abundant life here on earth. But let me ask you this: Is this something God has to prepare, or is it already made?"

"It's already made," mouthed Sylvia. "I know it's not something God has to prepare."

Sure enough, the speaker confirmed her thoughts.

"No, God is not a chef, the life He gives in John 3:16 is something God has prepared for the believer. It comes out of His Treasury of prepared things. Here's the clincher: Accessibility. If I see something sits in His Warehouse — already made — it has great accessibility. It's like someone handing you something. Here, take this. It's called grace."

What a change, thought Sylvia, this would make in her prayer life. I could stop begging for things. I could quit waiting. I know I have received, I know if I put my prayer under a microscope I would always be shouting, "I have received! I have received!" That's how I would see it.

"Now," the young man went on, "you have believed in a promise. You see it as already made and ready to take! You have used God's great accessibility. Your faith shouts, 'It's in my life! I have eternal life.'"

"Let us move on from the receiving of eternal life to the needs in the believer's daily life. The Word says you and I go from faith to faith, so we go from the faith of receiving life — eternal life — to the faith for living our new life."

He paused, "Has your answer to your prayer come into view? Has your answer shown itself in your life? Has it manifested itself? Here's where your faith fights the good fight of faith."

"Look at this way. I know I have received what I prayed about, but it hasn't made its appearance in my life."

Sylvia asks herself, "Well, how long would that take?"

As though he knew her thoughts, the speaker went on. "It may not come into view for days. Maybe weeks. There are those who have waited for years to realized their promise."

"I think of one young lady," reiterated the speaker, "year after year she testified she had been healed. Obviously from her appearance she had not been healed. Her faith spoke, not her sight. Finally she said in prayer, 'heal me as a blessing for those who walk by sight.' The next morning she awoke — healed."

Sylvia's mind drifted back — He'll always do what He says He'll do. If I fail to see an answer to my prayer, it doesn't mean it isn't there. I keep my eyes on the promise. The answer — prepared — is there, the answer simply hasn't shown itself. Like the lady in the story, I'm not walking by sight. He'll always keep His Word, whether it is now or later.

"A lady asked me a question this morning I would like to answer," the speaker went on. "She said she has loved one who is coming to visit her. She'll be driving in from one hundred miles out. Now here's the question; how do I pray her?"

The lady's question continued. "If I say I know she will arrive safely, I feel like I'm taking something for granted."

"If she said," enlarged the speaker, "bring her safely here 'if it be thy will.' If she prayed that phrase, obviously she has no clue to the will or mind of God."

"To reiterate, she has a friend or loved one driving to see her. She wants to support this one in prayer. More precisely, she wants the joy of knowing her prayer is filled with faith."

The young speaker paused. A smile crossed his face. Sylvia knew he savored the moment. He was going to answer: "How can I pray in faith for someone on the highway?"

"Turn to the Treasury. Turn to the Warehouse. You and I know," he went on, "the Lord loves that person. It says so in His Word. God has also decreed He will never leave this one. He also has given that person wisdom."

"Do you see where I'm going? To enjoy faith for the traveling loved one, I have to say about her what the Word says about her. Then my faith has the foundation — the backing — it requires."

As Sylvia listened she knew she had a truth she could take home. Again she mused, He has already made what I pray for. A take-home point we all were waiting for.

The meeting came to an end and the auditorium filled with the buzzing of talk. Sylvia remained seated. She tried to mentally digest what the speaker had said. She mused, "Everything for the Christian life has already been made." She chuckled to herself at the thought — God is not a chef. Sylvia glanced about. Most of the crowd had left. Soon she would step out into the sunlight of Saturday morning, and into a new sunlight in her own spiritual life.

God Looks on the Heart

How do you see Jesus? Do you picture Him as many artists do? They see Him as a man raising His right arm and saying "Peace." He stands aloof from life. He's distant. Not engaged. He looks more like a renaissance monk. The Bible paints a different picture. His actions say:

I'm here to have you face the facts.

I'll demonstrate love to you.

I'll unveil for you the nature of God.

What did He look like? The Bible is silent on this question. Why? Mankind looks on the outer appearance. God the Father looks on the inner man — the heart. Character defines the man. To see Jesus you and I have to look at what He did. You and I see Him through words and deeds.

At the age of twelve Jesus traveled to Jerusalem with His family. On the return trip to Nazareth His parents could not find Him. Three days were spent looking for Him. The distraught parents discovered Him with the scholars in the temple. He listened to them and sought answer to His questions. Jesus explained His absence with these words, "I must be about my Father's business." As the oldest of seven children we see a determined boy. He was conscious of Who He was, the Son of God with divine power.

I again see Him as a man in the Temple. He looks about: money changers, cattle dealers, stalls of business.

What are these commercial people doing in the Temple? Don't they know this is a house of worship?

He fashions a whip and drives the defilers from the Temple.

He had to be a Man of great physical strength as well as undisputable authority. He crossed the Sea of Galilee one day to face the feared Gadarene demoniac — a wild man who lived in the tombs. Everyone stayed clear of him. He fell on his knees before Jesus. He spoke to a storm at sea and it abated. He faced the specter of death and ordered Lazarus to come out of his tomb.

Many said, "He does what others are afraid to do."

He tackled hypocrisy. I think of the night He sat on the Mount of Olives and talked intimately with His disciples.

"I want you to be very careful that no man deceives you." He knew Satan was a master counterfeiter. Satan loved the word "illusion" — to believe in something which is not true. So the target of this master deceptionist became the Bible. Here's what the devil said:

"If I can get people to think they know the truth, when they don't, then I've won the battle."

The Scribes and Pharisees in Jerusalem — the Sanhedrin — were the leading hypocrites.

They shouted, "We are guardians of the truth. History is on our side. Tradition is on our side. After all, aren't we in power? We have the inside track."

A long chapter in the book of Matthew *(Matthew 23)* details Jesus' expose of the Sanhedrin. It pictures Him as a warrior against false beliefs. He saw behind their charade. He paraded them as blatant hypocrites. He warns His disciples and the multitudes,

> These men lived in the make-believe work of pretending to be something they are not. They are not what you see. They are fakes.

Jesus' great indictment *(Matthew 23)* against hypocrisy came in the last week of His life on earth.

> You claim to be that which you are not.
> You love to be called, Rabbi. Rabbi.

Insights

You parade long prayers. All the while you steal the houses of widows.

You fight for converts you can indoctrinate.

You obliterate the spiritual world with your reverence for material things.

Sure you pay a tithe, but you leave out love.

You want the world to applaud your cleanliness. Inwardly, you are filthy.

You are white washed tombs.

Inside is death.

You are descendants of those who murdered the prophets, how can you escape the damnation of hell? *(Matthew 23:33)* Much talk is made of life after death in the Bible. Four words in the New Testament describe hell: "sheol," the unseen state; "hades," the unseen world. "gehanna," the valley of Hinnom (a burial ground); and, "tartarus," to cast down. The great judgment of hell lies in eternal separation from the Lord Jesus Christ.

Some will say they have eternal life because of their Church membership. Another declares, I'm going to heaven because I was baptized. Thousands affirm, I'm going to heaven because I have lived a good life, I've earned it.

> "Man believes with his heart and becomes right with God, and with his lips he openly testifies to his salvation." *(Romans 10:10 literal)*

I Act on What God Says

Jairus threw himself at the feet of Jesus. His daughter had died. He had heard the Master preach in his synagogue in Capernaum. Would he "act" on what he had heard, while surrounded by unbelief?

"She's gone!" The teary-eyed doctor spoke with the only voice he could muster.

"You can talk louder," spoke up Jairus. "My wife has to know about her only daughter."

Fever like a forest fire had swept through the body of Ariel.

"How can I stop something that hit her so fast?" Dr. Immer unveiled his helplessness. "What was it? Three days?"

"She could run like a gazelle." Tears rolled down the cheeks of Michelle, Jairus' wife. "I can't believe it." She glanced out the window to a world teeming with life. "Only twelve. Everything to live for."

Death took the role of fellow traveler for Jairus. He had buried many as the ruler of the synagogue in Capernaum. Now he and Michelle journeyed for themselves in the dark country of mind-numbing grief and permanent loss. It was killing to look at the mother of their daughter and to know her laughter was gone forever.

"I can't say good-by." Jairus refused to accept Ariel's departure. Searching for an answer, he scarcely heard the doctor slip out.

"Michelle ..." Jairus broke the silence.

"Yes."

"There is hope." He paused before his pronouncement. "You remember the itinerant preacher who taught in my synagogue?"

185

"Of course."

"There wasn't anything He couldn't do. I know He has the power to make Ariel live."

"We're asking the impossible," the mother observed.

"He arrived this morning from the opposite side of the lake. I can ask Him to see Ariel. There are those who will ask; why is the ruler of the synagogue seeing this Man? I'll tell you, Michelle. Who am I? My daughter is gone. I am less than Nachim the beggar."

Jairus found Jesus at the fishing docks besieged by a large crowd.

"I have to see the Master. I have to see the Master."

Heart wrenching hurt threw him at the feet of Jesus. "I beg of you. I beg of you, Master." Jesus knew the powerful man kneeling before Him with clasped hands. "Ariel has died. There isn't anything you can't do. You can bring her back to life."

"Let's go." Jesus quickly followed Jairus, but frequent interruptions brought the retinue to a stop.

News of Ariel's death brought a crowd of relatives and friends to the home of Jairus.

"Where's Jairus? The mourning has to get under way."

"He's with the Master." Michelle spoke up. "He left two hours ago."

"He's got to be kidding!"

"He belongs here!"

Several left to find Jairus. When they found him they lashed into him.

"You shouldn't bother this Man. Ariel's been dead for several hours. There's nothing He can do."

"Don't listen to them." Jesus interceded. "Do you believe?"

"Absolutely!" Jairus was emphatic.

"That's all that's necessary."

I Act on What God Says

"I have to see this!" A man in the crowd laughed. "She's already dead!"

At the home of Jairus the mourning had reached a crescendo. Weeping, wailing, and doleful instruments created a pitiful lament.

"She's sleeping!" called out Jesus. "She's not dead."

Jeers and catcalls drowned Him out. "You gotta be out of your mind!" A wall of scorn cried out, "She's dead! Any dummy can see that!"

"Out! Out! Out!" Jesus ejected all the scoffers from the house. He knew they would prevent the mighty work He intended to do.

"Come, Jairus. You too Michelle, Peter, James, John … come along."

In hushed reverence they entered the room where the girl lay. Michelle cupped her hands over her mouth as Jesus took Ariel by the hands. A moment of silence passed, then Jesus commanded, "Maiden, arise!"

Immediately she sat up. She looked into the face of Jesus. "What's going on? Have I been in a dream?"

"Hallelujah!" slipped past the lips of Jairus.

"She'll need something to eat." Jesus spoke to Michelle as she walked her daughter around the room.

Jesus sowed four words into the heart of Jairus: "I can do this … " and Jairus saw his daughter raised from the dead.

See Matthew 9:18-34; Mark 5:21-43; Luke 8:40-56.

Tear Up the Roof

"I act on what the God says."
 Background: Many idolized Jesus for healing, but He knew His message was why He had come. So for several weeks He left Capernaum to preach in the towns and villages of Galilee. At this time, He had five disciples: Peter, Andrew, James, John and Philip, but he chose a sixth, Matthew. Being a rich man he threw a banquet to honor the return of Jesus. Religious leaders had come from great distances to "check out" this Man who was creating such a furor. When they saw Jesus eating with sinners at Matthew's banquet, they criticized Jesus for hobnobbing with sinners. Jesus replied that these were the ones who saw their need to repent.

Our scene opens in a modest home in Capernaum. A young man, Benjamin, pounds on the door of his friend.

"What!? What!? What!?" Sam flung open the door with agitation.

"What's all the ruckus about, Ben, with all that banging?"

"Haven't you heard?" Ben said breathlessly.

"Heard what?"

"He's back."

"Who's back?" Sam was impatient.

"Jesus, its Jesus, the Master."

Both young men immediately thought of their friend Danny. Together they had enjoyed their adolescent years, but Danny became paralyzed.

"There's no way he can get himself to see Jesus," stated Ben,

Tear Up the Roof

"it's up to us."

"Where is the Master staying?" asked Sam.

"At Peter's place."

"Let's put him on a cart and wheel him over there. We'd only hurt him if we tried to carry him that far."

"Let's go for it."

"We've come for Danny," Ben announced to the startled Mom.

"You've what?!" she cried out.

"Yeah! We've come for Danny. He's at Peter's house. If we can get Danny there the Master will heal him."

"You're wonderful; I know what Danny means to you ... " a tear formed in her eye. "He's so helpless, I don't want him hurt."

"We'll put him on a cart," protested the two.

"His two brothers are due back from fishing, you need more help."

Sam glanced down the street. "Wait, wait." He knew he and Ben could use their help. "I see them coming; yes, that's them."

With the help of Danny's brothers they loaded Danny on to the cart and set out for Peter's home. The anxious mother watched from the doorway as she saw the apprehension in Danny's eyes.

"You guys are something else!" grinned Danny as he flashed a confident smile but his eyes were like a frightened doe.

But the scene that greeted them at Peter's house wiped all hope from their faces.

"Oh no," cried one of Danny's brothers, "You can't get close to the house. There must be a thousand people mobbing the place."

As they eyed the brick wall of a crowd, it was Ben who spoke up, "Comin' through! Comin' through."

The crowd parted reluctantly to the four young men with a man on a litter. "Comin' through! Comin' through."

They met their match at the entrance to the house. "Oh! No, there's no place for the gawkers to go."

"And we were so close," lamented Sam above the hecklers.

The four good Samaritans appeared to have had their dream, to see Jesus, bashed.

"I'm glad Mom's not here to see this," whispered Danny under his breath.

"The stairs!" cried Ben, "get to the stairs!" They muscled their way to the outside stairway.

"Watcha doin?! Watcha doin?!" cried an irate bystander. "He's not on the roof! He's in the house!"

"Excuse me! Excuse me! We're going up those stairs. Stand back!" Onlookers gasped as the four staggered stair by stair with their burden.

"Now that you're up here," taunted an incensed man, "watcha goin' to do?"

"Take up the roof" ordered Ben. "Take up the roof!"

Tile after tile came up as Danny lay helplessly to the side.

"That's good! That's good! We can get him down through that," cried one of the brothers. "You go down first Ben, to catch Danny."

"Comin down! Comin down!" Ben dropped to the floor of the house. "Let down Danny!" he cried.

With arms that had hauled in many fishing nets they gingerly lowered Danny to Ben's waiting arms.

Startled spectators scrambled out of the way of the madcap scramble. As the tumult subsided Jesus looked at Danny and his friends. An expectant hush gripped the room as everyone fastened their eyes on Jesus.

"What will he do?" one woman put her hand over her mouth. "Will He heal this paralytic intruder? Will he order him out of the house?" You could hear a pin drop.

"Son," Jesus broke the silence, "because of the faith of you and your friends your sins are forgiven and you are pardoned."

INSIGHT

Jewish leaders from far and wide had become concerned with the sweeping popularity of Jesus. Who is He? Who does He think He is? Is He a threat? Will He give us problems with Rome?

When Jesus tells Danny that his sins are pardoned and forgiven they fly into a rage.

One Pharisee shouts, "You can't forgive sins. You are a blasphemer! Only God can forgive sins. You can't claim what belongs to God."

Jesus saw into their hearts and asked, "Why do you think evil and harbor malice in your hearts?"

Ben turned to Sam with frustration, "I wish the Pharisees had stayed out of this. Now Danny isn't healed."

Jesus saw their impatience, but He wanted to use this opportunity to proclaim His duty to these men so steeped in tradition.

Jesus faced these men of self-importance. "Let me ask you a question: Which is easier to say: Your sins are forgiven, or, Get up and walk?" (The answer: It is easier to heal than it is to forgive).

Jesus continues, to the delight of Danny and his four friends. "In order that you may know the Son of man has authority on Earth to forgive sins." At this moment He turned from the Pharisees to Danny, "Stand up! Pick up your pad and return to your home." Jesus demonstrated to the Pharisees that His power to heal showed He also had the power to forgive.

"Danny! Danny! Stand up, you're healed." Ben spoke the joy for the five of them, and Danny did stand up to the dismay of everyone. Some were afraid, others were in awe. They recognized this as a work of God and were filled with thankfulness. Danny walked home in a cloud, arm in arm with his friends, eager to share his new life with his mother.

INSIGHT

If Jesus had remained silent, nothing would have happened. In the book of Genesis God had said, "Let there be light," and there was light. He used words that are alive and filled with divine power to create light.

In our story Jesus says "Stand up!" These two words are impregnated with the power of God. His words "Stand up!" are containers. They have the capacity to hold the substance of faith, which Danny received.

If Danny had continued to lie on the floor he never would have been healed for he would have disobeyed the command of Jesus.

He could have said, "I can't get up. I've tried that a thousand times. Can't you see I'm paralyzed? My friends see that, I'm not crazy, you know."

Here's another scenario: Danny says, "I take you at your word. I have been healed. Thank you." But he does not stand up. Has he been healed? The answer is no because he lacks spiritual faith. His profession of faith is in the head — not in the heart. He failed in this case because he did not act on what Jesus said.

To these impostors Jesus spoke sharply. "Not everyone who says to me, 'Lord, Lord' will enter the kingdom of heaven, but he who *does* the will of my Father." He emphasized the word *does* (Matthew 7:21).

"Many will say to me," His voice rang with authority, "on that day, 'Lord, Lord, we prophesied in your name. We cast out demons in your name. Yes, we performed many miracles which demonstrated the very power of God.'"

"It was all done," exposed Jesus, "from the head — you want to pretend to be something you are not. If you cannot allow my Word to change your lives, get out of my sight.

"Here is how I picture this truth. If a sensible man hears my words and carries them out in his life, he will be like a man who built his house on a rocky cliff.

"A violent rainstorm came, and torrents, with ripping winds, but the house did not collapse because it had the rocky cliff for a foundation.

"On the other hand, if you hear what I am saying, but you refuse to let it change your life, you would be like a foolish man who built his house on a sandy beach. When a violent rainstorm came with ripping winds, the house fell with a thunderous roar because it rested on shifting sand."

Jesus pictures two men hearing what God has to say.

They could read:
> Throw all your worries on Jesus, because He cares about you affectionately and watchfully.

The sensible man remembers the verse.
> You have set your love upon me, and you watch over every detail of my life. In response to this I throw the burden of my anxieties upon Jesus. I rest on the Rock of your word because I do what you tell me to do.

Jesus calls the second man — the foolish man — who has heard what the verse says, he may say it, but he doesn't take action.

"OK," he says, "I think that's true."

But he continues to carry his backpack of worry, because he refuses to believe *in his heart* that Jesus loves and watches over him. He fails to execute what God wants him to enjoy. He has broken a spiritual law, and he suffers the penalty worry brings.

Insights

Timothy, the spiritual son of the apostle Paul, built his life on the foundation of the rocky cliff. Paul commends him on his unpretentious faith.

"I haven't seen you," writes Paul, "for some time, but I'm anxious to get together that I might be filled with joy as I observe your un-hypocritical faith." Just this word of encouragement says Paul:

> "God has not given us the spirit of fear. But He has given us the Holy Spirit's power, love and soundness of mind."
>
> I know I have received the Person of the Holy Spirit:
>
> As to power:
>
> He uses God's words to augment God's power in my life.
>
> As to love:
>
> I know Jesus watches over me affectionately.
>
> As to self-control:
>
> I enjoy the disciplines (to disciple) of my life in Christ.

I cannot pursue freedom from fear alone. When I have these three: power, love, and the disciplines — fear flees out the front door. In other words, if I am under the tyranny of fear, I have to allow the Holy Spirit to revive me in these three.

A young Christian says, "I have been listening to what you say, and I come to this conclusion: if I build on the rocky cliff, I will find no worry in my life."

One elderly lady testifies: "The moment I see fear in my life I fly to the Word and find the antidote. No wonder it says that His Word is healing and healthy to my body."

"Have the kind of faith," Jesus shared with his disciples, "that God has."

One cynical believer replied, "Who could ever have the kind of faith that God has?"

Jesus went on to demonstrate, "Mountain! Get up! Throw yourself into the sea!"

"What's He talking about?" queries a businessman.

"If I have impossibility in my life," says a student, "that's a mountain. It's something that can't be done."

"Humanly impossible," adds the elderly lady. "He speaks to the impasse, He sees it uprooting itself, and throwing itself into the sea!"

"I find this interesting," observes the cynical man, "that I speak to worry. I address fear as though it has ears. And by giving voice to my faith I am a doer of the Word." Giving voice to my faith is part of the sequence.

Reify — I See the Unseen

Ted and I hadn't seen one another in a while, so we set up a luncheon to catch up on things. After a sandwich he wiped his mouth with his napkin and posed this question.

"Norm, did you ever hear of the word 'reify'?" He studiously printed the word on a piece of paper. "R-E-I-F-Y. That's a verb."

I spelled the word R-E-I-F-Y, and said the word a couple of times; reify, reify. "I'm afraid I'm in the dark," I admitted.

He spelled it again, "R-E-I-F-Y," funny little word, but it is like a hidden gold mine.

"Rich in meaning. Now I suppose you want me to tell you what it means?" We laughed together.

"You wanta' take a stab at what it says?"

"Yeah. No harm done," I agreed. "How about refit. Ya' know, like something a machinist would do?"

"Good guess," Ted complimented, "the noun for 'reify' is 'reification.'"

"How about 'to rebuild'?" I was interpreting by the sound … reification, to rebuild.

Ted smiled at my struggle to be a linguist. "I won't keep you in more suspense; the dictionary says it means to see as real."

"Ya' mean like in magic?"

"I don't know about magic, but let me see if I can come up with a definition. Reification says I see something invisible as a concrete material object."

"Let me see if I get it," I ventured. "If I reify something I can't see, it is turned into something I can see. Something visible. Is that right? It is said of Moses he endured as seeing Him who is invisible." *(Hebrews 11:27)*

"Exactly. You know," he laughed heartily at his own thought, "You and I have to reify reify. I think we have to make reify real."

I joined him in the fun of his double entendre.

"You recall," Ted sought to bring reify into the open, "the story of the woman who touched the hem of Jesus' garment with her fingertips?"

"Definitely," I responded, "she was healed instantaneously."

"Yeah. She suffered from a blood disease. It had been going on for twelve long years. Her doctors took what little money she had. All to no avail, she continued down hill."

"As I recall, she lived in Capernaum, by the Sea of Galilee."

"Right," confirmed Ted, "Jesus loved that city. He often returned there."

"The woman we're talking about," I added, "would have heard from time to time of a healing in her own home town."

"When she first became ill," observed Ted, "she asked herself, 'What's happening to me?' As her suffering increased she faintly thought of healing. It was not tangible."

"I think I see where you're heading. As she heard of the healings in her own home town, she began to ask herself, 'Why not me?'"

"What had been a dream, a mere thought, was becoming real." Ted appreciated my input.

"In her reification — making real, she was now saying, 'He could heal me.'"

"Faith comes," I quoted Romans 10:17, "and comes, and comes, by the hearing of the message concerning the Person of Christ."

"Right on! Her healing became so visible she began to talk

about it."

I joined in, "Yeah, I can hear her tell a neighbor lady, Jesus is going to heal me too!"

"It had moved from far away to something she could touch. She made it real or alive. Her faith had a voice, in other words her faith came out in the open. Her story challenged me personally. Really." It was like Ted was making an admission.

I took a sip of coffee and listened quietly as he finished.

"She acted," he weighed his words. "She took a course of action. This frail, sickly woman, joined a stampeding mob. Can you imagine that, Norm?"

His eyes moistened. She could have lost her life. The two of us sat in quietness.

"I think of the wrong things she could have said like:
'I'm destitute.
I'm worse off than ever.
All hope is gone.
I'm going to die.'"

"And there were those who told her she would be trampled to death. But she countered with words:
'I'll make it through the stampede.
He has healed many.
I'll find a way to Him.
I know He can heal me.
I'll enjoy a new life.'"

I smiled at Ted as we got up to leave the coffee shop. "Ya' know, Ted, sometimes the things we believe in are more real than the physical things around us. I like your word, reify."

Mary Magdalene

Jerusalem slept. Darkness gave way to dawn as faint streaks of light appeared in the east. A small group of huddled women moved cautiously along the silent street. Sleep had eluded them since they had witnessed the crucifixion and burial of Jesus. Now the Sabbath was passed and on this first day of the week their destination was the tomb where they had laid His body.

They represented the once splendid movement of the young man from Nazareth. Their dreams had suffered a stinging defeat as they witnessed His murder and burial. No battle flag led this helpless few. No band played where history was written in each face. Thousands once lined these streets just to get a glimpse of a Man who would change the world. These solemn faces were a shadow of the thousands who looked to a new world. Some were rich. Others poor. The powerful. Outcasts. Enemies. Followers.

Now what? Where do we go from here?

"Are you sure, Mary, that we have enough spices?" Joanna pushed back her hood as she framed the question to her friend Mary Magdalene. Though she lived in a palace, Joanna saw herself as a devoted disciple of the Master. Her husband, Chuza, was a steward in Herod's household. Now this bold lady wanted to know if they had enough spices to anoint the body of Jesus.

"I think I have enough, Joanna," Mary wrapped her arm around the shoulder of her friend, "but my concern is the huge stone slab His accusers put over the tomb. They were worried we'd steal His body and then claim He was resurrected."

Joseph of Arimathea, a rich Jewish follower of Jesus, owned

property at the foot of Calvary hill. Here he had hewn a tomb for his own burial. He begged Pilate for the body and he finally relented. The handy garden sepulcher was a convenient place for the Roman soldiers to deliver the body.

As Mary trudged along the dark street she reflected back to her childhood in Magdala, a fishing village on the shore of the Sea of Galilee. Tears flooded her eyes as she pictured the scene the day the Lord healed her, and how she threw herself into His ministry. Just as there was that inner circle of men — His disciples — there was also an inner circle of women who looked after His health. "A woman of Magdala named Mary" played a keystone role in this group.

Many questions flooded the minds of the committed women. The mother of the Lord asked, "Do you think the guards at the tomb will arrest us as collaborators?" And her sister wondered if the disciples might be there. The stone plate covered the tomb and the guards continued on their posts, but suddenly a cataclysmic event took place. An earthquake shook the ground and an angel appeared before the women. His face shone as lightning and his garments were as white as snow. The guards were so terrified they froze in place, unable to move because of fear.

"Do not be afraid," the angel spoke to the women. "I know you are looking for Jesus. He is not here. He is risen, as He said He would do. Come see the place where He lay." With those words he rolled aside the stone that sealed the grave.

"I'll go in," volunteered Mary Magdalene. She saw the empty tomb and the linen in which they had wrapped His body.

"He is not here. He's gone," she reported to her fellow believers. Before he left the angel bid them, "Go quickly now. Tell His disciples He has risen from the dead, and behold, He will go before you into Galilee. There you will see Him. I have told you. Leave." They left the tomb immediately bearing the historic news

Mary Magdalene

with great joy, and ran with the news they couldn't hide, but as they ran they were met on the road by the risen Lord. He greeted them and they fell prostrate at His feet in worship. After this joyous encounter they hurried on their way to tell the disciples what they had witnessed. Mary Magdalene was given the privilege of bringing the thrilling news of the resurrection. Peter had thrust himself forward as the designated leader, and then turned on Jesus to say he never knew this Man. In ego-driven ambition the disciples argued who was the greatest among His followers, and brave Mary was the one He selected to be His news bearer.

Everyone knew Mary and loved her. I have selected a few of her co-disciples to express their friendship with Mary. Joanna has this to say: "Though I lived in a palace and Mary was from a fishing village, we became bonded sisters from the early work of the Lord. My husband, Chuzza, was a steward in the household of Herod. I saw a lot of phonys, and I gazed on excellence from time to time, but with Mary, I would say to myself, 'There goes one classy lady. When she spoke she had something to say. When others spoke she looked at them and listened to each word.'"

Mary, the mother of Jesus, had this to add. "Mary Magdalene belonged to the generation that came after mine, but we were like mother and daughter. If I were asked to picture Mary with one word, I would say love. We watched the Savior being crucified from a distance. It was a terrifying experience. Each one felt abandoned and helpless, but one by one Mary shared the tears."

"My name is Salome, and I am the mother of two of Jesus' disciples, John and James. My husband is Zebedee. He is the patriarch of all these fishermen. Mary, the lady from Magdala, and I sought accommodations for the Master in the city of Capernaum. We met this nobleman in the marketplace."

"Hafed, what a joy to see you." Mary knew everyone, and she enquired of his son who the Master had healed.

"'I'm delighted to see you,' assured Hafed, after Mary made sure he knew who I was."

"The crowds have kept me from the Master, but I was hopeful He would spend the night at my place."

"Consider it done," Mary smiled.

The Lord had healed Mary of seven demons who had robbed her of a fulfilling life. Her release from this imprisonment gave her great thankfulness and this led to splendid faithfulness.

Immediately after the resurrection Mary Magdalene reported to the disciples the appearance of the Lord. "At first sight I thought it was the gardener, but then He opened my eyes to understand what had taken place."

"I find this hard to believe," spoke up one of the disciples. Another was harsh. "That can't be! I've never heard such nonsense. I think the ladies are overcome with grief."

But Mary and the others were adamant. "You don't have to take our word. Go and see for yourself." Peter jumped up, "I'll take that dare. I'll go and see for myself." Peter jumped up and took off on the run for the garden where Jesus was buried. But John, the faster runner, passed Peter in his excitement to see for himself the glorious miracle. Out of breath, they discovered that Mary was right — the tomb was open. Cautiously they entered. No body.

"He is gone!" whispered Peter as he looked at the linen clothes carefully folded. Together they stood in the tomb trying to patch together the conflicting possibilities.

At that same time, a Sunday, which was the first day of the week, two disciples were walking to Emmaus. The two-hour walk from Jerusalem gave them ample time to get into an animated conversation on the death of the Lord.

"I never thought the Master would be crucified," stated Cleopas.

"I find that being naïve," countered his friend, "He did say the Son of Man would be in the earth three days. Do you remember that?"

"Are you saying this was inevitable?" queried Cleopas.

As they aired their sadness over the death of the Lord, a Stranger took up the hike with them. Their eyes were restrained from recognizing Him as He asked, "You two seem to be in an argument. What's it all about?"

Cleopas and his friend came to a standstill by the side of the road. Their downcast faces mirrored the crisis of the last seventy-two hours.

"You must be new here," cited Cleopas, "seeing you do not know about the world-shaking events that have happened here in the last few days."

Jesus enquired, "What sort of events?"

And they said to Him, "The things concerning Jesus of Nazareth, a great Man, a prophet mighty in deed and word in the sight of God and all the people. The chief priests and our rulers delivered Him to a judgment of death and crucified Him. What we had in mind when He was living is that He would be the one who would gain freedom for Israel. Three days have passed since our hopes were dashed by His death."

"But wait, this is not the end of the story. Certain women of our number brought astonishing news."

"What was that?" Jesus asked.

"You won't believe this, they went to the tomb early this very morning and the burial place was empty. His body was gone."

"Isn't this amazing," chimed in the friend of Cleopas, "but it's not the end."

"No," continued Cleopas. "Angels appeared also at the tomb. They declared that the Lord was alive. So several of our group checked out what the woman said they'd seen. They're right. He was gone, and He was no place to be found."

You can get the picture. Three men standing by the side of the road. Two of them trying to sort out the bewildering events of the last few days. They did not know the one they talked to was the risen Christ Who now reprimanded them.

"You men should really be scolded."

"Why is that?" asked Cleopas with resentment.

"For your ignorance," replied Jesus.

The friend of Cleopas couldn't believe what he was hearing.

Jesus continued, "The events of the past days were predicted by the prophets, but you didn't believe them. It was necessary and right that Christ the Messiah suffer all these things before entering into glory."

Then Jesus began with Moses and went through all the prophets explaining and interpreting the Scriptures in reference to Himself.

Toward evening they entered the town of Emmaus and Jesus took steps to continue this travel, but they urged and insisted that He stay with them.

"We've had a big day," urged Cleopas, "and the hour is late; why don't you stay the night?"

As their house guest, Jesus reclined at a table with them. He took a loaf of bread and praised God, gave thanks, and asked a blessing. He broke the bread and gave to the two men. In that moment their eyes were opened and they clearly recognized Jesus, but in that instant He vanished from their sight.

"He's gone!" gasped Cleopas to his friend. It then broke upon them that their new found friend was the risen Christ.

"Ya' know," reflected Cleopas, "my heart burned within me as He talked with us along the road, and He opened for us the Scriptures."

"We have to let the folks in Jerusalem know about this," responded the friend of Cleopas." Though the hour was late they walked the two hour trek to Jerusalem to report the startling events of the day.

See Luke 24.

Jesus Speaks to the Storm

Sunday school children listen with awe to the story of Jesus stilling the storm on the sea of Galilee. You and I can study this harrowing event from the inside and see for ourselves the majestic power of His faith. By His action He says, I will demonstrate for you the critical cog in implementing the faith that slumbers like a giant within you.

We begin our journey on the west shore of the Sea of Galilee. Jesus spoke in parables as He preached to the great crowds who were assembled there. He talked about the bread of life, and called our attention to the harvest we reap from the seeds we plant in the earth. He sketched mind-pictures of the lost sheep, the lost coin, and the prodigal son.

Jesus took His disciples into a house for a break before they crossed the sea. James addressed Him: "You talk about birds, and sheep, and the water we drink." He paused as he looked for words. "… Sometimes … I don't get it. Is that ok? I know there's a lesson, but I have to be honest, too often it goes right over my head."

"I appreciate your honesty," replied the Master to James, and then He expounded on the meaning of the earth, the seeds, the coin, and the lost sheep, but He cautioned them, "To you I give this special insight so you might understand the mysteries of the kingdom of heaven. Let me add," He went on, "you will be held responsible to share these secrets with others."

An evening storm seemed imminent as the ensemble left the house for the crush of people on the seashore. As Jesus looked at the sky to the west, He was approached by a sharp looking young man, a scholar, and one had studied the sacred scriptures.

"Teacher," spoke up the one who saw this as an opportunity for advancement, "I'm ready to cross the lake with you. Wherever you go I'm willing to travel as your disciple."

Jesus, knowing the heart of the man, turned him away with this reply: "Foxes have burrows, birds have nests," He paused for emphasis, "but the Son of Man does not have a place to pillow His head."

The sea Jesus wanted to cross was an inland body of water that was prone to violent storms. It lay 500 feet below sea level and was surrounded by high hills. Thirteen miles long and up to six miles wide, the Sea of Galilee welcomed the Jordan river on the north end. Andrew observed, "It should take an hour for a sailboat to cross the lake in favorable conditions. I should know," he chuckled, "I do have a fishing business here."

Jesus said, "I need to sail to the eastern shore, for I have a strategic work to do there."

"Do you have any idea what that is?" Peter asked John.

"No," answered John, "He hasn't told me anything, but it must be important, for it will soon be dark."

Across the lake lived an unkempt man in a graveyard. He made his home in the tombs, and was known throughout the region as "the wild man of Gadara." Fearful travelers took lengthy detours to avoid his domain. Jesus would heal this man and send him forth as an evangelist to the displaced Greeks who lived in the ten cities of Decapolis.

The tiny sailboat was only three miles out when the storm hit. Winds of hurricane proportions soon swamped the hapless craft. You and I can listen in to the words of the disciples.

"This is the end! We'll all drown!"

"Did you hear that? The boat is breaking apart!"

Above the roar one said, "I'm going to be thrown out of the boat!"

One man cried in his paralysis.

Jesus slept while His followers anticipated their deaths.

INSIGHT

Many years later one of the men (John) would write (1 John 11:18): " ... perfect love casts out fear." Jesus slept through that roaring violence because He grasped how much the Father loved Him.

"Wake Him! Wake him!" cried Peter. "Wake Him before we all perish!"

John thought, Peter's right someone has to do something before this boat goes under, so he clawed his way through his friends to the Master.

"Master! Master!" stammered John. Jesus opened His eyes. "We're going under!" John shouted above the screaming storm. "If you don't do something we'll all perish!"

Jesus sat up and rubbed His eyes. "What's the problem?"

"We're going down!" shouted Andrew.

Jesus could hear in their works that they had no faith, so He chastised them. "Why are you so frightened? Where's your faith?" At that moment He turned His face into the fury of the storm and commanded it, "Be still!" That's all He said — just two words, "Be still!"

He could have said, "Men, I think this is an excellent moment to call a prayer meeting."

He could have raised His hands in repudiation.

He could have said, "That's nature. We'll ride it out."

He could also have scolded the men; "You're a bunch of wimps! Stand up like men!"

He did none of these. He used the power of the spoken word.

"Be still!"

In another setting He instructed His disciples to speak to the mountain. *(Mark 11:22-24)*. He spoke to a tree. He spoke to a demon. In John 11, Jesus speaks to a dead man (Lazarus). In creation He talked to light. Let there be light, and light was *(Genesis 1:3)*. A skeptic could say, "That was Jesus. You are only you. Your words fall to the ground." In Mark 11:22 Jesus commands us to exercise the kind of faith God exercises.

Back to the story. At the command of Jesus, the wind ceased and there was a great and wonderful calm on the sea. John studied the Master's face and asked himself, "Who is this Man? Who is this Man? Even the wind and the sea obey Him?" The writer of the book of Hebrews (1:1) answers the question when he says, "He is the sole expression of the glory of God. He is the very image of God's nature. He guides and propels the universe through the power of what He speaks."

Words

*When I leave out spoken words I allow
my faith to die unborn.*

In the beginning, before all time was the Word, Christ, and the Word was with God, and the Word was God Himself.

And the Word, Christ, became a Person in the flesh, and lived among us, we actually saw His glory, the glory as an only begotten Son, full of grace and love (John 1:1, 14 amplified).

The Words that God speaks contain divine life, and are filled with His power *(Hebrews 4:12)*.

Every Scripture is given by God's inspiration *(2 Timothy 3:16)*.

Death and life are in the power of the tongue *(Proverbs 18:21)*.

Eternity is determined through words.

God reveals Himself to mankind through what He speaks.

The Father has willed to you and me the utilization of His Words.

His Words contain the power to move mountains.

We pray with words.

People fall in love with words

We marry with words.

Divorces are the consequences of words.

Wars begin with words.

Wars end with words.

If there is no written history, the peoples are forgotten.

Social relationships thrive or fail because of words.

Achievement happens because of words.

Failures are blamed on words.

Set a guard, O Lord, before my mouth; keep watch at the door of my lips *(David's prayer, Psalm 141:3)*.

Faith speaks the above verse:

"You have set a guard, O Lord, before my mouth; You keep watch at the door of my lips."

The Word is the sword of the Holy Spirit.

The Word is a seed containing Life.

Job asked, how long will you torment me and break me in pieces with words? *(Job 19:2)*

The natural man rejects the Words of God because they can only be understood by those who have the Holy Spirit. *(1 Corinthians 2:13,14)*

I see my faith as a pilgrimage to a far country. Each town along my journey calls for a unique faith because the challenges are different. Picture with me the following scenario. In town number 1 I received eternal life. We could name the town New Life. My faith was grounded in John 3:16. I move on.

I arrive at town number 2, "Worry." That's the name of this town. From town number 1 I learned the mechanics of faith: I'll need a verse from the Word, and I'll have to act on it. As you can see from the name of the town, the new challenge is worry. I am unaware of what the Bible says about worry, so I am helpless to exercise my faith.

As a horse eats hay and oats, so faith gets nutrition from information. I'll have to do my homework. What does God say about worry and anxiety? When I find this I'll have the hay and oats — the information — to back up what I believe.

> Casting the whole of your care (all your anxieties, all your worries, all your concerns, once and for

all) on Him, for He cares for you affectionately, and cares about you watchfully. *(1 Peter 5:7, amplified)*

Aha! I'm delighted to find such a verse here in Worry town. Take your worries I am told, and put them like a backpack on to Jesus. I can do this for one reason: He affectionately cares about me. Gone! See them as no longer existing.

How can I internalize this truth? How can I make it a part of myself? I understand His Word is a seed and I plant it by saying it.

You tell me in Your Word to throw all my worries on to the back of the Lord Jesus, because He cares about me affectionately.

Faith comes from hearing what the spirit has to say about worry, but in saying it, I also hear myself reaffirming the truth. I can write it in a journal or a flashcard.

Here's my problem, says the reader: I settle my worries on Wednesday, but on Thursday they're back. What do you do about that? Do I go back to Wednesday and re-believe 1 Peter 5:7?

If you do that you are saying the faith you first declared was counterfeit faith. Genuine faith has received the promise in the verse.

So what do I do on Thursday when worries resurface in my life? I remind myself of a fact that has taken place in my life.

Kenneth Wuest taught New Testament Greek at Moody Bible Institute. In his expanded translation he brings joyful enlightenment on the power of what I say.

> I have not received the spirit of the world system but the Spirit Who is of God, in order that I might know (if I know not, I can't believe) the things which the Father has bestowed on me in grace, which things I also put into words, not in words taught by human philosophy, but in words taught by the Person of the Spirit Himself, fitly joining together Spirit revealed truths with spirit taught words *(1 Corinthians 2:12,13)*.

It takes a spiritual being to impart spiritual life. Seeing my eternal life came out of the creative power of God's Words, when I change my words I change my life. I live by Holy Spirit power because I use Holy Spirit Words. The joyous realization of my faith comes about through the creative power of what God says.

Five Thousand Fed

Jesus spoke to His twelve disciples, "I want you to go on an evangelistic crusade that will take you through the cities and towns of Galilee."

Peter glanced at his brother Andrew, "I suppose you and I should pair up."

Jesus continued, "You will tell the people the insights I have been sharing with you. We'll go in different directions but I'll join you before you're finished."

Jesus had landed on the north shore of the Sea of Galilee and looked forward to some rest in the fishing village of Bethsaida, but He no sooner set foot on land before crowds engulfed Him. His deeds were on everyone's lips. "Have you seen Him?" "Have you heard Him?" "I saw Him heal a blind man."

It is no wonder that the ruler of Galilee became concerned about this man creating such an uproar — his name: Herod Antipas.

One advisor informed Herod: "I think this preacher making such a fuss is John the Baptist."

"No. No. No. That can't be. I had him executed."

"I know. I know. But I wonder if he is risen from the dead."

Herod listened with a wary smile across his face.

"This is Elijah the prophet. They said he would reappear."

"I would like to meet this man everyone talks about, but I'm a busy man. Your speculations only make more of His miracles for me. Who knows? Maybe He's a magician. I might even catch Him in his deception." (Herod knew John the Baptist personally,

Five Thousand Fed

but he would never see Jesus before His trial).

John the Baptist accused Herod of stealing his brother's wife.

"It is not lawful for you to have her," persisted John. So the Baptist was a prisoner for more than a year in the gloomy castle of Machaerus on the shores of the Dead Sea. In an unguarded moment Herod was tricked by his mistress into granting her the request of the head of John the Baptist. He was beheaded in prison and his disciples lovingly placed him in his tomb.

Herod Antipas was the son of Herod the Great. The father can be remembered for the slaughter of the infants when Joseph and Mary hid with their baby in Egypt.

Who are these people — the Herodians? They are a Jewish political party that favored Greek customs. They are descendants of Abraham through Ishmael and Esan, which makes them half brothers with Jacob. Often called Bedouins, there has always been bitter enmity between them and the conservative Jews of Jerusalem. Herod played out the role of a viceroy, serving as a deputy for Rome.

Back to our story. The twelve, as ambassadors with credentials, returned from their travels in Galilee and filled in Jesus on all the things they had done. They had hoped to rest on the banks of the Jordan River. Instead, they looked out on a sea of people.

"I was sure we would get a break," observed Andrew without stretched arm, "look at the crowds. Thousands. Yeah. Thousands." But Jesus welcomed them and taught them about His vision. He healed those who were in need.

As the day began to wane Peter noticed, "It is time to send these people to the farms and villages to put up for the night and to scrounge for something to eat."

"They look to me," said Jesus looking at the people, "like they need something immediately."

Andrew felt foolish when he said, "There is a youngster here

215

who has a bag lunch, five barley loaves and a couple of small fish. But what good is that when you look out on the endless crowds?"

"Have the people lay down," Jesus ordered, as they do at their home meal, in dinner parties, about 50 to a group." The disciples carefully seated the throng as Jesus had commanded. Jesus took the five barley loaves and two fish and asked God's blessing on them. He broke them into pieces and gave to His disciples to set before the hungry, and everyone ate to his complete satisfaction. What was left was picked up and deposited in twelve hand baskets. Five thousand men were fed, but with women and children the number could soar to two or three times that count.

When it dawned on the men in the crowd what Jesus had done they said, "We know for sure that this is the foretold prophet that should come into the world."

Jesus saw that they were going to take Him by force and make Him king, so He slipped away to a hillside where He could be alone.

"For ever since the creation of the world His invisible nature and attributes, that is, His eternal power and divinity, have been made intelligible and clearly discernable in and through the things He has made (His handworks)." *(Romans 1:2)*

John 1:1 says the Word (Jesus Christ) was God Himself, and as Jesus feeds the multitude He graciously pulls aside the veil to reveal His Godhead. When he created the world He spoke the thing desired — the world. When He created light, He spoke the thing desired — light. When He fed the multitudes by the Jordan, He spoke the thing desired — food for the hungry.

See Matthew 14:1-23; Mark 6: 14-46; Luke 9: 7-17; John 6: 1-15.

Anisa and the Pharisee

How beautiful upon the mountains are the feet of Him who brings good tidings. (Isaiah 52:7)

Three lives collide in this story of insidious deceit, heart rendering repentance, and declaration of deity. Simon was a Pharisee in Capernaum. Anisa (as I named her) lived in the world of prostitution. Jesus meets trickery with a lesson on love. Luke is the only writer in the New Testament to share this incident *(Luke 7:36-50)*.

Two young ladies laughed and giggled as they shared intimate stories of their lives. I said "ladies." I was misleading. They were not ladies, but two young women who had lost their way. Perhaps their excessive makeup was telling. Their language also gave them away. You see, these two women sold their bodies for money. You and I are interested in the younger of the pair — Anisa. She's nineteen, but looks like she is thirty. She will be on stage in our story as she meets Jesus. We begin with her encounter with Simon the Pharisee.

"I was told," relates Anisa with a quizzical look, "that this Pharisee wanted to see me. I had no idea what he had in mind. Was he going to preach to me? Maybe he wanted me to stop working on the Sabbath. Has this nice home up on the hill, but the word on the street is that you can't trust him.

"I'm tough when it comes to money. You have to be. I've been cheated too many times not to wise up. Up front. Up front. I always say. Let the money soothe the palm of my hand. If someone were to ask me if I was a shrewd business woman, I would say yes. They could be rich or religious, young or old, trust no one. Believe me."

"Did you go to see him?" Anisa's friend wanted to know the rest of the story with the Pharisee.

" Yeah. Yeah. I went to his house. Pretty fancy."

"Did he want your services?"

"No. No. No. Not in the least. That's what so queer about it. He's planning a dinner with lots of guests, but he wants to target one man in particular."

"What d' ya mean, he wants to target someone?"

"It's Jesus. Have you seen Him?"

"Yeah, I couldn't get very close to Him."

"Simon wants me to stand by Jesus."

"Have you any idea why he would want you to do that?"

"To embarrass Him. To make it look like He runs with whores. He thinks this will make Jesus the laughing stock to His followers."

"Give me a clue, Anisa. Did you take this job? People can think we're scum, but we never stoop that low. Right?"

"Yeah. I told Simon I would do it, but I'll tell you why. I heard Jesus speak one day, and I have to confess, I'm a follower — at a distance, of course."

While Anisa and her friend talked, a lad had delivered the dinner invitation to Jesus.

"Tell Simon I accept his offer."

Jesus entered Simon's house at the appointed time and seated Himself at the table. He took no notice of the fact that a young woman had positioned herself behind Him. It was Anisa. Two women put their hands over their mouths in disbelief.

"What is He doing with that horrible girl behind Him? How did she get in here? Simon should be ashamed of himself. No man in his right mind would ever want to be seen with her. Look at the makeup. She looks like a clown. And that long hair falling over her back makes her look cheap."

What went on in the minds of Simon's guests was nothing compared to what went on in Anisa's heart. She looked on the back of the Man reclining before her. He gave no indication that He knew she was there, for He never looked at her.

"I think the first feeling I had," testified Anisa," was the sublime sense of His holiness. No sin was present. I felt like I had stepped from darkness into light and I saw a way out from the world I had known. I wanted to reach out Him and be washed from head to toe. I understood on the inside that He would forgive me. Someone had told me He could make a new Anisa. I believed it. Someday I could walk down the street and hold my head high. When I looked at Him I saw love. I saw the Messiah. I saw God.

"As these thoughts ran through my heart like a bubbling creek — you won't believe this — I found tears rolling down my cheeks. I felt no shame. My heart had taken over my life.

"I moved cautiously to my knees at His feet. I cradled His feet in my hands as my tears fell like rain to wash the dust from them. I dried His feet with my hair, and gently massaged them with the precious ointment I had with me. Again and again I kissed the feet of the One I worshipped."

Simon spoke to an aid, "I'm disgusted. If He were a prophet He would be aware of what sort of woman is touching Him." (When Simons says, "if He were a prophet," he spoke unbelief.) "Doesn't He know everyone shuns her, and He associates with her."

As Simon reveled in his scheme, Jesus interrupted, "Simon! I want to bring a truth to your attention." Jesus did not "beat about the bush" when He faced this wall of evil. He did not conciliate His host, but He placed Simon below Anisa.

Simon, surprised by the candor of his guest, smirked, "Teacher, say it."

Jesus pointed to Anisa. "Do you see this woman? Do you see what she has done?"

"Everyone has seen that." Simon smiled at his aid as though he had won the day.

Jesus went on. "A certain lender of money had two debtors who owed him money."

"I hear what you're saying," listened Simon.

"One debtor owed him five hundred denarii, and the other debtor owed him fifty denarii. Neither debtor was able to pay the lender his debt, so he freely forgave them both. So, here's the question for you. Which debtor will love him more, the one who owed him five hundred denarii or the one who owed him fifty denarii?"

Simon felt relieved that he knew the obvious answer. "I take it," he smiled knowingly to his aid, "the lender would be loved the more by the debtor who owed him five hundred denarii."

"You have answered correctly," cited Jesus, who turned to Anisa.

"Do you see this woman?"

"Yes."

"When I came into your home, you gave me no water for my feet, but she has washed my feet with her tears and dried them with her hair. You did not give me a kiss, but this woman from the time I entered has not ceased to kiss my feet tenderly. You did not anoint my head with ordinary oil, but she has massaged my feet with expensive ointment."

"So! What are you saying?" Simon growled impatiently.

"Her sins ... Many... Many," Jesus paused in reflection, "are forgiven her because she has loved much. If one shows little love, he receives little forgiveness."

With this pronouncement Jesus faced tearful Anisa. "Your sins are forgiven."

"Who does He thinks He is?" whispered one of the belligerent guests. "He should know only God can forgive sin. Blasphemy. That's what I call it."

Jesus turned to Anisa. "Your faith has saved you. Enter into the domain of peace you have longed for. You are free from the enslavement of a life of sin." Jesus looked inside Anisa, past the world of shame and saw a heart filled with faith and love.

Many people came to Jesus. One came as a son. Another came as a daughter. One came through an army officer. There were those who came through John the Baptist. Anisa came alone — hidden behind a deceptive plan to discredit Jesus.

She stood up with a tear-stained face to embark on a new life. A smile —long forgotten — beamed across her face. Where did she go from here? History hides this. She returned home, I'm sure, to tell her mother and father what happened to her. She could have gone to Gadara to join the movement of "the wild man" in proclaiming the Messiah. Was she at the cross? She could have been. Her love and faith could easily have brought her there with other women.

Miracles, by themselves, were not the astonishing deeds of the Lord Jesus Christ. After all, false prophets also performed miracles *(Revelation 13:13)*. The miracles He worked were a spokesman to His deity for they were predicted with precision. There is forgiveness for you, Anisa, for we read: He comes with forgiveness *(Psalm 130:4)*.

See Luke 7:36-50.

Transfiguration

Four months before His death, Jesus spoke to His disciples.
> I want to make it clear to you that I must go to Jerusalem and suffer many things at the hands of the elders and the high priests and scribes, and be killed, and on the third day be raised from death. *(Matthew 16:21)*

Jesus said He "must" go. Why "must"? He "must" to fulfill the prophecy, but He "must" go to provide atonement.

> Grace from Jesus Christ, the faithful and trustworthy Witness, the First born of the dead [first to be brought back to life] and the Prince of the kings of the earth. To Him who ever loves us and has once and for all loosed and freed us from our sins by His own blood. *(Revelation 1:5)*

"Some of you who are standing here," spoke Jesus, "will not die before they see the kingdom of God." The record of Christ's transfiguration in each of the first three gospels is preceded every time by the above quote.

In response to His declaration of a kingdom, the people said, "Ah! He will go to Jerusalem and set up an earthly kingdom. Of course, He will be our new king. Then, we shall be freed from the yoke of Rome and their lackeys, the Herodians."

Jesus also said something at the same time which the people could not understand. "The Son of Man must suffer many things and be rejected by the elders and chief priests and scribes, and be slain, and be raised the third day." *(Luke 9:22)*

Up to this time, four months before He died, the events in His life centered on His work, but preceding His trial and death, you and I get a better picture of who He is.

We find Him one hundred and twenty miles north of Jerusalem in the picturesque valley that is a source of the Jordan River. Snow-crowned Mount Hermon rises ten thousand feet above the city of Caesarea-Philippi.

"I'm taking you, Peter," Jesus spoke, "and the brothers James and John."

"What do you have in mind?" interrupted Peter.

"We're going up on Mount Hermon," answered Jesus. "I'm sure you'll enjoy a season of prayer."

"I'm game," chimed in James.

A week had gone by since Jesus had informed His disciples of a kingdom. Now we find three disciples with Jesus on Mount Hermon. What occurs there — the transfiguration — becomes a monumental revelation of the Lord Jesus Christ. While He prayed, His face changed and began to shine like the sun. His clothing became dazzling white as with the brilliance of lightning flashing. To the disciples' astonishment, two men appeared enveloped in a brightness that blinded the eyes. One was Moses and the other was Elijah, and they talked with Jesus at length about His impending death.

INSIGHT

A thing may be "transformed" by a light shining on it from without.

In transfiguration, the light is shining forth from within. The glory did not shine upon Jesus, but shone out from Him through His clothing. He drew the veil aside to reveal who He was all along.

Peter, James and John had gone without sleep for a long time so they dozed off, but when they awoke, they continued to see His splendor, majesty, and brightness.

Insights

When Moses and Elijah were departing, without thinking, Peter, true to character, blurted out, "Master, it has been thrilling for us to be here. Here's what I propose: We'll build three huts, one for you, one for Moses, and one for Elijah." While Peter was babbling off the top of his head, a cloud began to envelop the mountain, and the disciples were terrified.

From out of the cloud, a voice thundered, "This is my Son, my Chosen One, my Beloved. Listen to Him." At the beginning of the voice, the paralyzed disciples fell on their faces. When the rumbling of the voice and the cloud had evaporated, Jesus softly laid His hand on them and whispered, "Get up, but do not be afraid." After a few minutes of gaining their senses, they stood up and looked about and saw Jesus by Himself.

"Men," Jesus turned to the three who had seen who He was, "our work here on the mountain is finished. Now we'll go back down to where the others are waiting for us, but first let me caution you, tell no one what you have seen until the Son of Man has been raised from the dead."

The three carefully and faithfully kept the transfiguration to themselves, but they questioned and disputed with one another what raising from the dead might mean.

"Hear, O Israel, the Lord our God is one Lord." *(Deuteronomy 6:4)* And in Ephesians 4:6, Paul the apostle says there is one God. The Father speaks out of the cloud in the transfiguration and says, "This is my beloved Son." Jesus speaks of the Father, the Son and the Holy Spirit. *(Matthew 28:19)*

Question: Is Jesus as much God as is the Father?

Answer: The whole fullness of the Godhead bodily dwells in Christ giving complete expression of the divine nature *(Colossians 2:9)*.

Question: To whom do I pray?

Answer: I pray to the Father, in the name of the Son, under the unction of the Holy Spirit.

Question: How many Gods does Christianity have?

Answer: One.

Question: Why there are three distinct personages?

Answer: Personages help us to understand the complex manifestations of the One God.

Two times in the New Testament *(Romans 12:2* and *2 Corinthians 3:18),* the word for 'transfiguration' is used for the believer. They say, "Change your outward expression to one that comes from within and is representative of your inner being. We all, with uncovered faces, reflect as in a mirror the glory of the Lord, are changed from one degree of glory to another by the Lord."

"Listen to Him," says the Father in the transfiguration on Mount Hermon. When you and I say His word about the situations in our lives, we are listening to Him.

Peter, James and John witnessed the transfiguration of Jesus. Fifty years later, John recalls the splendid hours.

> The Word was made flesh and dwelt among us, and we beheld His glory, the glory as of the only begotten of the Father, full of grace and truth. *(John 1:14)*

John calls Jesus "the Word." We have to back up several verses *(John 1:1)* to find out who the Word is.

> In the beginning, before all time, was the Word, and the Word was with God, and the Word was God Himself.

Transfigured before His three disciples, Jesus reveals Himself to be God, for only God could make known His true identity. When He lay in the manger as a baby, He could have closed down the Universe with the flick of His hand.

Our First Baby — A Miracle

The more Sue and I talked about the problem, the greater the problem grew. We wanted a child. But time — four years — produced nothing. Bluesville. I can't remember all the roads we traveled in our quest. We were sure of one thing — we had exhausted our resources. We persuaded ourselves that we were destined to a childless marriage. No way out. Looking back I can see we were doing everything from a "human" point of view. It never occurred to us to make a 180° turn to resolve this crucial need in our home.

As you read this I can hear you saying to yourself, "I know what he's going to say. Accept your circumstance. Look on your childless marriage as God's will for your lives. Stop fighting it. Submit." Absolutely not! On the contrary, now is the time to start fighting.

The beginnings are not clear. I can't recall the date or place where it began to dawn on me how much God loved Sue and me.

Are you thinking: "Oh, Oh, pass me a dog-eared tract?" Hang in there. You'll find it illuminating.

This was different. He *had* to send His Son. Yes, He *had* to. He loved us — and you too — so much that His love pushed God to give His Son. (You can verify this insight in the Amplified translation of the Bible, Ephesians 2:4.)

Our lack boiled down to this: If God loved us so wonderfully and intensely — our wanted baby was also the recipient of His love!

We discovered a resource we had been blinded to all along. Up to this time we had been saying:

"It's no use."

"It's not in the cards for us."

It's a funny thing, and you'll get a kick out of this, the first sin mentioned in the Bible concerns speech. In essence it says this: do not say about a situation what God does not say (you can check this out in Genesis 3:1). In other words, say about a condition what God says about it. Simply put, we were saying words about our scenario which were contrary to God's thinking. So, what did we do?

Instead of: "It's not in the cards for us."

We began to affirm: "God loves Sue and me in a very personal and intimate way."

At this same time someone brought to our attention that "we learn to be victims." "We learn to be victims." I had never thought of that before. It seemed to say: I invite defeat. I mulled that over in my mind for a long time. In that ruminating process a verse from the Bible came to my attention:

> The Lord said, "my thoughts are not your thoughts, neither are your ways my ways." *(Isaiah 55:8)*

Hey! I was on a roll. I had stopped saying:

"It's no use" and "It's not in the cards for us."

Why not start making God's thoughts our thoughts? And why not start making God's ways our ways?

I can just hear you say, "Oh. Oh. Now we can't even have a beer!"

Nope. That's not the road we're traveling. We're not on the "No No Road." We're on "Abundance Highway."

Sue called my attention to a verse from the Bible.

> And God blessed them, and God said to them (Adam and Eve), Be fruitful, and multiply,

and replenish the earth. *(Genesis 1:28a)*

You might ask: "What did you see in this?"

God's intent. In His love for us He could give us our first child.

"Aren't you pushing the verse to squeeze that out of it?"

No. I don't think so. It says it is God's will that children replenish the earth.

"Is this God's will for every young couple?"

No. There are many reasons why some couples go childless. Our marriage was unique. We believed God wanted us to have a child.

Other verses helped to change our thinking. Ephesians 3:20 was instrumental in bringing about the 180° awakening:

> "The action of His power is at work within us. He is able to carry out His purpose and do superabundantly, far over and above all that we dare ask or think — infinitely beyond our highest prayers, desires, thoughts, hopes or dreams." *(Ephesians 3:20, amplified)*

Our attitude changed. We were learning to think God's thoughts. Despair was replaced by faith. Who's a victim? Certainly not us! What happened to that stupid resignation: "It's not in the cards for us?" And what happened to all that talk about a problem — (or was it a crisis)?

We realized that it wasn't simply a "human" dimension, but a spiritual dimension as well — THIS is what we had left out.

Jason came. As you can guess, well and with open eyes; our hearts were filled with thankfulness.

The Significance of David and Goliath

A long time ago people from this nation said a Messiah would someday visit mankind. They also told us the family through which He would come. That nation was Israel, and the lineage came through David.

> And the angel said to her, Do not be afraid, Mary, for you have found favor with God. And listen! You will become pregnant and give birth to a Son, and you shall call His name Jesus. He will be great and will be called the Son of the Most High; and the Lord God will give to Him the throne of His forefather David.
>
> *(Luke 1:30-32)*

Both of the parents of Jesus came through the lineage of David, so we readily see the importance of becoming acquainted with this man. Paul said God found David to be a man after His own heart.

DAVID AND GOLIATH

Once upon a time there lived a giant. His name: Goliath. He was a wicked man because he tried to destroy the army of God. When he fully dressed in his armor, he weighed over five hundred pounds, and stood over ten feet tall. He looked like one of King Arthur's knights when he dressed for battle. To protect his head from the blow of an ax he wore a bronze helmet. His body armor — weighing close to two hundred pounds — was made of flexible loops of interlocking chain that had been fashioned by his blacksmith.

"I need more protection," clamored the giant. "Look at my

legs. Look at my shoulders. Nothing. Nothing. Can't you shape something to protect my legs? While you're at it, mold something across my shoulder." His artisans in bronze perfected the coverage of the giant's shoulders and legs. To bring down His enemy he carried a spear with a designed tip that weighed twenty-one pounds. For close hand-to-hand combat, his sword rested in its sheath which hung from his belt.

"I have a shield," roared the boisterous giant, "but it's so big it takes a soldier to carry it. He considers it a great honor to march before me into battle. He doesn't do the killing. He leaves that up to me." Again the hulk enjoyed his sadistic humor.

"One man! Choose one man!" The voice of the giant echoed off the hills of the Valley of Elah. "Let him come down to me. We will fight. If he kills me," here the giant paused to enjoy his humor, "if he kills me, my army, the Philistine army, will become the servants of the army of Israel." His laughter made the Israelites shudder in terror, and his shield-bearer danced like the opening act of a stage play. The cowardly giant enjoyed making a spectacle of himself. His diatribe went on: "But," he emphasized the word, "But if I kill him then the army of Israel will become the slaves of the army behind me." At this the Philistine army cheered their gladiator.

Every morning. Every evening. This berating had gone on for six weeks. He set the conditions of battle. Two or three good soldiers could easily have felled the giant, but the army of Israel was so disoriented by fear it couldn't act. The Philistine army was so scared that they let Goliath fight for them.

"I defy the proud army of Israel!"

"Give me a man! Give me a man today!"

"Are you people deaf?"

"Why don't we scamper for our lives," whimpered a stalwart of Saul's elite.

The Significance of David and Goliath

"We can't do that," pled a sergeant, "they'll hunt us down like dogs."

Socoh was the city near the valley of this impending "battle to the death." It lay fifteen miles west of the town of Bethlehem. The Israel army under King Saul encamped on a mountainside, and the Philistine army under their spokesman, Goliath, camped on the opposite mountainside. The no-man's land that separated the two forces was the valley Elah.

The stalemate between the two armies had now been dragged out to six weeks. This war of attrition had been won by Goliath. He would stamp forward with the clank of his armor, and his lackey shield bearer going before him, and then he would taunt King Saul's army.

"Why aren't you drawn up for battle? You live in holes like rabbits." Then he would laugh in derision.

"I don't know what to do!" implored Saul. "No one wants to be killed by this gorilla of a man."

So smart, keen young soldiers were transformed into cowards with tails between their legs. One corporal said, "We have surrendered to terror." Another chimed in, "Are we without shame?"

Three men in the army of Saul were brothers. Their family would have sustained a terrible loss had they all been killed in battle. Eliab, Abinadab, and Shammah were the three oldest sons of Jesse, a patriarch from the town of Bethlehem. He had ten children in all, eight sons and two daughters, Zeruiah and Abigail. Nothing is known of the wife or wives that Jesse may have had. His youngest son, David, twenty-three, served as a shepherd for his father's sheep.

Jesse called for David. "I want you to do something for me."

"What would that be, Father?"

"Your soldier brothers are in need of food. Take corn and bread from our warehouse and go to the valley of Elah where they are arraigned in battle. I think it will go better for everyone concerned if you take ten cheese rounds for their regiment."

"Good idea," volunteered David.

"And one more thing."

"And what is that?"

"Find out how everything goes, I mean about the battle and army life, and then when you return you can fill me in on all the details." Early the next morning at the break of day David loaded his donkey with what his father ordered and set out for the battlefield in the valley of Elah.

"Don't worry, David," Monas his replacement for the care of the sheep spoke, "I'll look after the sheep like you did."

"I know," answered David, "I know, Monas."

As he traveled westward he waved as he crossed paths on their way to Jerusalem. He could see the city of Socoh off in the distance, and he enjoyed the forests and rough terrain as he talked to his donkey. He found the supply depot for the army of Saul and deposited his food there. A soldier directed him to where he could find his brothers, and he lost no time in finding them.

"How are things going?"

"Have you had enough food?"

"Have you been injured?"

"Are you homesick?"

"Wait. Wait. Wait." Interrupted Eliab, "You're drowning us with questions."

"Your father wants to know. He told me, Bring me news of my boys." As the brothers brought David up to date on their well being, Goliath cursed his way to forefront of the Philistines. All eyes riveted on him. A frightened hush moved over the valley of Elah.

"Who's he?" David broke the silence.

"He's the giant." Abinadab volunteered.

"Why aren't you drawn for battle?" taunted Goliath.

"One man! Choose one man! Let him come down to me. We will fight. If he kills me, my army, the Philistines, will become the servants of Saul's army. But if I kill him you will become our slaves." The giant relished his own humor as the Philistines cheered the one who would give them the victory.

"Every morning," David's brother, Shammah, spoke with fear in his voice. "Every morning and every evening he parades before us."

"How long has this been going on?" Queried David.

"Six weeks," confessed Eliab. "Can you believe it? Six weeks. He curses us by gods."

David quietly studied the peril to Saul's army and explained in dismay, "I can't believe my eyes. You're running like rabbits fleeing from a dog. He's only a man. He's making a mockery of the army of the living God. The word will go out for all the world to hear that a single man defied the army of Saul."

The soldiers saw David's courage and hurried the news to Saul. "There is a young man here, not a soldier, but he has said that he is not afraid of the giant."

"I can't believe it. Is he still here? That's the first good news I've had in a long time." Saul secretly thought to himself, "How can any man in his right mind volunteer for a suicide mission? Certainly he will be killed. His family will turn on me. My people will rise up in rebellion. They will cry out, 'Why did you let this young man be slaughtered?'"

"Let no man," David spoke with conviction to Saul, "be afraid to fight this man. I have no fear to meet this infidel in hand-to-hand combat."

"I hear your words! I hear your words! Sure!" Argued Saul, "Look at you. A shepherd. Not a warrior. Look at you. What do you know about warfare? This man's a killer. That's all he's ever

Insights

known. He began his training when he learned to walk."

Look at what Saul said. You and I can see Saul's heart through the window of his words. He could have said, "David, the living God of Israel will deliver Goliath into your hands." He was ignorant of that truth so he could not put voice to the truth; instead he spoke of defeat.

"You can't fight this beast, he will kill you." But David persisted. "True. I am a shepherd. You're right, I'm not a professional soldier like this man, but I have fought wild animals."

"Tell me about it," encouraged Saul.

"One time a ferocious bear came after my sheep. Another time it was a hungry lion."

"And what did you do?" Saul listened intently as he sized up the maturity of the young man before him.

"I caught them by the nap on their neck and rescued the lamb from their jaws."

"Go on." Saul was intrigued by the quickness David narrated.

"These foolish intruders tested my watch so I had to kill them. You understand, Sir," David emphasized, "just as I killed the attacking lion and the ferocious bear so shall this juggernaut of the Philistines go down. No man should allow him to mock the army of the living God."

"I enjoy stories." Saul slapped his knee.

David sensed that Saul was thick-headed about the spiritual power of conflict. "It is clear to me it was the Person of the Lord Himself Who gave me victory over the lion. Likewise it was the Person of the Lord Himself who gave the bear into my hand. I don't go into battle alone, the Person of the Lord goes before me, and He is the One through Whom I shall prevail."

Saul thought to himself, "I'm learning from this common shepherd. I don't think I've honored the Person of God. Look at the mess my people are in. He has been battle-tested with the wild beasts. He can use speed, but first he must get past the shield bearer. I don't see how he'll do it. He says over and over that the Lord is with him."

Saul had been looking out the tent door pensively; now he turned to the expectant David. "Young man, you have great confidence."

"Yes Sir, it would be foolish for me to fight him if I wasn't certain I could kill him."

"All right. All right." Saul spoke reluctantly. "Fight the man. If you must. If you lose we'll be their slaves. The outcome of the battle rests on your shoulders. The Lord be with you."

David had taken only a few steps from the presence of Saul when he heard, "Wait. Wait." Saul had an afterthought. "You can't fight Goliath dressed like a shepherd."

"Are you sure?" questioned David.

"Yes. Yes." You need the armor of a combatant. "Here is a sword; you'll need that. I also have here a helmet of bronze, and this coat of mail."

"I'll give it a shot," conceded David in deference to Saul's authority.

He donned the items Saul gave to him but soon confessed he felt imprisoned. "I can't move. I can't see. All of this will impede me."

"It's up to you," spoke Saul in resignation.

With Saul's blessing he left the tent dressed as a shepherd. He had his hardwood staff to fend off the blows, and he stopped at a stream as he descended the hill to the valley floor. He selected five smooth stones which he put in the kidskin pouch slung from his shoulder. In his hand he carried a sling, a piece of leather tied to two strings. The object was to put a stone in the leather saddle, whirl the strings, and release one string. The stone in the saddle would fly like a bullet at the target. David had spent hours each week practicing with the sling and he knew he could hit a coin at thirty paces.

David walked to the forefront of the army of Israel. In this moment of cut-throat violence no prisoner would be taken for this was a fight to the death. All eyes were on him including the eyes of the shield bearer and Goliath. The giant looked about to see if there was a soldier to fight him.

"Who are you?" He roared in laughter to David. "You have no armor! Where's your helmet? No mail! No sword! A kid with a stick! Don't you know who I am? I'm not a dog!" With disdain, Goliath cursed David by his gods and hollered, "Come to me, sonny boy, and I will give your flesh to the birds of the air and the beasts of the earth." The giant rumbled forward.

David testified, "You come to me with a sword, a spear, and a javelin. I come to you in the name of the Lord, the mighty God of the ranks of Israel."

The giant leaned forward on his sword and enjoyed a belly laugh at the words of David.

"Your threats and cursing have made a fool of us for many days so the hour has come when the Lord will deliver you into my hand."

"Did you hear that?" Goliath smirked to his shield bearer.

David shouted, "I will not only kill you. But I will also cut off your head and give the bodies of you and your compatriots to the birds and beasts. All of this will happen for one reason: that everyone may enjoy the knowledge that there is a living God in Israel."

With the stone in the pocket of his sling David sprinted with lightning speed before the giant could react. His sling whirred above his head like a propeller and he released one string as he had practiced thousands of times, and the stone found the mark he sought: the exposed forehead of his enemy. Goliath pitched forward on his face with the clanging of his armor. He had been knocked out, so David ran forward and stood on him. He drew Goliath's sword from its scabbard and decapitated him as he had promised. The shield-bearer and the Philistines fled for their lives on the death of their leader.

INSIGHT

There are those who read the story of David and Goliath and see it as another story. Others see it as history. Some compliment its literature. "Prophecy," says another reader. For the believer today it goes far beyond another story, history, literature or prophecy, for in it you and I can see the dynamics of faith.

Jesus taught us to speak to the mountain (Mark 11:22-24). You'll recall He also spoke to a dead man, to a tree, and to the sea. In that Mark passage we learn that the God-kind of faith speaks about things which are not in existence, as though they were in existence. David's faith spoke to the giant about his death as though it had already happened. The Holy Spirit penned this account that you and I might see a model of faith in action. You and I have been given the authority to speak about things which have not been made as though they are already in existence. That's the God-kind of faith Jesus says you and I should have (see Mark 11:22). Be patient. Simply say what God says about your situation.

They Closed Their Ears

I was interested in a column I saw the other day.
Coming Spiritual Events was the heading. Underneath I saw some of the meetings that were happening in town.

Our City Council Reviews a Church Site

Women and the Workplace

Who Picks Your Synod Leaders? How About a Woman?

As I looked at the seminars I asked myself some questions. What are people looking for when they attend these sessions? Is it knowledge? What about fellowship? Could they want a voice in what's going on?

And I employed these questions to myself as I began another essay. What would I be looking for? I would hope that I would find a very personal lesson from The Holy Spirit, something that would challenge my faith, something that would couple the daily happenings in my life with what the Bible said about them.

I had these thoughts in mind when I looked at Israel in the year 1490 B.C. God had just taken them miraculously through the Red Sea and they found themselves stranded at Kadesh-barnea (Numbers chapter 13). One million people. Herds. Flocks. A mixed multitude of followers. Through their forefather Abraham, who had lived five hundred years earlier, this great throng had been promised the land of Canaan. So it stood written in their Scriptures.

Before we go into this land, said the people, we want to know what we're getting into. Their words defied what God said. If we go pell mell into Canaan we'll all be slaughtered. Think of our children. Here's what we propose. Send someone up there. They can check out this land, we'll know what we're getting into. They threw out God's promise. They wanted to walk by sight, and not by faith.

In his weakness, Moses gave in to the people. So men were selected. One from each of the twelve tribes. Now we can have peace of mind, agreed the people, these men will bring back a reliable report of their search of the land.

We'll take a break from our narrative to point out something. God had already spied out the land for them *(Deuteronomy 8:7-9)*. So this act was a big step in doubting the Lord. They failed to trust what God had said, so they took matters into their own hands.

They complained, "it's God's fault we're stuck here in Kadesh-barnea." Their deliverance across the Red Sea was quickly forgotten, a miracle of the past.

"As far as we're concerned, God is dead."

"We need someone we can trust."

In their fear they set themselves up as gods of their own making.

So Israel, rejecting God's counsel, selected twelve men to do a search of the land that had been promised to them. These men were leaders. The cream of the crop. They had an excellent track record.

After forty days, the chosen twelve returned from scouting out the land.

Shaphat, of the tribe of Simeon reported to the people. "We came to the land to which you sent us. Surely it flows with milk and honey." And he showed the people the fruit they brought back. They could see it was a land that flourished with abundance.

But Palti spoke up with a trembling voice. He represented the tribe of Benjamin.

"Don't forget to tell the people about the cities."

"Yes, oh yes," said Shaphat, "the cities are large and are heavily fortified."

"But what about the people," shouted someone from the crowd, with fear in his voice. "What are they like?"

Sethur of the tribe of Asher answered, "We saw the sons of Anak. Giants. Great Warriors. Courageous fighters."

Israel spent the night in tears at the report the twelve brought back

"We should have died in Egypt," they screamed. "God has brought us to Kadesh-barnea to be slaughtered by the sword. We're a doomed people!"

But two men faced the rebellious crowd. "Let us go up at once," shouted Joshua and Caleb. "We can take this land."

But Nahbi, a scout from the tribe of Napthali screamed, "Joshua, Joshua, how can you say that? You saw these people with your own eyes. I'm telling you, they could fight gods. I saw myself as a grasshopper when I looked at them."

He saw himself as a grasshopper

"He saw himself as a grasshopper," mimicked the frightened people.

Joshua seized the moment. "Let's go up! Let's go up at once! Why wait?"

At this cry, the crowd began looking for rocks.

"Stone 'em! Stone 'em!"

Moses intervened to save the faithful two. In their defiance what did Israel forfeit?

"I had something wonderful for you," God had promised. "A land lies before you; a land between the Jordan river and the Mediterranean sea, a land which I gave to you many hundreds of years before, under Abraham. I had pledged to do this for you."

"We'll all die taking it!" Cried the people.

"No. No. No. I will fight for you as I did at the Red Sea, and you shall see My power with your own eyes." *(Exodus 14:14)*

At the beginning of this essay I asked the question: how can I profit from this study? Here's something that brings me to my feet.

> I do not need to ask for something God has already given to me in His Word. I pursue a course of action triggered by His promise. God pledged to Israel: I have given you the land. I will wage the warfare.

If Israel had said — "We speak from our hearts of Your presence and power. In faith we march into the land you have promised. We know we'll be victorious" — then they would have avoided the judgment. In their defiance of God's promise, this generation died in their forty-year sentence in the wilderness. Joshua and Caleb would have led them into the land of God promised to Abraham.

The One Who Sees Beyond

What happened to the wonder of childhood?
Joyce Kilmer said:
I think that I shall never see
a poem, lovely, as a tree.

He saw beyond. Beyond what? Beyond the obvious. Beyond what most of us see. A tree stirred Joyce Kilmer's feelings, his passion. The juices of appreciation flowed.

Don't you think those who see beyond put the magic into life?

A neighbor said to me, "Put your arms around this tree."

Pointless. My arms went less than halfway around the giant elm that tried to touch the clouds.

"Before the Civil war," he revealed, "this baby struggled to be as big as a man."

The colossal base flared out to support the towering tree — looking so much like the flying buttresses of a grand cathedral.

He whispered respectfully as he laid his hand on this living statue, "This rugged bark — have you ever seen such depth?"

I touched the tree with the reverence of conversion.

"What would the tree say," he queried slowly, "if it could talk? Indians, settlers, passing families, children, admirers and the blind snow storms. She's seen it all."

You and I can see beyond in people as well as things of nature. When you say to another, "You've got it in you to succeed" — you are seeing beyond. You're calling his future. You're sprinkling him with angel dust.

Where would the doers of history be if they had listened to the detractors? Behind every successful person stands one who has seen beyond.

This ability to see beyond — where does it come from? It's not innate. It's learned. It's a skill. How can I get it? It's the simplest thing in the world. One word — OBSERVE.

Jesus talked about seeing beyond in spiritual understanding:
> Whoever sees beyond shall be given more. And he shall have insight in abundance. But for the one who fails to see beyond, what little he has shall be taken away from him *(Matthew 13:12 literal).*

Paul the apostle saw beyond when he testified how the Holy Spirit had opened his own spiritual eyes.
> I do not look at the things which are easily seen, but I gaze upon the things which are not seen. For the things which are so easily seen are always changing, but the things which are not seen — they are eternal *(2 Corinthians 4:18 literal).*

Why Me?

I received a phone call from my friend Ted.
"Have you got time for lunch?"

"Sure," I replied. As Christian friends it was our pleasure to see one another from time to time.

"What does Friday look like?" Ted asked.

"Looks good on this end."

"Say 12:30. Usual place."

"I'll be there."

We met at the restaurant, and after some chitchat he brought me up-to-date on difficulties he had experienced in his personal life. As the waitress took our orders I reviewed in my mind his surgery and the financial hurdles that followed. As the waitress left I assured him that I had been walking in faith on his behalf during those testing days.

"Thank you. I banked on it." He paused, with a look out the window, then he asked, "I know you were speaking a verse as you brought me before the Father, what verse was it?"

"It was a verse in Isaiah Forty."

"How'd it go?"

"He gives power to the faint and weary. Verse twenty-nine. Here's how my prayer went."

> Father, You say in Your word You give strength and power to those of us who are going through a time of the testing of their faith. Ted is experiencing such a time in his life. You always do what You say You will do, so I know You have given Ted power just as you promised.

"Thank you." A tear came to Ted's eyes. "I experienced the very strength you prayed for. Ya' know, Norm, you and I have so much to be thankful for."

"I can say Amen to that."

"When you're talking about the Word," Ted took a sip of coffee, "I did chew over a verse in the first chapter of the book of James."

"When you say that word 'chew,' excuse the interruption, it reminds of a cow chewing her cud."

"Yeah," Ted smiled. "She ruminates on her cud. She doesn't gulp it down."

"So you chewed over a verse in James?" I moved on.

"I did," he answered. "Here's the verse, but I preface the verse with my own name to make personal claim to its promise."

> Ted, when you find yourself surrounded by trials be filled with joy. Why? Because this is the hour you make the fantastic discovery that you have genuine faith.

"That's a big order….to be filled with joy when the chips are down."

> Ted, when you find yourself surrounded by trials be filled with joy. Why? Because this is the hour you make the fantastic discovery that you have genuine faith.

Ted repeated the verse slowly. I listened to each word and then I said, "I can hear those words tumbling around in the drums of your mind."

He chuckled at my picture. He went on, "Here's what I hear the Father saying in this verse: 'Your faith means everything to me.'"

"Good insight."

"He goes further." Ted paused to look out the restaurant window. "He not only says it means everything to Him, but I also understand, He wants me to have the joy that I have genuine faith."

"In other words, he wants you to say, 'I have genuine faith.'"

"Correct."

"A bystander could ask," I observed, "did God put the trials in your life to prove your faith?"

"No. No. No." Ted hurriedly answered, "I looked at my medical problems and the financial crisis that followed as part of the drama of life. In the midst of my scene the Father was looking at my faith. You recall the Lord's Last Supper."

"I certainly do."

"In that final hour Jesus said to Peter: 'Simon, Simon, listen! Satan has begged me to give all of you to him. I have prayed for you that your faith fail not.' (Now here's the Lord's faith) 'When you are established, strengthen the brethren.'" *(Luke 2:31,32)*

"The Lord knew," Ted elaborated, "that when He was gone their faith would shout, 'He lives!'"

I rejoined him, "Great! Life and death hang in the balance of our faith."

Ted grimaced as he said, "Satan hates faith."

"I have to confess," I looked Ted in the eye, "that all too often when the going gets tough I'll ask, 'why me?'"

"One of the first things I had to learn," Ted paused in search of the right words, "is that trials are as much a part of life as breathing."

"I hear what you're saying. Don't be surprised." We sat quietly for a moment, "chewing the cud" on what had been said.

"I learned an important lesson," Ted broke into our rumination.

"What was that?"

"You can't pick tulips out of the air."

"You've lost me," I said, as I took a sip of coffee.

"I'm saying this, that the joy requires a source."

"In other words," I filled in, "your words require authority, and how do you do that?"

"This is what the Lord said to me when I lay in the hospital."

Ted, I have personally carried away your sickness (Matthew 8:17).

"The source of your joy, as I grasp it, sprang out of what the Lord assured you."

Ted went on, "Here's what I did. After I read that verse in Matthew, I mentally put my sickness in a boat."

"I picture it."

"Then I pushed it out to sea."

"Gone. As far as you were concerned, I can see why the Bible says, 'It is alive,' when you pictured in your heart that your sickness had been carried away ... "

"Simple. The Word said so."

" ... and this knowledge gave you the joy James speaks about."

The waitress checked our cups as Ted spoke. Another verse came to my mind as I faced financial hurdles.

"Interesting. I would guess it would be the testing of your faith."

"True."

"How'd it go?" I asked.

"Ya' know the early church took a hammering."

"I think of Stephen's martyrdom."

"They learned how to face suffering. Peter talks a lot about trial in the five chapters of his first book. This verse is found in the first chapter."

"Be filled with joy, Ted, that you have learned for yourself that your faith stood firm under testing." (verses 6 and 7)

"This discovery, that your faith withstood the attack, is more precious than gold."

"That's my literal rendering of the verses." Ted chucked at himself.

"I like your use of the word 'discovery.'"

"I had to learn," he went on, "that my spirit requires the food of God's Word. I found spiritual nourishment for my financial predicament from Psalm one."

"I recall that Psalm says the man who delights in His word shall be like a tree planted by the river."

Ted took over, "… he shall bring forth his fruit in his season, and he shall prosper in all his ways."

"You began, I take it, to look at your situation through the eyes of God."

"It was simple. I embraced what the Father guaranteed in Psalm one."

"You took Him at His Word. And your financial picture?"

"I soon found out. I could keep current."

"That's good."

Ted rejoiced, "I'd like to shout the lesson I learned from the housetops!"

" … In a word that would be?" I asked.

"He keeps this Word!"

INSIGHT

It was midsummer in Galilee, early in the brief three-year ministry of Jesus. He had enjoyed many pulpits. One day he preached from a boat. He also taught in the synagogue. Once He was in a private home when some desperate followers tore off the roof to get their friend to him. He taught on the side of the road. In our story He spoke from a hillside and the title of His message is The Sermon on the Mount.

Jesus pictures two men building two different houses. One

Why Me?

man digs deep till he hits rock. That will be his foundation for his house.

The other builder says, "that's too much work to dig for rock, so I'll use the sand as a foundation for my house."

So the two houses are built. Time passes. Both men are doing fine but nature shows her terrifying side. The winds blew. Storms batter the houses. Floods. The house built on the rock foundation stands like the day she was built. The house built on the sand foundation crumbled to the ground.

The house built on the sand pictures the life lived without the new spiritual life God gives. So Jesus poses this question: "Who shall enter the kingdom of heaven?" (Matthew 7:21-27)

"There are those among you" Jesus continues, "who say things like this: 'Lord, Lord, we have prophesied in Your Name. Yes, we have cast out demons in Your Name. It is true we have done miracles in Your Name.'"

"From a square I will declare," says Jesus, "I never knew you! Get out of my way! (You are trying to save yourself with your works)..."

"Now," Jesus says, "I will tell you the answer to this question: Who shall enter the kingdom of heaven? He is like a man who built his house on a rock foundation. When the storms of life come his house stands firm. He has done the will of My Father. He has heard the Word and acted on it. With the heart you and I believe unto righteousness." (Romans 10:10)

Practicing the Three Secrets

THIRTY-ONE PERSONAL PROFESSIONS OF MY FAITH

God used words to create light.
And God said, Let there be light, and there was light.
(Genesis 1:3)

Other Bible verses are vested with the same creative power when they become one with the believing heart. Light enables my eyes to see. What God says gives sight to my spirit.

Jesus doesn't have to return in person to work supernaturally in my life. Instead, He has lavished upon me words — promises — pledges — guarantees — a blood contract in writing.

He created light with words. He creates spiritual life with words. I enter the Christian life through the doorway of what God says. In the same way, the only sustenance for the Christian life comes from what God says. Faith must be united or joined to something to live. When I speak in faith the words that God has spoken, the Holy Spirit activates their divine power in my life.

This chapter plays the right chord for the one who says, "I don't know where to start. I don't have the foggiest idea how to find a promise, and worse yet, how in the world do you frame it into a profession?"

The love of God, I'm sure you'll agree, gives us our starting point. From this jumping-off point, the 'professions' aim at building the life of faith. Each profession contains a lead-in statement, a Biblical promise, and the profession of faith that the verse summons.

One can become a Christian from a handful of words, such as John 3:16. Millions have done so. Other verses as I mentioned above — in their striking brevity — contain the same life-changing power.

God has given everything to you and me that pertains to life and godliness *(2 Peter 1:3)*. In other words, God has done all He's going to do. Someone asks, "Doesn't He have an ongoing workshop?" No. Another brings this up: "I'm waiting for that 'go-ahead' feeling." Feelings lack reliability to be a repository for my faith. God always talks about knowing. He has given me the answer for every need of life. He expects me to find it, know it, and profess it.

Seeing that God expects me to know my inheritance, my life faces several transformations. I no longer beg God to do something; I realize He has already done it. Once I find it I can stand resolutely on His gift to me. I know His will on the matter from what He says.

Now that I have found these words that form the wellspring for the dynamic Christian life, what do I do with them? Under the teaching of the Holy Spirit I frame these commitments of God into a spoken personal affirmation.

Why does it need to be spoken? One said, For a word to 'live' it needs to be uttered (it needs to be gotten out). I know God loves me because He says so. A stifled word dies unborn. God speaks. In the same way, my faith speaks. My inner man listens to what my mouth proclaims.

The Thirty-One Professions translate circumstances to God's viewpoint. New vocabulary — God's Words. New speech — saying what God says. What I say with my mouth now enters a new dimension — words impregnated by the Person of the Holy Spirit.

Say a profession a day. Jot it down on a dated card and keep it handy. Review it from time to time with an audible voice. Write your own responses on the card.

Be patient. Don't look for something overnight. You are taking a giant spiritual step and your life will be dramatically changed. You will find it the best investment you ever made. Begin today to enjoy the supernatural life God wants you to have.

Thirty-One Personal Professions of My Faith

1. I start out with the sublime truth — God's love.
    > But God! So rich is He in His mercy.
    > Because of and in order to satisfy the great and wonderful and intense love with which He loved me ...
    > > *Ephesians 2:4 (Amplified translation).*
    > > *(Second profession goes to Ephesians 2:5).*

    I profess: Your great love for me flows out of who You are.

2. I have a new beginning.
    > Even when I was dead, slain by my own sins, He made me alive together in fellowship and in union with Christ. — He gave me the very life of Christ Himself, the same new life with which He made Him alive.
    > > *Ephesians 2:5 (Amplified).*

    I profess: Through this love you have given to me the very life of Christ Himself.

3. How can God give to me the life of Christ? The creative power to do this lies in the power of God's Words.
    > I have been born again, not of a seed which dies, but of a seed — God's Words — which live forever.
    > > *I Peter 1:23*

    I profess: You have created this new life in me through what You say — Your Words.

4. What does God expect of me in this new life?

Insights

> The just shall live by faith.
>
> *Romans 1:17b*

I profess: You have given me this new life to enable me to live by faith.

5. Is it acceptable to simply *acknowledge* God? No.
> Without faith it is impossible to please God.
>
> *Hebrews 11:6a*

I profess: You expect me to live by faith.

6. Seeing that God expects me to live by faith, where can I find this faith?
> Faith comes (and comes, and comes) out of a source of that which is heard, and hearing by the Word of God.
>
> *Romans 10:17*

I profess: Your Word is the wellspring for my faith.

7. Can I find a model in the Bible of the kind of faith I'm supposed to have?
> Have faith in God (King James margin: Have the faith of God).
>
> *Mark 1:22b*

I profess: Jesus instructs me in this verse to copy the kind of faith You practice.

8. I picture God as having a faith that would be out of my reach.
> (By faith) God calls into existence the things that apparently do not exist.
>
> *Romans 4:17 (last phrase).*

I profess: As I study Your faith, I see You use Words to bring things into manifestation.

9. How does the Bible picture God's faith?
> And God said, let there be light: and there was light.

Genesis 1:3

I profess: In this verse I see the awesome power of Your spoken Word.

10. How did Jesus tie together this God-kind of faith with my faith?

> Whoever says to the mountain, "Mountain, get up and hurl yourself into the sea!" Now the one who says this sees it as done because he has no doubt in his heart.
>
> *Mark 11:23*

I profess: When I have heart faith I receive the answer immediately.

11. God's dynamic faith belongs to me!

> And this is the confidence which we have in Him: we are sure that if we ask anything according to His will He hears us. Since we positively know He hears us, we also know with settled and absolute knowledge that we have as present possessions the requests made of Him.
>
> *John 5:14,15*

I profess: To pray Your will I pray Your Word. I know I possess in advance that for which I believe.

12. Jesus reaffirms this startling insight as to how God believes.

> ... believe that you have received (beforehand) and you shall (automatically) have them.
>
> *Mark 11:24b*

I profess: I delight in this truth that to believe is to have received.

13. What else can I learn from these verses in Mark 11?

> ... whoever says to the mountain.
>
> *Mark 11:23a*

I profess: I have been given authority to address the thing

desired.

14. God created with Words. He sees my words as the key to my heart.
> Death and life are in the power of the tongue, and those who love it will eat its fruits (for death or life).
> *Proverbs 18:21*

I profess: I speak Your Words which are alive. Through them the Person of the Lord Jesus Christ lives in me with power.

15. Do my words expose who I am?
> The mouth speaks what's in the heart (Jesus speaking).
> *Matthew 12:34*

I profess: I change my words and I change my life. I sow Your Words into my heart so I can speak faith when I talk.

16. Can I shout, "I have it now!"?
> He who believes in me now possesses eternal life.
> *John 6:47*

I profess: If I can know I have eternal life, I certainly can claim in advance I possess what You promise for my day to day living.

17. How can I find supernatural power in what I speak?
> We have not received the spirit of the World system but the Spirit Who is of God, that we might come to know the things (His promises) which God has bestowed on us in grace.
> We put these "promises" into words, not in words taught by human philosophy, but in words taught by the Holy Spirit Himself, fitly joining together Spirit-revealed truths with Spirit-taught words.
> *1 Corinthians 2:12,13 (Wuest)*

I profess: You have given me Your Words. With my mouth I mix what You say with the desires of my heart.

18. Why are God's Words different from ordinary words?
> Because God's Words are a living thing they are filled with divine spiritual power.
>
> *Hebrews 4:12*

I profess: I use the Words You have bestowed on me because they alone impart spiritual life.

19. Why are God's Words a living thing?
> God is not a man that He should lie, or a son of man that He should change His mind. What He promises He does. If He has spoken it, He will carry it out.
>
> *Numbers 23:19*

I profess: Your Words are alive because You transform them to divine power in the believing heart.

20. What else makes His Words live?
> When God made His promise to Abraham, He swore by Himself, since He had no one greater by whom He could swear.
>
> *Hebrews 6:13*

I profess: I see by this verse that You are under divine oath to carry out Your promise in the believer's life.

21. Can I be certain I have the right to use these living and powerful Words?
> The Father has lavished upon us His great and precious promises (or guarantees), that through these I might share in His divine nature.
>
> *2 Peter 1:4*

I profess: I am indwelt by Christ. He lives through me when His Words energize my life.

22. Why are words a telltale window to my heart?
> The Word is near you, on your lips and in your heart...

Romans 10:8a

I profess: My speech attests to the presence of the Lord Jesus Christ in my life.

23. I wait for the manifestation of the promise. Nothing happens. What went wrong?
> Hold fast to the profession (saying the same thing as God says) of your faith without wavering (for He is faithful Who promised).
>
> *Hebrews 10:23*

I profess: I continue to say what You say, even in the face of refuting circumstances.

24. I see that the promise may not be realized overnight.
> Abraham remained absolutely convinced (he waited twenty-five years) that God would do exactly what He said He'd do.
>
> *Romans 4:20,21*

I profess: Like Abraham, I keep Your promise before my eyes.

25. I can't set the time for the realization of the promise.
> You have need of patience, that, after you have done the will of God (to see the promise "in place" in my life) you might "carry away" what He has given.
>
> *Hebrews 10:36*

I profess: I have Your guarantee in writing — it stands written with finality.

26. If I have to wait for the promise, where can I look to find the creative power to bring the promise into realization?
> I have spoken it, I will also bring it to pass; I have purposed it, I will also do it.
>
> *Isaiah 46:11b*

I profess: I see the creative power to bring Your promise to fruition lies in the promise itself.

Thirty-One Personal Professions of My Faith

27. How could Abraham have had such life-changing faith?
> God bound Himself by an oath on the basis of Who He is to carry out His Word to Abraham.
>
> *Hebrews 6:13*

I profess: Your oath gives me greatness of faith.

28. Trials will try to tear down the ramparts of my faith.
> Receive trials joyfully. You know from experience your reaction to them proves the authenticity of your faith.
>
> *James 1:2-4*

I profess: Trials give me the opportunity to embrace Your Word firsthand.

29. Give me a verse you would turn to during your testing.
> Christ is able to do superabundantly beyond all I ask or think (or even dream), according to the power that works in me.
>
> *Ephesians 3:20*

I profess: I know that Christ has already worked this matter out.

30. I notice your functional use of verses in the Bible.
> The sword which the Holy Spirit wields is the Word of God,
>
> *Ephesians 6:17*

I profess: Thanks be to God Who always causes us to triumph in Christ *(2 Corinthians 2:14).*

31. You must see your life of faith as a warfare.
> Fight the fight of the faith, which combat is marked by its technical beauty (Wuest). Take possession of the life you have been summoned to. Continue to boldly say your precious confession.
>
> *1 Timothy 6:12*

I profess: I use weapons, unlike human warfare, that are mighty in God's warfare for the destruction of the enemy's strongholds *(2 Corinthians 10:4)*.

Part II

Collected Stories and Essays

A Great Man

I can see a summer evening — 1928 — with dusk wrapping its arms around "The Old Castle." Dad named our home in memory of his boyhood days at Friesenborg Castle in Denmark. Our open front porch held a half dozen neighborhood rag-a-muffins where Dad held forth as the Hans Christian Andersen of South Minneapolis.

"I don't believe in ghosts," Omar Norheim gave notice. (His nickname was "Kisser.") He thought he had donned a bulletproof ghost vest for what was to come.

"I'm like you," Red Marcy laughed nervously, "there are no ghosts, but I'd sure run like heck if I ever ran into one."

Everyone laughed, releasing repressed fear, each trapped in a graveyard of his own making.

Dad made his way through this obstacle course of comments with a mischievous smile playing on his face. No sir, these ghost story Scrooges couldn't detour him. He ran his hand distractedly through his graying hair. All eyes riveted on him in expectancy.

"I can still see the house in Lading." Oh! Oh! Here we go again. You could have heard a pin drop. "Lading is a village in the tiny land of Denmark — far across the sea."

All of us stood in our minds in front of this house in the small town of Lading. Roguishly he transported us to this far away fairyland. Fear numbed each one. Hands gripped tight. We knew something bad was about to happen.

"I know why she haunted this house there in Lading," he announced with certainty. This laureate conductor of the macabre had a phantom gargoyle peeking around the corner of the house. "A wo-wo-woman ghost!" stuttered Peg Nielsen who always walked with a limp. "I n-n-never heard of a wo-wo-woman ghost."

"Oh sure." stated Dad emphatically. His stentorian voice carried as much authority as that of big Pastor Bartsch. "She was looking for the grave of her baby."

"Looking for the grave of her baby?" echoed a barrage of voices. A female spectress walked among us to lay her hand on a small shoulder.

"Why wasn't he buried in a cemetery?" queried Red Marcy. And Harry Nielsen blurted out with amusing innocence, "I've got a porch."

"I don't know why he had been buried under the porch there in Lading." Dad threw his own apprehensive look about the porch. All eyes followed his.

"Nobody's buried under our porch," Lloyd said flatly with questionable assurance.

"That's hard to tell," opined Dad suspiciously. He gave them a moment of silence to listen to their hearts. He snapped off the silence like the breaking of a twig. "Have you ever seen a troll?"

"Wait! Wait! Wait!" all hollered. A cacophony of protest met his change of subject. "What about the lady ghost and her baby?"

"Oh. Oh. Oh," the beguiling storyteller chuckled, "the people who lived in that house began to dig under the porch."

"Was she — the lady ghost — was she watching?" asked Dave Pace with studied interest. Dave knew dusky gremlins and goblins were prowling beyond the porch rail. He also knew the ghost police didn't patrol this street tonight.

"No, she wasn't watching," filled in the storyteller, "they were digging in the daytime. You can see ghosts only at night."

"I'm glad they didn't ask me to dig," one laughed excitedly.

"Me too," chorused another.

"Finally they found the bones of the baby," announced a relieved yarn spinner.

"Wow! a little skeleton!" exclaimed Dave. "The people of Lading had a funeral," Dad uttered like a newspaper reporter, "and the little baby boy was given proper Christian burial in the churchyard cemetery." This gave the story credibility.

"Did the lady ghost come around anymore?" Elmer wanted to know.

"No, no," answered this guide to the gruesome, "all along she wanted this baby buried with her."

"Boy!" quipped a relieved Omar, who didn't believe in ghosts in the first place, "I'll bet they were sure glad to get rid of her."

A face peering through the spindles ventured in a quavering voice, "I've never seen a troll." He was baiting Dad.

"They lived in the forest. Nobody has ever seen 'em in town. Anyway they lived in the forest of Friesenborg castle. I played there when I was a boy like you. This is in the tiny country of Denmark."

One would swear he knew the trolls on a first name basis, but he never stated outright that he saw one. Often he left us suspended as he ignited our imaginations. He tip-toed through our childlike openness. He talked about Hulgar the Dane who would someday save Denmark when there were not enough men left to stand around a barrel. On his magic carpet he took us to castles and dungeons. He helped us to hear the chains dragged back and forth in the attic.

We entered twilight swashbuckling and daring, but when darkness descended there was no pretense to naked bravery. How welcome the volunteer chaperone.

"Anybody goin' my way?" sounded one in veiled friendliness.

"If I walk you home, who's gonna walk me home?" countered

a nervous voice.

Our neighborhood had become a graveyard policed by a woman ghost. She took no hostages. For sure I'm gonna pull the covers over my head tonight.

I want to jump ahead now to 1970. I sat with my two brothers and two sisters in the family room of the funeral home. Dad had just died.

Pastor Johnson asked us, "How would you characterize the life of your father?" He searched for words that would make Dad live again. In forty-eight hours he would publicly eulogize this ninety-year old man. What would he say? He looked to us.

Lloyd spoke up first. "I suppose you're looking for something that would help you picture this man, something that would help you see him as we see him."

Pastor Johnson nodded. Each one of us faced the question — How would you characterize your dad? — with hallowed feelings. Words seemed such feeble tools in a room pervaded with that Lenten atmosphere. Our minds traveled back in time.

I thought to myself. His death constitutes more than an end to an era. His departure closes down a micro-civilization. Not even a vapor. It's gone. Disappeared. I find it sobering.

When I peek into the sanctuary of a departed loved one's life — motion pictures — sacred pictures — dance across the slate of my memory. Imagine this: I am a trustee of his legacy.

Elmer broke the hushed reverence. "I think of all he saw across the years from eighteen-eighty-one to nineteen-seventy."

Each one saw Dad's life — glinting — from another facet of the diamond in this moment of solemn reflection.

"He loved America." Evelyn jogged us back to the moment. That started a torrent of comments.

"Dad was never a complicated man." appraised Betty.

"That's for sure," agreed Lloyd, "he never lost his childlikeness."

"Everybody liked Dad," I interjected.

"I think the reason for that, Norman," Elmer rejoined with feeling, "was because he never talked about other people."

"Do you remember," chimed in Betty, "that he never allowed gossip around the dinner table?"

Pastor Johnson leaned forward as he began to see the colors for the portraiture of this man. He said to himself, "I wish I had known this man more intimately."

"He whistled a lot" recalled another. "Don't you remember him whistling in the bakeshop?"

"Oh yeah," reminisced Evelyn, "he loved all kinds of music."

"Talking about music," said Elmer with a broad smile, "what about that song 'The Bells of Hell Go Ting a Ling a Ling'? That was a World War I song."

"And what surprises me is that he knew all the words," recollected Betty. "And what about 'How Much Is That Doggie In The Window?'"

"Oh, that was by Patti Page. He loved Patti Page."

Lloyd mentioned how hard Dad had worked in his life.

"You can say that again," responded Elmer, "He was a roll-up-your-sleeves kind of a guy."

My thoughts kaleidoscoped and tumbled through the years of my father's life. I projected myself into a veritable hymn of fatherhood. Memories unleashed lyrics that are ineradicable.

"As I listen," reflected the minister in a moment of quiet, "your father impresses me a great man."

"He sure was," exclaimed Elmer and Lloyd in unison. All of us felt a kinship with the insight of the pastor.

For each one the minister had sounded the right note. No one could have strummed a finer phrase. I can still hear the first words of his eulogy to a packed chapel: "We have come together today

A Great Man

to say farewell to a great man."

I mulled the sentence over in my mind ... We have come together today to say farewell to a great man. A great man. A great man. What made him great? I've spent some time thinking about that since that morning in the funeral home. How do you measure a man's life? I can't use the measuring stick of money ... or success ... or power ... or status. None of these help me ascertain the dimensions of his life.

If you had the privilege of meeting him you would have noticed his voice first. Rich and baritone with a beguiling Danish accent. At five foot nine he stood erect with a strong build. His posture was that of a military man.

"Stand as straight as a candle, Stron," was his admonish to me. A wisp of a smile played across his face as if he was up to some mischief.

Pronouncements came with such finality such apocalyptic certainty — a voice from the clouds.

"Stron, yop this is the Yellowstone Trail."

I stood open-mouthed at the small concrete bridge between Lake Calhoun and Cedar Lake. A small sign identified the rail line — Yellowstone Trail. Oh yes, as an eight-year-old boy I thought it was God Himself speaking. Nothing could be added to this proclamation. How could I know it was nothing more than the name of a rail line?

Dad entered this world in the deep of winter in Denmark. He was born two weeks after Christmas, January 6, 1881, the second son to Laurs, age 32, and Kirsten, age 25.

I can picture the day when Kirsten said, "Laurs, today he crawled for the first time." Or, "Laurs, today he took his first step."

Out of deference to his wife, Laurs named him Rasmus. Kirsten's maiden name had been Rasmussen. Laurs also had a half-brother named Rasmus. I wonder if somebody kidded Dad about his name when he came to America?

"Hey, Rasmus, you better get moving."

He dropped the name and went by the initials "RC" or the name "Chris" from his middle name, Christian.

"Do you know how the fox gets the porcupine to turn over?" he would ask us as he taught us about forest lore. "He would pee on him." Then he would laugh in embarrassment. He spent his boyhood in the forests of Friesenborg Castle. Here with his four brothers and dog Thor he enjoyed an idyllic childhood. He watched his dad care for the horses and coach of the Count. After an eighth grade education he left this charming life to travel to the town of Hamel.

So at the age of fourteen, in the year of 1895, weighing only sixty-four pounds, he commenced his bakery apprenticeship. In 1899 at eighteen he achieved the coveted title of Master Baker.

"You boys," Dad later admonished his sons, "have to have a trade. I'm not raising you to move pianos all your lives."

At eighteen he began the life of an itinerant baker. He put on his seven league boots to see the world. When he landed in a new town he went to the office of the baker's union.

"Here are my credentials. They show me to be a master baker."

He always found work. Between 1899 and 1912 he traveled through Denmark, Germany, and Norway. He and a good friend became bicycle racers.

"I'll never forget that day," he would laugh, "this farmer kid leaned out from the inside rail to see us coming. Wham! We collided heads. I went sprawling on the track but I wasn't hurt. I never did find out what happened to that big kid."

Many times he stood on the winner's platform to be decorated for his achievements on the track. A drawer of medals gave credence to this, but he talked little about those badge-filled years. I wish I had asked him more about his years as an adventurer.

America. America. At first, no more than a word. Then it moved to acquaintanceship. He perked up his ears when America was mentioned. A new life. New adventures. New opportunities. His dream passed from "I could never do that," to "Why not!"

This Gulliver with a dream in his pocket landed in the Norwegian harbor city of Trondhjem in 1912. A dandy of thirty-one with a straw hat, cane in hand, a sharp dresser with a clipped mustache. A lovely brunette with olive skin caught his eye, and they talked America as they hiked the forested hills that smiled down on this fjord city.

They crystallized their dream with Dad sailing first for America in 1913. He landed with his hands full of ambition but little money in his pocket. In desperation he took a job in a tire factory in Racine, Wisconsin. He hated it. It was not the picture his mind had painted on those pine-covered hills overlooking Trondhjem. Mom came over a year later and they were married in South Minneapolis in the spring of 1915.

When Dad was fourteen years old he started to work for Mr. Christiansen. A dignified man, an important man, a man who always wore an expensive suit — he owned the town bakery. Mr. C. became his life-long role model. Even though Dad often worked harder than an underling the persona he had of himself was that he was Mr. C. If he looked at himself in the mirror he saw himself as a successful Mr. C. This perception became the core to everything he did. He owned more than twenty-five different bakeries in his lifetime.

Dad enjoyed telling the story of his appearance before the draft board in 1917.

"How tall are you?" barked the sergeant to Dad.

"Nine foot five!" blurted out Dad in his anxiety. He could laugh at himself. But he was thirty-six years old, had two children, so they excused him from service.

1918-1923. Dad co-owned a bakery in Osage, Iowa with a Mr. Engstrom.

"Never have a business with a partner," was the only thing he had to say about those years.

In 1923 he bought The Old Castle and moved back to Minneapolis.

"I have moved thirteen times," he reminded us, "and I'm not moving anymore." And he didn't. He lived there forty-seven years.

By 1925 five children were scurrying about The Old Castle. As each child grew, to around the age of two, Dad fed the child on his lap during the dinner hour.

He never learned how to drive a car. Of course, he never owned a car. He never took a vacation. He never ate in a restaurant. He never swore. He never talked politics, sex or religion. He never was a churchman, and he never read books.

He possessed a robust common sense, a shoe-leather philosophy all his own. A number of phrases served as mileposts in his journey. One was "Stay away." If he saw a hopeless situation that would spell nothing but trouble he simply stayed away. His counsel contained two words: "Stay away." I've used those two words like a pair of shoes through the years.

"Aw ta dickens." Another verbal tool from his vocabulary tool box. Who cares? Or, it's only a bunch of humbug. As far as he was concerned the difficulty didn't amount to a hill of beans. No wonder he never lost a minute of sleep worrying about a problem.

"Pyot." A Danish word pronounced pee-yot. "That's a lot of pyot." Pyot would mean gibberish or nonsense. So when Dad said, "That's a lot of pyot," he was saying that talk doesn't mean a thing.

How can one forget "Skock" Johnson? Skock meant chess in Danish. Chess Johnson. He and Dad loved to play chess. Several times a year they would sit in the little telephone room and play till 2 a. m.

"How can you get up at five a.m. to run a bakery when you don't get to bed till two o'clock?" Mom would quietly ask.

"Skock" Johnson looked like an old prospector. Mom was always leery of old man Johnson. He had clued her in one night that he had no use for Christianity.

"You shouldn't have anything to do with that man. Don't you know that man's an atheist? He has no use for God. You shouldn't have anything to do with a man like that."

Dad taught everyone in his family how to play the game of chess. After World War II young men —Pierre Virite, Howard Revac and Bob Comer — joined Dad and the family for an evening of chess. To this day they speak fondly of their memory of "Chris."

"I don't like to talk about dying." Dad's whimsical smile vanished from his face. "I don't want to die. I don't want to buy a cemetery plot."

His fear of death shadowed him most of his adult life. He spoke about it frequently.

His large open Bible lay on the chest of drawers in his bedroom. In the last decades of his life he closed his day with the reading of a Psalm. I can feel the heat from that 60 watt light bulb. I can see him standing ramrod straight in his pajamas. And I can hear his voice, still strong, reading aloud in reverence and meditatively.

> Some trust in chariots.
> Some trust in horses.
> But as for me, I will trust in the Lord.
> *Psalm 20:7*

His formal education took him through the eighth grade. He

never walked the hallways of a high school. He knew nothing of Shakespeare or the so-called "greats" of the literary world. Now he stood in the company of words that were seeds. Seeds because they possessed life. He exchanged his fear for a new found confidence.

> One thing have I asked of the Lord, that will I seek after, that I may dwell in His presence all the days of my life, to behold the beauty of the Lord and to enquire in His temple.
>
> *Psalm 27:4*

Alone he came to the discovery that these tiny words — these seeds — possessed the awesome power to change him. He saw himself in a mirror. As he gazed he was lifted out of the fear of death that had haunted him all his life. After that he never again talked about the fear of dying. He drew a line in the sand. Quietly he purchased six gravesites at Lakewood Cemetery. Now he joined the thin ranks of spiritual nobility who know that

> ... the one who dwells in the secret place of the most high, abides under the shadow of the Almighty.
>
> *Psalm 91:1*

I can hear him mutter " ... the secret place." He taught us how to live, and he showed us how to die.

I think back to that morning in the funeral chapel. We brought his life into focus so we could see it better. Again and again the phrase echoes and reechoes through the halls of my memory. Your father was a great man. Your father was a great man. Isn't there music or an angelic choir for such an hour as this?

I shiver when I think on that winter day so long ago when Kirsten gave birth to a baby boy. He runs with his brothers in the forest of Friesenborg Castle. I groan with pain when I see him crashing into the farm kid while leading the bicycle pack.

He strolls the foothills above Trondhjem and enthralls Mom

with his dream. That's him at the ship rail with a faraway look in his eye as he sails for the land of his dreams.

Oh so clear, him holding me on his lap and feeding me at the dinner table. Only yesterday we stood under that small railroad bridge and he declared, "Yop, Stron, this is the Yellowstone Trail." Now the porch of The Old Castle has fallen silent.

Memories are more precious than rubies. They light the darkness of where I came from, and they help me to see who I am. Gee! I wish I had learned more about him when he was here to tell me. And I wish he knew how much I thought he was a great man.

    God's gentleness has made me great.
Psalm 18:35

Insights

John

It has been titled the wedding in Cana of Galilee. A family affair, simple, but Jesus turned it into a stunning story that has been the delight of everyone who reads it. You find it in the gospel of John *(2:1-11)*. Before you and I enjoy the "wedding," we will look at this man, the disciple John, who was an eyewitness to the wedding in Cana of Galilee. He refers to himself as the disciple who Jesus loved. I'm sure Jesus loved all of His disciples, so what nugget can we mine in this? John says he has a special kinship with Jesus and this was borne out on the cross when Jesus enlists John in the care for His mother. At the last supper John lay his head on Jesus chest; he was an affectionate person.

The distinguished Christian scholar Lewis Sperry Chafer said John's gospel is the most important literary production ever composed. He wrote these things, he tells us *(John 20:31)*, that you may believe that Jesus is the Christ, the Son of God and that through believing in Him you may have life through His name (who He is). John writes that before there was time Christ lived, that He was with God and that He was God Himself *(John 1:1)*.

To size up John we first take a look at Jesus. Who was this Man called Jesus? What did He look like? Often we picture what He looked like. Was He tall? Was He short? If we look at what Jesus did, you and I have a picture of a strong man. He drove the moneychangers and bird sellers from the temple. No one questioned His authority. Often He would spend the daytime in ministry, and His nights in travel. He was likely a tall man, maybe 6'2", to garner the respect He commanded. You and I could picture Him a bearded man who carried Himself with authority. He would have exuded an unmistakable aura of power, which inspired respect, awe, and devotion without bounds.

So what kind of a man would be drawn to Jesus? Jesus would have enjoyed a man who could see ahead — a visionary, someone who was teachable, but finished what he started. John had been a disciple of John the Baptist before he joined Jesus at His transfiguration. Often we picture John as a lonely fisherman (together with his brother James) at Capernaum. This is not true. He was a successful businessman who hired employees *(Mark 1:20)*. Not only did he own a second home in Jerusalem *(John 19:27)*, but he was, alas, a personal acquaintance of the high priest *(John 18:15,16)*. John was the same age as Jesus, thirty, a smart young businessman with a sparkling future.

The apostle John was a cousin of John the Baptist; that would also make him a cousin of Jesus. "He will be great," announced the angel Gabriel at the birth of Jesus, "and will be called the Son of the Most High; and the Lord will give to Him the throne of His forefather David" *(Luke 1:32)*. Certainly John knew of the angelic announcements, such as this one from Luke, about Jesus and John the Baptist, so he acted on that knowledge.

His array of carefully crafted writings shows John to be gifted intellectually as well as spiritually. I, II and III John, the gospel of John, and Revelation paint a portrait of a man filled with the Holy Spirit. Jesus nicknamed John and his brother James the Sons of Thunder. You and I are given no clue to the meaning of this name. John's mother's name was Salome, in Hebrew *Shalom*, meaning peace. She was the sister of Mary, the mother of Jesus, and is one of the women at the cross. No mention is ever made to the wife of John.

Back to the wedding in Cana of Galilee. It has been three days since His baptism in the Jordan River when Jesus arrives to celebrate a wedding. Five young men accompany Him: John, James, Peter, Andrew and Philip. Other disciples would be added later. You and I are never told the names of the bride and the groom, but owing to Mary's responsibilities, a relative was likely involved.

This miracle took place at the beginning of His ministry. Only days before, you and I know He had gone through His trial by Satan. In baptism He had received the Holy Spirit, the time being early spring, four months off before He would proclaim His ministry at Passover time.

Evidently the bride and groom were well liked for it was a grand affair with the town of Cana well represented. Eastern weddings can go on for days so you and I can easily understand shortages in provision.

I can see the picture. Jesus quietly chats with friends or His disciples when His mother comes to see him. She alerts Him to the fact that the party has run out of wine. Why would she bring this shortage to His attention? I think the answer can be found in the Holy Spirit crafting a miracle. She certainly had a sense of His divine power.

I can hear her say, "I'm sorry to interrupt Your talk with Simon, but they have run out of wine."

In terms of respect and endearment Jesus replies, "I don't know if that's our concern, Dear." At this point Jesus felt the problem lay with the person in charge of the festivities.

He continues with His mother, "If you feel it is our concern I'll do something about it. The timing's wrong. It's way too early. I was looking to later this spring."

You do not find that Mary argues with Him at this point. She finds substance (and we know faith is a substance) for her faith in Him when He says. "If you think it is our concern I'll do something about it," Her faith came by what she heard, and her hearing by what He said *(Romans 10:17)*. She puts words to her faith when she says, to Hared the headwaiter, "Whatsoever He says to you, do it and do it promptly."

Six stone water pots stood nearby. They were used for ceremonial washing as the laws of purification demanded. They could hold about twenty-five gallons of water apiece, which would be about a half a barrel.

"Fill these empty water pots." Jesus instructed Hared. "By the way," He went on, "fill them to the brim."

Hared did what Jesus requested. He filled the six water pots with water, and returned to Jesus.

"I have done, Sir, that which You asked," said Hared, when he returned to see Jesus. "All six water pots have been filled to the brim with water."

"Hared," Jesus spoke to the headwaiter, "I have more for you to do."

"And what is that?" Asked Hared.

"Take a wine glass and fill it with the water from the water pots, and present it to the gentleman who is presiding over these festivities."

Hared did as he was told and brought the wine to the one Jesus indicated. He took a sip of the water turned into wine. He had no knowledge of where the wine came from, but Hared knew. Smiling from ear to ear the head of the feast summoned the groom.

"Sir," he boomed, with a hearty laugh, "everyone else serves his best wine first, and when the guests have drunk freely, then he serves the inferior wine. You surprise me. You have kept back the superior wine till now. I can't believe it."

As I studied John's story of the water turned into wine I was surprised by the amount. The stone pots held at least one hundred and twenty-five gallons of wine. The incident opened John's eyes to the greatness and power of the Lord Jesus Christ. He is the one who wrote most eloquently of the deity of the Lord Jesus

Christ. "Before all time was the Word. The Word was with God. The Word was God Himself. And the Word became flesh and lived among us." *(John 1)*

At this time, four hundred and fifty years had elapsed since the last public miracle of the Old Testament. Daniel was spared, you and I can read in Daniel six, from the mouths of the lions.

I can hear His disciples after the water has been turned into wine. One would say, "He showed us the power of God." Another, "I can easily see He is no ordinary man." Simon Peter exclaims, "I can understand why John the Baptist says, He is the Light of the world." John the Baptist also says, "I saw and bare record that this is the Son of God." Jesus reached out to the heart; to the spirit He wanted these men to believe. He knew faith comes from knowledge, so He provided them with the information to believe.

Spend It, Baker Boy, Spend It

"Spend it, Baker Boy, spend it!"

Gertie spoke wringing words from aborted pilgrimages. Our story goes back to the thirties. Harry and Gertie Rothenberg had a pa-and-ma Red and White grocery store on Twenty-Seventh Avenue and East Lake Street in South Minneapolis. A couple doors from them Dad had a bakery. Whenever Dad ran out of a spice or whatever, I'd run over to their grocery store to pick it up.

"Here comes Baker Boy," they'd say with a twinkle in their eyes.

Decades passed. I hadn't thought about Harry and Gertie in years. And where should I run into Gertie? She's a bakery clerk at the Lincoln Del in St. Louis Park, a suburb of town. I jolted her memory a little.

"Gertie, my dad had a bakery a couple doors from you on Twenty-Seventh Avenue and Lake street."

She studied the face across the counter. What had been a sixteen year old boy had turned into a man. Fifty years had gone by. She scanned the photo gallery of her memory. Her search found what she was looking for. A warm smile of recognition splashed across her face.

She exclaimed, "Baker Boy! You're Baker Boy!"

We chatted about the old days. She was plucky. Still as trim as I remembered her. Compassionate. Her smile never left her face. Tough willed and outspoken in a friendly way.

Whenever I stopped at the deli she always greeted me as "Baker

Boy." One day my wife was with me and Gertie gave me my customary salutation, but she added, "So this is your wife, Baker Boy?" Her question had an air of expectancy. And her pronunciation of 'wife' seemed to start with the letter 'v'.

"Yes, Gertie, this is my first wife," I said teasingly.

"Yeah. Yeah." she laughed, "I can see you two have been together a long time. That's nice." She told Glorian how pleased she was to meet her.

"Baker Boy, let me ask you ... " she tiptoed gingerly into her question, "Do you have a little set aside?" She drew in a breath of air. "You know ... a few dollars?" Only those who hold a special place in your heart can ask a personal question like that. No one had ever asked me that before. I found it strikingly fresh. I hid my surprise to avoid her embarrassment. She traveled a road and I wanted to go along for the ride.

"Yeah, Gertie, we have managed to tuck away a few dollars through the years."

This time she didn't dillydally around.

"Spend it! Baker Boy, Spend it!

"I'll tell you why (again I could hear a 'v' in the word 'why'). In the winter times Harry would say, 'In the spring, Gertie, we're going to travel. When the weather gets nice, Gertie, we're going to take a trip.'

"April came. 'Harry, I would say, we better get over to triple A to plan our trip.'

"Harry got flustered. 'Vell, I'll tell you,' Harry would gently explain, 'I can't pass up this Contract for Deed. It's a money-maker, Gertie. We'll travel later on.'

"'Harry,' I'd say, 'I heard that last spring, and the spring before that. There's always another Contract for Deed. We have enough money, Harry. Why do we need more?'

"Harry always thought the Contract for Deeds were more important than enjoying our money. We never took a vacation. It's been two years since Harry died.

"I want to ask, 'Harry, where are the memories?' Where are the pictures? Where are the stories of faraway places?'

"You can see why I say if you have a little set aside, spend it. Don't put off your dreams. Enjoy your money while you can."

Days passed. A couple of years went by. I noticed I didn't see Gertie at the deli anymore. So I asked about her one day.

"I haven't seen Gertie around for a while. What has happened to her? Is she in a nursing home?" I was hoping to visit her.

"No," solemnly replied the man behind the counter, "Gertie died this past winter."

"I'm sorry to hear that," I said sadly, "she was such a lovely lady."

What was Gertie telling me? Like the Indian of old, I put my ear to the ground to hear the life-impacted message. She and Harry obviously had two conflicting views on money. She saw money as something to enjoy. Money, to Harry, had an end in itself, something to save. To Gertie, money was a commodity, something to exchange for a higher value. For Harry (I trust I'm not too harsh in my appraisal) money could have taken on the proportion of a god.

Did Gertie's summons to sensibility affect your life? Yes it did.

I hope I had not been tight-fisted up to meeting her, but since that time if I catch myself being skimpy, I say, "Spend it, Baker Boy, spend it!"

I have given some thought to what Gertie unveiled to me about Harry. I never knew him well enough to say he showed a certain pattern of behavior. I have observed three life styles you will find interesting.

Thrifty Tom

This gentleman has an intelligent thrift plan. He enjoys his money and has good financial management. He pays his own way and practices generosity. Gertie would have found him compatible.

Parsimonious Pete

He buys as cheaply as possible to stash away his money. He has a savings goal. When he reaches it, he sets a new one. Words like tightwad — stingy — frugal — all apply to him. Pete refuses to spend money. Though he will deprive himself of the necessities of life, he always pays his own way.

Frank the Freeloader

Here we have the least likeable of our three personalities. Frank the Freeloader lives off you and me so he can add more money to his savings account. He wants others to pay for the ticket that transports him through this life.

With seven hundred thousand dollars in his savings account, he will sponge off from one living from hand-to-mouth on Social Security. He's ruthless and resourceful. He loves only himself. Money owns him, not the other way round. Though he thinks about money all the time, he refuses to talk about money. He doesn't want to expose himself.

People come by money through work, investment, a gift, finding it, borrowing money, and, lastly, through thievery. Frank the Freeloader comes by some of his money by stealing it from others.

You're out for dinner. It comes time to pay the bill. If he doesn't excuse himself to go to the washroom, he will sit with head down looking into his lap. When he sees there are enough twenties to cover the bill he heaves a sigh of relief.

One brazen individual tells him to catch the tip. He says the smallest he has is a twenty. He goes home and banks that twenty dollars into his savings account. That twenty dollars was stolen money!

You ask, how does he get by? By the politeness of others. Most of us feel it is embarrassing to appear cheap. Frank the Freeloader says, I don't care about appearing cheap as long as I can sock the money away.

Does the freeloader suffer any consequences? Yes he does.

First of all, he does not live by faith. If he did he would exhibit more Christ-like behavior. He misses out on the blessing of the spiritual law of giving; give and it shall be given to you *(Luke 6:38)*. As others find out about him they will shun his company. He disdains common sense, because Christ-like behavior takes into consideration the other person.

Galton

His home: Samaria. His name: Galton. His religion: mountain gods. His importance: he met Jesus only days before He was crucified.

Galton had leprosy. And he couldn't remember when the disease invaded his body. What he did know was his isolation. After he was pronounced leprous, he was sentenced to live alone.

"You have a contagious disease," he was told, "so we can't let you contaminate others." But a few cared. They would leave leftovers from their table for Galton.

"What gets me," said Galton, "is the loneliness. Outside. Outside of town. No friends. No one to talk to. This is what gets to me. I am not allowed in the market place. People won't even touch my money. A life of wandering.

"I have to chase people away. True. I'm told to warn people I'm a leper. They can't see the sores on my arms, so I must let them know I have a contagious disease. You ask, 'How do you do that? What do you do if someone approaches you?'"

"If someone comes near me I have to holler: 'Unclean! Unclean!' Then the traveler knows he has to stay his distance. You might ask how this comes about. Why do I have to holler a warning?

"It's the law. When I first contacted the disease I showed myself to a priest, and he informed me I had leprosy. They tell me he is skilled in the detection of the disease. And when I am healed I will have to get an OK from the priest saying I am healed.

"'But,' you say, 'you are a Samaritan, one who is not a Jew. Why are you subject to Jewish law?' Good question, and this came about through my isolation. There came a day when I fell in with a Jewish gentleman. He also had leprosy and he was lonely. Our religion barriers crumpled. We bonded on our common tragedy.

"Sometimes he would holler 'Unclean!' Other times it would be my turn to holler 'Unclean!' And then we would laugh about our turns to holler. Gee! It was good to laugh again. We suffered hunger together. We talked about our children. After all, it was for their good that we lived outside of town.

"We used to say, 'We live the good life!' It was our way of looking tragedy in the face. I don't know if animals can laugh. We did. I guess you could call it hope. In all my filthiness, rags, and dog's life, I knew I would someday be back home. Once more I would work in my carpenter shop, and once more I'd be home with my loved ones. But right now I seem to be going backwards. 'How's that?' you ask. In addition to my Jewish friend, other Jewish lepers have joined. What a raucous bunch. We doubled to four. Soon another. So they came. Lonely men. Outcasts. Spurned by society. Now, believe it or not, there are ten of us. You could call us the dirty ten.

"And we knew all the news. Some gossip. But our talk centered on an itinerant preacher from Nazareth. They say He heals the sick, and that would mean us. But this is not His territory. You see, we're on the border of Samaria and that's out of His way. They say he goes to Jerusalem, but the Jews there want to kill Him.

"I'll never forget that morning. Spring was in the air, and we had picked up another rumor. One of a thousand. 'He's at Sychor! He's at Sychor!' Fat chance. I'm not going to give in to another disappointment. When He comes we'll know it. They say crowds follow Him. I don't mean seventy-five people, I mean hundreds. Thousands. It's always a mob scene. And we can't join 'em. 'Keep your distance. Don't spread your germs.'

"Like I said, it was a spring morning. I didn't know this day would change any life. For three years we had been hearing stories of Jews. One man said he saw a blind man healed. Another man came by and said he was known as the wild man of Gadara. He shared with us his new life. Long before he came we knew He could do what some thought was impossible.

"'Keep your distance! We don't want your disease!'

"It was no different this morning.

"It started out with people running. Some were running south. Others were running north. I picked up the words, 'He's coming! He's coming!' And He was. People moved in waves. A thousand voices. Some crying. A choking dust made the scene obscured. I think everyone of the dirty ten saw Him at once, but He was so far away — lost in the masses — Maybe He could hear us.

"'Jesus! Master! Have mercy on us!'

"Did He hear us?

"'Jesus! Master! Have mercy on us!'

"We hollered in unison at the Man Who had healed so many. He came closer. He was looking at us. The crowd parted as He made his way toward us.

"I looked at this Man who had the land in an uproar. I was taken back by His presence. With all the expectancy surging through me, I studied Him as He moved with authority. His disciples had all they could handle in keeping the mob back. It crossed my mind that they might trample Him.

"He stopped. I saw Him looking at the dirty ten. Compassion was written across His face. Then He spoke.

"'Go! Show yourself to the priests.'

"I knew this meant we had been healed, for it was the priest who pronounced us clean. I stopped back. My body tingled. I glanced at my arms, gone! The leprosy was gone. I shouted to myself: 'I'm healed!'

"'Galton!' One of the ten cried, 'Are you healed?'

"'Yes! Yes! What about you?'

"'Yes. We have to show ourselves to the priests.'"

But Galton turned and fell on his face before Jesus. In a loud voice that all could hear he glorified God. Over and over Galton glorified God.

Jesus saw faith in what Galton said. Jesus commended him for his faith. "For," He said, "Your faith has made you well. I have restored you to health because of what you said."

"I healed ten," said Jesus. "Where are the other nine?"

Nathaniel spoke up, "They went to the priests to prove their healing."

"Ironic," stated Jesus. "Out of the ten only this foreigner, this outsider, recognized Who I am."

Galton knew the nine were thankful, just like he was, but they failed to say so. In their absence of words they revealed their absence of faith. Jesus read their hearts by their words. If they had nothing to say they had no faith in their hearts. Jesus did not censure them for unthankfulness; He judged them for a failure to believe.

Galton sat alone on a stone wall. The tumbling crowds had disappeared to the south. He was filled with worship. Tears welled up in his eyes as he pictured the Savior.

"I have seen the Messiah. He has given me a new life. My joy will be to share with others what I received from Him."

See Matthew 19:2-20 & 28; Mark 10:2-45; Luke 17:11-18 & 30.

Self Pity

*The Father loves me and places divine
value on me. I should see myself
through my Father's eyes.*

Mom always said, "I can't stand self-pity." She employed this phrase when she heard one of her kids feeling sorry for himself. "I can't stand self-pity." I wouldn't be surprised if one of my siblings said, "I think I heard Mom say that a hundred times." Her Norwegian accent brought it out more forcefully, "I can't stand sel' pity." she would leave the "f" out of self. The missing "f" heightened her contempt for feeling sorry for yourself. She lived the hardscrabble life of an immigrant, but I never heard her complain. She lived her admonition. She never felt sorry for herself.

The other morning Mom's credo was trashed when my self-blame wrestled for attention. I joined the gang beating up on myself. You deserve an F for yesterday. I saw in the mirror of my memory a rascal who said the wrong thing. After all, you can learn to say nothing. On and on, tossing and turning was on a treadmill. My self-importance blew down the street. Am I over-tired? There may be a prescription for mental self-abuse. So the hand-to-hand combat continued. In the midst of this struggle I heard Mom's voice bouncing off the walls of my memory. "I can't stand sel' pity. I can't stand sel' pity."

I suppose a psychologist would say this is the mind's mechanism at work. Perplexities are thrown into the mind's tumbler.

Some are kept, others are thrown into a dumpster.

Mom's injunction was like a stop sign. "Stop" feeling sorry for yourself. Her credo has no medicinal value, which is what I needed. I found some healing in the encouragement! Be kind and gentle with yourself. I asked myself in my introspection: "What about your words? Words like 'You deserve an F.'" When my self-blame wrestled for attention it fought with the guns of words: "You're a nobody." My adversary uses words, so if I change my words I can win the battle.

Words shape the week before me. I understand one can prepare himself for failure with the wrong words. I also know words are seeds; they'll bear the fruit of that which is said. Jesus taught me to speak to the mountain. With my ears I listened to the words I speak. Solomon, reputed to be the wisest of men, said that death and life are in the power of the tongue. I knew that God had created the universe with words, and He allows you and me to see who He is with words. He bequeaths to you and me His Words.

If I want to stop this "sel' pity" business, I need a new vocabulary. The old words will be thrown into the dumpster. Replacement words will work on my self-image. In my contemplation I recalled the words of Jesus, "You should love your neighbors just as you love yourself." The riveting truth that slammed into me said, "You shall love yourself." This wasn't an option; it was a spiritual command. "You shall love yourself." But why? But why should one love himself? Is it because he sees himself as thoughtful? Or honest? My thinking wondered up a tributary. "You shall love yourself" danced around in my head. Then it broke on me like a revelation, an epiphany, you should love yourself because God loves you!

I changed my words. "Norman, you love yourself because the Father loves you." John 3:16 came to my mind: "Norman, I love you so much. I sent my Son to die for you." This new insight brought life into new focus; instead of looking into new circumstances through my own feeble spectacles, I now saw them through God's eyes.

The replacement words have been found. The medicinal value has been realized. I could walk down the street with the knowledge that I was someone special. This was not self gloating. I was not thinking more highly of myself than I ought to think. I was looking at things as the Father sees them. I thought He might say, "Ya' know Norman, your mother was right, I can't stand self pity either." It's like a Christian with the spiritual repository of my word. With these vast reserves he foolishly says, "I'm broke." When I felt sorry for myself I was only listening to what I had to say. God wasn't in the picture.

You will recall I found myself locked in, "You're a loser." My words drove me into the ground. Mom's admonition lacked the medicinal remedy I sought. Then in a hallelujah moment, it dawned on me. He has set His love on me. He says I'm special to Him.

You could ask, "Did you hear this in a sermon?" No. Another asks, "Did this illumination come from something you read?" The answer is yes. It came from the words Jesus spoke to Nicodemus *(John 3:16)*. "For God so loved the world." Instead of the word "world" I made it personal. I inserted my own name. I also used the amplified translation. So it says, "For God so greatly loved and dearly prized Norman that He even gave up His only begotten Son ... "

These Words contained divine spiritual life and power. With my new freedom and release from self-incrimination, I cast about for other words I could use as replacements in my vocabulary. The word "heir" caught my attention. Just think of it: All that belongs to Christ also belongs to you and me! Mind boggling. As I meditated on being an heir, I recalled the story of the Ray

Bosley. He lived on skid row. He found food in a restaurant's dumpster. He pillowed his head at the Mission. In the midst of his destitution, unknown to him, Ray was a wealthy man. How could that be? An aunt in a distant city had made him the sole heir of her estate. He knew nothing about it. He never received what had been willed to him. What I have learned from Ray's story is that I have to know and I have to act on what has been willed to me in Christ.

Paul the Apostle spoke about being an heir when he said, "You see clearly the grace of our Lord Jesus Christ, that though He was so very rich, yet for your sakes He became very poor, that through His poverty you might be rich." *(2 Corinthians 8:9)*

Jesus told the story of a rich farmer who was poor.

"My harvest," exclaimed the farmer, "overwhelms me. What am I going to do? I need more storage. Aha! I know what solves my problem. I will tear down my existing barns. Then I will build bigger barns." He left God out.

As he was basking with his smugness God confronted the man, "You fool! Tonight the messengers of God will demand your soul! You trusted in your harvest. What worth does it have for you now?" *(Luke 12:16-21)*

God saw the farmer's heart through his words: "Soul, you have provided for yourself." His words gave evidence that God did not exist in his thinking.

I shared with you the story of the foolish wealthy farmer who failed to find in life the love God had for him. He trusted in himself alone.

Then I will say to my soul, "Soul, you have provided for me for many years. Now rest in your security."

I started this essay with Mom's no-nonsense words: "I can't stand self pity." I found refreshment in "Be kind and gentle with yourself." Words, I reminded myself, put on parade the pictures in my mind and I can use them to change who I am. I can see myself in a mirror and say, "Norman, love yourself because God loves you. Norman, the Father said, 'I love you so much I even sent my Son to die for you'."

Widow of Nain

She was a widow who lived in a small town. That we know. She, on the other hand, didn't know she would have an encounter with Jesus. But she did — brief and sudden — but life-changing.

The story starts when her only son dies. He was twenty, an apprentice carpenter, like Jesus, when he died of an unknown illness. It had been different when her husband died. She had a son as a companion. Now that he was gone she was alone. Oh, she had shoestring relatives and a town that loved her, to be sure. But with Ereck's, her son's, death much of her livelihood had been stripped away.

She lived in Nain. Her story has been titled "The Widow of Nain." A town of eight hundred, it sits in the mountains west of the Jordan river. Nain was a good day's hike, south and west, from the sea of Galilee. Jesus had healed the Centurion's servant boy on a Thursday — that was in Capernaum. So he walked from the north shore of the Sea of Galilee to Nain — to be in Nain on Friday.

Summer was marching into autumn when Jesus made this hike. And much of the time they endured the heat that fought stubbornly to hold on to summer. Jesus brought all of his disciples with Him when He hiked to Nain.

In addition to His disciples, a large group of followers accompanied Him. Some were interested in learning. Others wanted to see the spectacular miracles He did.

"You can never tell what's going to happen," said a neophyte

Insights

priest.

"Yeah," cited another, "I've seen Him heal a blind man. It was the most amazing thing. This guy was by the side of the road, and he kept hollering to Jesus to heal him. And Jesus stopped and touched his eyes. At first, things were blurry, but in a short while he began to shout, 'I can see, I can see.' You can understand why I'm part of a band, there must be five hundred of us, who feel we're a part of history."

So you have at Nain the meeting of two masses of people. One is a funeral procession. Only hours have passed since the widow's son died, but as the custom prevails, they have the funeral the day of the death. All of Nain had turned out for Ereck's funeral. Some were carrying flowers. Others wore black to picture the sorrow in their hearts. A sister of the widow sought to sustain her as she tried to realize the impact. It was like a dream. "This can't be happening to me. Is this true? Am I in a nightmare?"

Stumbling on to this scene comes the rumbling crowd following Jesus. "What's going on?" Jesus asks His disciple James. "It's a funeral, Lord. This widow has lost her son. He died last night."

Jesus saw the distraught woman in the funeral procession. He could see she was beside herself. People were shouting in defiance to the tumbling clouds of dust. The crowd of mourners walked in silence, while the crowd with Jesus fought to get to the front.

"How can I see anything?" cried out one young man. "Every time I get to the front, ten people rush in. I came here from Capernaum. I've been up all night. It must be one hundred degrees, and I'm always pushed back."

The crowd brought life, and the other crowd carried death. Hundreds of people collided. Mixed emotions. Expectations ran high. "What will happen?" asked one crowd. "It's a night of mourning," sighed the other. But then, something happened. Jesus saw the widow. He saw her grieving heart. His disciples filled

Him in on the grim theatre before Him. His heart was filled with compassion. Slowly He moved toward the woman.

Those who were carrying the coffin came to a standstill. He looked at the woman and spoke to her. She knew this Man. He was the One everyone spoke about. She was surprised at His youth as she met Him up close. His authority and presence commanded respect, but what could He do now? Ereck was dead. "Maybe He'll tell me Ereck will be in the resurrection. I know that."

In the new stillness that enveloped their meeting, she thought she heard Him. And she did.

"Stop crying."

That's all she heard in a voice that reached out and touched her. She stopped and studied His eyes. She had never seen eyes that mirrored so much love. Inside, in her spirit she whispered to herself, if anyone could do anything in this critical time, He's the one. She moved from one staggering loss, to one who knew love and life were yet in the world. As these thoughts filled her mind, the Lord stepped toward the coffin. Pallbearers — young friends of the dead man — watched with confusion. What's going on?

Jesus paused before the coffin. He reached out with His right hand and touched it. Jesus broke the silence.

"Young man, young man. I'm speaking to you."

An older woman whispered, "He's talking to Ereck! He's talking to Ereck!"

"Sit up!" Jesus commanded.

"He's told him to sit up," someone confided to Grandma.

To the astonishment of everyone, Ereck sat up.

"How can a dead man sit up? How could he hear?"

A friend of Ereck's found he had no voice.

Ereck's mother was passing out, but her sister grabbed her around the waist before she could fall. Many in the crowd held their hand over their mouth in disbelief.

"What am I doing in this coffin? Is this a joke?"

Jesus took him by the hand and led him to his mother. Tears and sobbing filled their embrace.

At this time, John the Baptist was sitting in prison, and he sent two of his disciples to verify the credentials of Jesus. So the men came to Jesus and asked, "Are you the One who is to come, or shall we continue to look for another?" Jesus answered not by telling, but by showing.

As the Baptist's disciples journeyed to back to John, they talked about the miracle they had seen. "John will be thrilled to hear we saw Him raise a dead man."

"True, but what can we tell John was His secret?"

"Words. Words filled with divine power. As I recall, He said two little words. 'Sit up!' Yeah, and the young man sat up. John will know we became believers when we saw what He did."

The Day I Ate What I Read

"I can lift it out like this." With his two hands Doctor Meyer made the gentle motion of lifting a baby out of its bath. He was demonstrating how carefully he was going to lift out my cancerous left kidney.

"If you're apprehensive," he went on with a concerned look, "I can help you along with a medication. I don't know, maybe you're the type who chooses to tough it out on his own."

I fell silent in the harsh reality of serious surgery. He told me what I had been suspecting for several days. I looked at myself in an invisible mirror and knew that something like this could not throw me into a personal tailspin. For, from the recesses of my spirit I heard a voice. It was not audible, but I listened carefully. It appeared to wrap warm loving arms around me. I know who you are, you're the Bible verse I was chewing on just a few days ago. I repeated the phrase slowly to myself:

" ... I will never leave you or forsake you."

" ... I will never leave you or forsake you."

As I prepared to meet with Doctor Meyer, I had found these words in the thirteenth chapter of the Book of Hebrews. From their pledge the Person of Christ had become an integral part of me.

"It's up to you." The interruption of Dr. Meyer brought me back to the moment. "I can prescribe a sedative if you like."

"No, no," I mumbled distractedly, "I won't need any tranquilizers. I'm sure everything will go fine."

As I dressed to leave I scolded myself. Why didn't I share with

297

Doctor Meyer the words that welled up in me? After all, I had simply made an alliance with what God said. Was I ashamed of that? Would he think I had gone off the deep end? I knew Christ was not ashamed to be in my company.

Only the night before I had concluded that each of us owes it to those we love to share the legacy of being an over-comer. I'm sure all of us are apprehensive about trying circumstances, but I thought about what the Apostle Paul said. "Fight the good fight." When we face a crisis a battle takes place. Victory came for me when I ate what I read. I saw behind the words.

I checked into Fairview Hospital the next morning, and they set me up in my pre-surgery room. At eleven o'clock I got a final hug from my loved ones after my preliminaries were completed.

"Mr. Sinclair." Two young men stood at the door.

"Yes, that's me."

"We're ready to take you to pre-op."

As I placed myself on their bed in the hall, I saw a small group of people at the end of the corridor. I could tell by the looks on their faces what they were thinking.

"There goes some poor guy to surgery. I sure feel sorry for him."

"Little did they know," I whispered to myself, "that the Person of Christ was living in me at this moment." Could I expect them to see that? Pity was the furthest thing from my mind. I think they should envy me. But how could they know how grateful I was? A handful of words had given me the picture that I was cradled in His arms.

Isn't there always music for such a moment as this? At least there is in the movies. For my audience down the hall I'm afraid it would have been a ponderous and sorrowful opus. Oh yes, I could hear the music. Majestic, filled with triumph and victory, and love. His presence was more real to me than the aids pushing

The Day I Ate What I Read

me through the scrubbed corridors.

"Well, how did the surgery turn out?"

"He lifted out that kidney just as he said he'd do."

"Are you ready to go home?" my wife asked, several days later.

"Oh yes."

I stood by my car in front of the hospital. Morning sunshine — warm and flaxen — flooded the entrance. Common place experiences took on a surprising elegance. I glanced up at the third floor window that had been my home for twelve days. Not only was I on the road back to health, for I was doubly blessed, my heart was filled with thanksgiving. As I looked at that window I muttered to myself, " ... I will never leave you or forsake you."

" ... I will never leave you or forsake you."

As I rode home in the car I asked myself, how had these words had such an impact on my life? I faced up to the fact that I had taken "squatter's rights" to this small band of words. I think I had wrestled with them till they became a part of me. I had savored each word as it formed an image in my mind. Relishing the pledge, I lost myself in the Author's faithfulness. They handed me on a platter my needed perspective on my upcoming surgery.

Look at the word "meditate." In the Hebrew language it means to mutter or growl. For example, when a dog growls as he goes after that morsel of marrow in a bone, that's meditation in Hebrew. You and I chew food for survival.

We masticate the food by grinding it to pulp. Our taste, teeth, tongue, saliva, and swallowing all get a workout. Spiritual energy comes from "eating" what God says, but I have to masticate it for entrance into my spirit. I mutter or chew over a verse so that what I see enters not only my mind, but also my heart. I do more than read the words, I give the Holy Spirit time to translate them for me. Eating those black specs on a page brought something into my life that wasn't there before.

Notice what Joshua said:
> This book of the law shall not depart out of your mouth, but you shall meditate on it day and night ... *(Joshua 1:8)*

Again we see the word "meditate." Growl over it. Mutter it. I can see it happening in my life. I see as God sees. I walk in God's shoes. I feel as God feels. Words that are chewed over, masticated, can touch chords in my spirit that release me from the taut strings of fear and worry. No longer do I simply admire the picture I see in my mind, now I step into it.

When I hear some of the ads on speed reading, I wonder if such vocal ruminating is shunned in today's rocket-propelled tempo.

"Now you can read that book you've always wanted to read in one evening."

"Speed reading — go with the flow."

"Why not read with the speed of light?"

"Read those corporate reports on your lunch hour."

Many race from page to page as starry-eyed zombies. Why? Do the spoils go to the one who simply finishes the book? I remember one woman who said, "My husband reads the book of Romans while I put on my shoes!" Biblical language comes concentrated. It uses magnificent brevity with license. It needs more than reading. It needs to be chewed over. I know a man who avows, "My problem in reading my Bible comes from not getting past the first verse."

No phrase in the book of Jeremiah comes with greater frequency than this: "Then the word of the Lord came unto me." No wonder we find in the book of Jeremiah:
> I have put My words in your mouth *(Jeremiah 1:9)*. God speaking.
> Your words (Jeremiah replies) were found, and I ate them, and Your word was to me a joy and the rejoicing of my heart... *(Jeremiah 15:16)*

The Day I Ate What I Read

His word was in my heart as a burning fire; shut up in my bones *(Jeremiah 20:9)*.

Ezekiel concurs with Jeremiah when he says:

He said to me, Son of man, eat what you find in this book; eat this scroll, then go and speak to the house of Israel.

So I opened my mouth, and He caused me to eat the scroll.

And He said to me, Son of man, eat this scroll that I give you and fill your stomach with it, and it was as sweet as honey in my mouth. *(Ezekiel 3:1-3)*

Jeremiah and Ezekiel allowed the Holy Spirit to convert into life that which they read. I'm sure they could have said, "we wholeheartedly agree with what you say, but more, what you say imparts life." No wonder a British historian said, "Words are deeds at great moments in our lives."

One naturalist said, "I went on a two week vacation; I got halfway across my back yard."

"I once discovered," said a student of the noted teacher, Louis Agassiz, "among the remnants of sand and debris in my collecting net, a curiously speckled, shell-like or seed-like object. I walked over to Professor Agassiz to show it to him. He would never identify the object because my privilege rested in finding it out on my own.

"However, in the eagerness of the moment I asked him what it was. He looked at it intently for a moment. His face took on a perplexed study. He took a magnifying glass from his pocket and began to examine the find with great care. Gradually a knowing smile spread across his features, and he chuckled faintly as he closed the lens and put it back in his pocket.

"He handed the specimen back to me with the remark, 'I'll give you three weeks to find out what it is.' He returned to his work as though nothing had happened.

"The following afternoon I accidentally discovered that my

specimen was the cornea of a crab's eye. It had become detached from a crab I had captured. It had remained in the bottom of the net after its owner had been removed. I have to say this about Professor Agassiz, that man could get more out of me in a few weeks than any other professor I was ever under in three years."

Professor Agassiz saw that our "school learning" has impregnated us with the idea that an "authority" must interpret for us. Do I need someone "in a uniform" to aid my understanding? Certain skills and information come through others, but we have to train ourselves to think on our own. I can hear Louis Agassiz mutter as he turned a specimen over and over in his hand.

Writing was an arduous ordeal for Earnest Hemingway, exhilarating, but demanding all of what he called his "juices." "I rise at first light, and I start by reading and editing everything I have written to the point where I left off. That way I go through a book several hundred times, honing it until it gets an edge like the bullfighter's sword. I rewrote the ending of 'A Farewell to Arms' 39 times in manuscript and worked it over 30 times in proof, trying to get it right." He appreciated the scope, insight, power, and life behind words.

God has chosen to unveil Himself to you and me through words, and He has anointed us with the Holy Spirit to give us spiritual sight. O, for the childlike wonder of peering at an anthill on our stomach!

The Devil and Mr. Kanatha

Choppy waves slapped the shore as Peter steered the ship inland. Little evidence was left of the storm that had roared during the night. Two curious sea gulls flew overhead, as a fast moving cloud threw shadows over the harbor.

"Take it to the right," shouted Thomas.

A scent from the ocean gave backdrop to this aromatic theater. To the south, the disciples could see the infamous cliffs throwing deformed shadows across the dunes.

"We're terrified."

"We've tried everything."

"How would you like a ten-year nightmare?"

A cacophony of voices slammed into Jesus as he alighted from the ship.

A nervous teenager said laughingly, "We even thought of killing him."

Jesus studied the cliffs when Matthew filled him in, "He lives in those cliffs."

"It's an ancient cemetery," said one. "The dead are buried in caves. Do you see 'em?"

One pointed a bony finger toward the caves while other's voices their common despair.

"He's naked, Lord."

"And dog-dirty."

"Shaggy hair falls all over his face,"

"And he looks at you with hatred."

"I swear he's got the strength of ten men."

"Yeah. We had him in shackles."

"And chains. He laureates himself with stones."

A woman said he was forever screaming.

"I think he's a man who is an animal."

"Or the other way around," laughed a teenager.

Jesus listened as another muttered, "We're helpless, Lord."

Jesus seated Himself and talked about the man these people feared.

One older skeptic mumbled to himself, "How can He help? Nobody can. He'll be surprised when the wild man attacks Him. What'll He do then?"

Two young men stepped forward. A slight smile played around their lips.

"Can we help?" one asked.

"How's that?" Jesus replied.

"I know you have disciples to assist you. We thought we might be able to bring this man to you."

"How could you do that?"

"I'll think he'll come with us. You see, we have sneaked bread to him."

"I see. Bring him to me."

"They're bringing him here," a frightened woman breathed to her mother.

"Will they be able to hold him?"

"That's the question," answered the daughter.

A man interrupted. "There'll be fighting. I'm getting out of here. He's a mad bulldog."

In a foul-smelling cave, the two volunteers found the feared man. He looked at them with surprise.

"We have not come with bread." He did not reply, but continued to study his intruders. "The Master wants to see you."

Silence. There was nothing they could do. It was up to him.

The Devil and Mr. Kanatha

One of the visitors extended his arms. He opened his palms in peace.

"Will you take my hand? The Master is waiting for you." They wondered how they could bridge the gulf. Anything could happen. It did. He stood up. A moment passed.

"Did he say something?" one asked as he heard a guttural sound. With an air of resignation, he walked forward and took the outstretched hands. A surprised crowd broke ranks as the three came down from the cliffs.

Jesus stood up as a hushed aisle formed before him.

The wild man saw Jesus from a distance. He released the hands of his caretakers and ran forward. In worship, he threw himself on the ground before him.

A disconnected voice, like the voice of a ventriloquist, frightened and high-pitched, gushed out of the man.

"What have you to do with me, Jesus, Son of the Most High God?"

"Come out of him!" Jesus commanded the demon.

"Come out of him!" The demon from Satan would not budge.

"I don't want to go back to hell. In the name of God do not torment me."

All the while the wild man lay prone before the Lord.

Jesus addressed the demon. "What is your name? I repeat. What is your name?"

"Legion. Legion," he stammered, so frightened he gave his number instead of name.

"Legion, for there are thousands of us."

"I order you to leave the body of this man. Now!"

"You have nothing to do with us!"

"Stop this nonsense," Jesus replied. "You have no choice but to vacate this man."

"Yes. Yes." spoke up Legion. "We're going. But to where? Again I say, Don't send us to hell. Put us in those hogs."

Over on the hillside was a herd of hogs. As Jesus pointed, the demons found bodies in the hogs on the hillside. Confusion followed as the hogs ran down into the sea. The hogs drowned and Legion and his troops returned to hell. Two fisherman joined the crowd to check out the excitement.

The changed man sat before Jesus. His nervous quivering had stopped. A quiet calm enveloped him. Eyes, once filled with hatred, now looked at his Savior with worship and gratitude. After his bath he was dressed and had some food.

He related a tender memory of a preferred education in the provincial town of Kanatha. He relived his success in the world of business, a wife and three children.

"I think my downfall started with over-preoccupation of myself. I failed to see how I was hurting others. I'm ashamed of the greed that consumed my thinking. I lost my way. Without direction I became homeless. I became fair game. Satan dispatched his henchmen."

Epilogue

This man became the frontrunner, the John the Baptist to the ten cities of Decapolis. His proclamation of Jesus as Savior preceded the feeding of both the four thousand and the five thousand.

The Quiet Time (QT)

Ted and I met today for an enjoyable lunch. He was a friend from the old neighborhood so we shared a number of common memories. I confess, we also talked about the who's who. In previous meetings I noticed that the conversation drifted to one subject. Today would be no different. Ted mentioned that a friend of his had attended a retreat.

So I asked, "How long did it run?"

"Five days."

"Wow, that's a long retreat."

"He said he had a wonderful time," filled in Ted.

"Did he say he would do it again?" I asked.

"He thought it could have been shorter. I presume it was a religious retreat. Right. He said it unscrambled his mind. I imagine his mind was overcrowded. Yeah, like a crowded elevator. No more room for unwanted drama." The waitress interrupted over meanderings with a fresh pot of coffee.

Ted went on, "I've been to something like that, but it jump-started me."

"I have an idea of where you are going."

"Yeah, I think all of us need to pull off the road once in a while."

"I agree."

"Five days is unnecessary. I am thinking of a daily time."

"Say twenty minutes. I think most people refer to that as 'my quiet time.'"

"That's it, a time to sort out the congestion."

Insights

The two men studied the street outside as they prepared to move on.

"Ok," I broke the silence. "Someone says, 'Ted, I have set aside my twenty minutes. So, where do I go from here?'"

"Of course, one should be alone."

"That's right."

"Except for the presence of the Lord."

"There you have it! Awareness."

"Sure, one has to be alert to what the Father says."

"I see; it's not casual. After all, I 'm in the company of the One Who created the universe."

"You prepare yourself with reverence."

Ted went on. "I'm before Someone Who loves me. I hear His voice in His Word. I listen. I understand His Words possess divine creative power. When I change my words, I change my life."

"We've prepared ourselves with deep respect as we enter our quiet time, so where do we go from here?"

"We have an open Bible in front of us." Ted flipped his Bible open to Psalm one.

"To many, the Bible is intimidating. Fifteen hundred pages. Sixty-six books. I don't know where to begin. Carefully constructed words. Brevity. Hidden meanings."

"It's almost like one needs a guide."

"There are nuggets. It's kinda like panning for gold."

"Are you suggesting we need someone to take us by the hand?"

Ted laughed. "No, I like to mine those nuggets for myself. I like to say the Holy Spirit is my Guide."

"I see several approaches,' I ventured. "Some read. Others memorize. Some specialize, like in prophecy."

"Whatever works."

"What d'ya mean by that?"

"Whatever gets into the spiritual bloodstream."

"Getting back, you mentioned the first Psalm."

Ted chuckled. "The best way to illustrate the quiet time is to go through one. This Psalm talks about the blessed man. This blessed man meditates on God's Words day and night (verse 2). I don't read more than a couple of verses. The word 'meditate' means mutter in the original language. I do that. I mutter the first two verses of the Psalm."

"What nugget did you mine in this digging?"

"Oh, that's easy. I answered a question."

"What's that?"

"Who is a blessed man?"

"And your answer ... "

"The blessed man delights in God's Words. He loves them so much he mutters them both day and night."

"So, you feel in your quiet time that God was talking to you."

"He was, in this first Psalm."

"I think someone would ask at this point, 'Is this quiet time for everyone?'"

"Definitely. Keep it simple. Listen. Ask questions. It's spiritual nourishment."

"Another entity I employ in my quiet time is to inject the first person."

"Ya mean like 'I' or 'me'?"

"Right. So I would say, as the blessed man 'I' delight myself in the Word you speak."

"I notice that you speak the verse out loud."

"Not only do I speak the verse, but I'll repeat it over and over."

"Then you hear it with your own ears and listen in."

"As to the time, that's individual. My brother-in-law likes to stop at a park on his way home from work. He spends twenty minutes at a picnic table and then finishes his trip back home."

"Five-day retreats are for those who have the time and the money, but just as we need food daily, it adds up that our spirit hungers for the manna from heaven."

"One thing we haven't mentioned," Ted went on, "is how much the Father enjoys our fellowship. I think I forget that once in a while."

"Yeah," I agreed, I paused. A verse came to mind. Paul the Apostle wrote that Jesus died for all, that they which live should not live unto themselves, but unto Him which died for them *(2 Corinthians 5:15)*.

"Another thing, Norm," Ted spoke with feeling. "In my retreat or quiet time I've had an audience with the very Person of the Lord Himself so as I take leave I thank Him for the awesome privilege He gave me."

Sarepta of Sidon

Jesus sought seclusion in Phoenicia. For two years He had worked out of Capernaum in the land of Galilee. The twelve had been called and served their apprenticeship. They had shared the message of the kingdom with the masses looking for the Messiah but Jesus marveled at the unbelief He encountered. King Herod watched Him carefully, thinking He was a resurrected John the Baptist, whom he had beheaded. The time had come to say goodbye to Galilee, to Capernaum, to the persecution in the synagogues, and the bitterness of the scribes and Pharisees.

From now on, all His work would be in non-Jewish territory, so we find Him traveling in the towns of Tyre and Sidon. He was well known there, for many from these towns had journeyed south — a two days journey — to hear Him. He could not be hidden for long, for His arrival leaked out and the needy reached out for Him.

Phoenicia looked back a long time. It was here in Sidon that the widow of Sarepta fed Elijah the prophet. That was in 875 B.C. We'll also name our heroine in this story Sarepta ... Her ancestry was Greek, and she comes with the tearful tale that her daughter has been torn by an evil spirit. Sarepta has heard many stories of the fame of Jesus, so she ventures forth on the testimony of others.

"Does He know," asked Sarepta, "anything about unclean spirits? Sleepless nights, tragic confrontation, warfare," Sarepta described her horrors with her daughter, "Nightmares describe my life, but I love Diana as a mother should. I look into her face and tell her she is beautiful, but she stares back at me with empty eyes. Abandoned."

"'Knock! Knock! Is anybody home?' Then she flees. At dusk I find Diana on her face on a dusty hillside, and I kneel beside her with my hand lovingly resting on her back. This wasn't the daughter I raised. This was a stranger from another world, a world of suffering and evil.

"They told me the Master was resting in this house."

"He is exhausted from His journey from Galilee. Come back another time."

"This was my moment. Why should Diana have another day of tears?" I thought to myself, "as a Jew He'll revere David, so I'll use David as my mediator."

"So I begged, 'O Lord, son of David! Have mercy on me. My daughter Diana is possessed by a demon!'"

One of His disciples reprimanded her, "Be quiet woman! The Master rests."

"I know. I know. But the demon in my daughter does not rest."

"The Master did not answer my cry," said Sarepta, "but I pictured my daughter and kept up my cry."

"You've got to do something with this woman," Nathaniel spoke to Jesus. "She's driving us crazy. We told her you were resting, but she didn't go away. She keeps on with the harangue about her daughter Diana. She's possessed with a demon. Can you tell her go away? She doesn't listen to us."

Jesus saw the embracing love the mother had for her daughter and addressed her.

"First, let the children be fed." By this He meant the children of Israel.

"It is not fair to take the bread that belongs to the children and throw it to the puppies."

Jesus tested her faith. Did she believe in her heart that He could heal her daughter? This persistence was what He sought of the Jews in Galilee. Now, here was Sarepta, a Gentile who saw His divinity and He reminded Himself of other Gentiles who had stormed the door for His healing. He thought of Priscilla, the Samaritan woman by the well. Through her, Jesus brought the good news to the city of Sychar. And then there was the nobleman of Capernaum. He couldn't forget him. He smiled to Himself as He recalled the Roman soldier, the centurion, who received healing for his servant boy. Of this soldier Jesus would say, "I have not found such great faith in my own people."

She thought of her friends in Tyre and Sidon. They had told her, "This Man is the Messiah. He's the fulfillment of Jewish prophecy. I saw Him heal a blind man." Another said He had the power to drive the demon out of Diana. From the testimonies of so many Sarepta knew He could heal her daughter. "You could say," she said, "that I have faith."

Her tearful and distressing plea had secured a hearing. At least He was now hearing her, but she had to let Him know she believed.

She took three steps to where she stood before Him. She fell down on her knees and touched her forehead to the ground in profound reverence to His Lordship. She thought of what He had said: It is not fair to take the bread that belongs to the children and throw it to the puppies.

Sarepta saw the face of Diana in her mind. She thought of what the Master said. He was right. It's not fair to take the children's food and feed it the puppies. She did not want to steal anyone's bread, she thought, I only wanted Diana freed. This Man can remove the chains of the devil. She thought of the change that had overcome her. A few moments ago she was the screaming woman His disciples were trying to chase away. Now she kneeled before

Him with the knowledge He was "the sent One" from God.

Sarepta spoke. "What you say, Lord, is right. It is not fair to take the children's food and feed it to the dogs, but sometimes the puppies eat the crumbs which fall from the children's fingers."

Jesus looked down at Sarepta and answered her, "Sarepta, great is your faith! Diana is healed. Your words have revealed your faith."

Sarepta stood up and thanked the Lord for healing Diana. She excused herself from His presence to hurry home to see her daughter. She found her lying quietly on the couch and the demon gone. Her love had wanted this moment more than she could speak, so the high drama now came gushing out. She found herself crying uncontrollably, with Diana in the role of the comforter.

"It's ok, Mom. It's all over. I'm healed. Now there are two of us to face the world. Maybe I can find the Master to thank Him for my healing. Like you, I'll fall at His feet in worship and praise."

A spectator to this heart-touching scene wanted to know how she revealed her faith. "As I watched this played out," she said, "I kinda missed how the Lord knew she had faith. Did you get it?" she asked rhetorically.

"Yah, I think I did," said a Canaanite woman, "it was when she replied 'the puppies eat the crumbs which fall from the children's fingers.' That phrase says, I believe. That's the way Jesus saw it for He complimented her for her great faith."

Another friend asked, "Where did she learn to believe? She's never been in a synagogue."

"Or read scriptures," interjected another.

"Her faith," an elderly woman chimed in, "came from words. All her friends were telling her about Jesus. How He healed a blind man."

"And a deaf man," said another.

That's all she's been hearing for the last two years.

She could have heard testimonies of those who have been healed.

See Mark 7:24-30; Matthew 15:21-28.

Headache

Ted told me an interesting story last Friday that I found life-changing. He told me his friend complained to him about recurring headaches. I thought Ted was blunt when he asked his friend, "I don't want to be preachy, but have you ever wondered what God thinks about your headaches?"

His friend had to catch his breath, then stammered, "What dya' mean, what God thinks about 'em?" Ted chuckled to shake off the embarrassment that was in the air.

"Yeah, this is what comes to my mind when I encounter a problem like you have."

"You mean you ask yourself, 'I wonder what God thinks about my problem'?"

"That's the idea."

Ted's friend went on "I'll go along with what you're saying, but I have to confess, I need some help. Honestly, I wouldn't know where to start. For example: Where do I go to find out what God thinks? God could use angels. Maybe He talks to me when I pray."

Ted was delighted to see his friend's openness. "It's in the Bible," he stated frankly.

"Ya' mean God talks about headaches in the Bible?" Now his friend chuckled.

"Not exactly," Ted smiled.

"What does it say?"

"When Jesus died on the cross," Ted chose each word carefully, "He healed us of our sickness." *(1 Peter 2:24)*

"Is this what ya' mean when you say God is thinking about my headaches?"

"Precisely. This is what He says in the Bible."

"I believe the truth you quoted, but this is my concern: how do I cross the threshold to make it a working part of my life?"

"You hit the nail on the head," Ted complimented his friend on his insightfulness. "This is a task," Ted agreed, "shared by many. You did say you believed this verse, so that sets in motion the answer for headaches. Let me share with you a little secret on activating the verse you believe in."

"I'm following!" exclaimed his friend. "Will I go *blink* when the light goes on?"

Both laughed at the needed humor.

"The first thing you and I have to ask when we look at a Bible verse is to ask, 'What is the message the Holy Spirit speaks?' I'm like an old prospector looking for a vein of rich gold. Here's the gold in our verse: 'By His wounds you have been healed *(amplified)*'."

"I notice the verb is in the past tense."

"True. God sees you as already healed of your headaches. This is the take-home point."

"Right."

"You can wear this certainty as a badge: I am healed of my headaches."

His friend chimed in, "I call that the new language of speaking from the heart. As I embark on my new journey, will I be healed instantaneously?"

"Very possible. In your new joyous outlook the Holy Spirit travels His own road."

"I understand."

"As you have internalized this verse you could feel led to see your doctor. Exercise, diet, and the rest are factors. After you have been healed you will see the road the Spirit took."

"I'm thankful already, as His Words are wrapped around me. Wait'll my wife hears this! I have learned a new language, the language of love."

A Rich Man Finds True Riches

*Time will lift a veil sublime,
To reveal it was His work all the time.*

His name: Zacchaeus. He was too old to be running, but he ran. As one of the richest men in Jericho he had no business to make a fool of himself by climbing a tree, but he did. What motivated this middle-age man to run? What drove him to climb a tree? Stories. Stories. Stories. Everyone talked about the young preacher from Nazareth. Maybe He'll throw out the tyrannical Herodians. What about Rome? They'd go too.

One of his employees told Zacchaeus, "I saw Him heal a blind man. He was not temporarily blind, this man had been blind all his life."

His wife brought home a cockamamie story. "You won't believe this, Zacchaeus, but I saw Him raise a dead man. It was a friend of His, a man by the name of Lazarus. It's true. I saw it for myself."

Then Zacchaeus heard the story of the ten lepers. "He healed them. Every one of them."

Now you know why Zacchaeus would run to be ahead of where Jesus was walking. He had to catch a glimpse of a Man who could heal a blind man, of a Man who could raise the dead, of the Man who had healed ten lepers.

Zacchaeus thought to himself, "When people talk about this great Man, I'll chime in, 'I saw Him! I saw Him!'" Stop for a moment to get a picture of Zacchaeus. As a tax collector he was

Insights

labeled a publican. Jesus classed publicans with harlots *(Matthew 21:31)*, and Zacchaeus was a chief publican with a staff of employees. He did not receive a stipulated salary but was free to collect all he could in commissions.

Zacchaeus would be the first to admit it. "I get no respect. I am not the most popular man in Jericho, he said with a wry smile. I blame it on the job. I am the highest bidder for the taxing stations in town, so when I walk down the street I see myself as a successful businessman. First of all, you and I know the people hate to pay taxes. And, second, the money isn't spent here; it goes to Rome. Sure people shout at me."

"You scumbag!"

"You gouger!"

"He's money-hungry," said the man in the street. "He's the wealthiest man in town, but he wants more. He over-charges, that's the problem, he tries to charge more than required."

"So," Zacchaeus said, "I made up my mind. I wanted to see this Man who could be the long-awaited Messiah. He's been preaching and healing for three years. He has a great following. He could set up a new government. I'm sure there will be bloodshed if He does. All of us are shaking in our boots. After all, Rome has a tight grip on us."

"I'm only five feet tall so my chance of seeing Him is small. I'd be lucky to get within ten feet of Him. I could be trampled by the crowd." Futility filled the mind of this ambitious man, so when he saw the throng that moved like sea waves, he watched from a hill. "Where will He pass? Will He swing to my right? I'd guess by that tree, but I'll have to run to make it." Out of breath, Zacchaeus scrambled up the branches of the sycamore. He peered out. "Yes, if He passes here I'll see Him." A group of teenagers pointed in derision at a businessman in a tree. The dust! O the dust. Swirling clouds of dust. Noise. Everyone seems to be hollering. Kids wander alone. He was right. The roiling mass encircled his tree, and there He was! His disciples formed a cordon for His protection.

Jesus stopped and looked into the tree. Zacchaeus froze. "He is looking at me. That can't be. I know. He wants to reprimand me for my work. No. Maybe He wants me to contribute to His ministry."

Then he heard, "Zacchaeus! Zacchaeus!"

He couldn't believe his ears. Who told Him my name?

"Come down! Come down at once!"

With that command Zacchaeus clambered down. He shivered with excitement as he stood before Jesus.

The Lord spoke. "Today I will be a guest in your home!"

"I'd be honored." Zacchaeus's voice trembled. He repeated to himself, "He's coming to my house."

As the entourage prepared to leave the shadow of the sycamore the crowd reacted.

"You can't do that, shouted a storekeeper, don't you know he's a publican? A cheat!"

Jesus looked at a young man who carried a baby. "Lord," he informed him, "he is a sinner."

Zacchaeus heard the scoldings and undertones. There must be something he could say in this embarrassing moment. He interrupted the hecklers.

Zacchaeus put his new-found faith into words. "Lord," he spoke imploringly, "half of my possessions I will now give to those who have little. And this, listen to this, if I have over-charged someone, I will now restore four times as much."

Jesus listened to his plea, but did not commend him for his new intentions; after all, he would only be following the law. Jesus looked at the taunters and said, "Today salvation will come to his home, this is his birthright, for he is a son of Abraham, and I have been sent to the lost sheep of the house of Israel" *(Matthew 15:24)*. For the Son of Man has come to seek out and to save that which was lost.

INSIGHT

You and I can glean some truths from the story of Zacchaeus as we remove layers and peer behind what happened that day. Jericho is a city of priests, but Jesus chose to be entertained in the home of a despised man. He spurned those who thought God could be found in a building, to teach that God works in that heart of man. Zacchaeus had been outside of the Lord. Now, he and his family became children of God because Jesus came to seek that which was lost (Luke 19:10).

If you and I had selected an evangelist to reach Jericho and beyond we never would have chosen Zacchaeus, but Jesus did. He sat by Jacob's well and chose a Samaritan woman, who could have been a prostitute, to bring the gospel to Samaria. One day he had a vision for the city of Capernaum, and selected a Roman army officer as his "go-to" man.

Travelers to Jericho would say, "I see a city of palm trees." Jesus said, "I see a city with people who are lost." In a matter of a few days Jesus would die for this hated man and everyone in Jericho. Paul the apostle wrote that faith expresses itself and works through love (Galatians 5:6).

See Luke 19.

ROMANS 4:17

I chuckle to myself when I think of what Ted said.
"I have a new name."
"What d'ya mean, you have a new name?"
"Yeah," he said, "you can now call me Romans four-seventeen."
That's Ted for ya; always kidding around.
"You know," he smiled with mischief, "Abraham changed his name."
"I recall he was called Abram. What prompted him to choose Abraham?"
"He was seventy-five, can you imagine that, when God told him he was going to have a son."
"Did he have any children at that time?"
"No," he clued me in, "none up till then. After that promise and though childless, for twenty-five years, he proclaimed he was the father of a multitude."
"I can hear him," I chimed in.
"Hey! Harry, you know what, I have a son."
"Abraham, you must be off your rocker. You don't have a son. I'll have to tell everyone old age has set in early."
"I have a name for him."
"You have a name for an invisible person?"
"Yep! His name is Isaac. As far as I'm concerned he's here in person. I can see him with my eyes of faith. Sometimes when I am with the camels, I tell 'em about Isaac."
Ted whole-heartedly agreed to the picture of Abraham. He saw

Insights

his childless situation through God's eyes.

"True. He could have said: 'Ya know what, I don't have a son. I wish I had a son. Sarah is too old.' By the way, what does the verse say?"

"It goes like this: 'God speaks of things that are not in existence as being in existence.' You could add, foretold and promised. Then it would read, 'God speaks of things. He has foretold and promised as though they had already happened.'"

This is what Abraham did.

"Yes," answered Ted. "He talked about something that could not be seen, a son, as though he were actually present."

I mentioned I had read that verse, and that I struggled to understand it.

"Abraham lived his life through the lens of what God speaks. What God said framed his faith. For example, he never said he could be a millionaire. God had never said he could be a millionaire."

"Ya know," I added, "I see a finality here, a spiritual law. I mean from God's point of view."

"I think," Ted went on, "He asks you and me to act on what He says in his Word."

"That's what I like about Abraham."

"Those years he waited for Isaac were filled with gratitude."

"I'm certain they were. 'Thank you for my son. Thank you for the promise. Thank you for your faithfulness. Thank you for your love.'"

"How did this spiritual breakthrough come about?"

"I like to think of it as a 'revelation.' In this case, the Spirit spoke through a speaker I heard on the radio."

"So you see these 'revelations' as the way the Holy Spirit opens one's eyes."

"Oh yeah. Maybe one's listening to a speaker on the radio.

Could be a book."

"Or a friend," I suggested. Sure.

"But it's a high moment. A time of refreshment. Wow! I never saw that before. Kinda like insider information. Sometimes I'll run and write it down before it slips away. I feel from this sunny message that I have been lifted from one plateau to a higher plateau."

"I think there's a verse that says I cannot know the things of God unless the Spirit shows them to me. Sometimes I feel like I have to take my shoes off. I'm standing on holy ground."

I chuckled and I pictured Ted without his shoes. "Arms uplifted. Looking to heaven."

"These Lenten moments have such worshipful quality to them. I like to think of these experiences like an exclamation point. For days I feel like I'm walking on a cloud."

"He says He loves us so you and I can enjoy this demonstration of His care."

"On these disclosures, spiritual breakthroughs, how often do you experience them?"

"That's a toughie. Sometimes I'll go for months without this spiritual discovery. They come unexpectedly. From what I've been told, they will happen as long as we live."

"That's good news."

"So you have pitched a tent along side of Romans four-seventeen and taken up squatter's rights."

Ted smiled. "I've been putting Roman's four-seventeen to work in my life."

"How's that?"

"I've been speaking of things He has promised things which are not seen, as though they're present in my life."

"Ya' know," I commented, "you can see that same truth in the man Noah."

"Sure," Ted agreed.

"Though he could not see the flood, he acts as though he can see it."

"Moses. Same truth. He took his people out of Egypt. He didn't fear the wrath of the king, for he endured as seeing Him who is invisible. I think the sublime example of this truth is seen in the Lord Jesus Christ who is the source of our faith. To obtain redemption for man, He endured the cross and is now seated at the right hand of God."

Lazarus

"I've never seen Lazarus so sick."
"I feel so helpless."

Martha and Mary talked about the sickness of their brother Lazarus.

" If Jesus had been here I'm sure He would have healed him." Martha aired her anxiety as she spoke her faith.

"No question about it." A tear ran down the cheek of Mary as she spoke what was in her heart.

"Do you have any idea where He's at?"

"Over by the Jordan river, so they say," Martha continued. "Abi, our neighbor, says he wants to help. You know he and Lazarus were as thick as thieves. I'll ask Abi to tell Jesus that Lazarus is slipping away."

"That's dangerous." Mary was frightened. "If Jesus comes to Jerusalem, the angry Jews will kill him."

With Mary's OK Martha talked to Abi. "It's a day's journey. Are you sure you have the time?" Abi sighed. He too was distraught over the sickness of his friend. He left immediately on his secret journey and delivered his note to Jesus. The note read, "The one you love so much is sick." One would think they would request His presence. They don't. They inform Jesus of His friend's sickness.

Jesus shared the news with his disciples, who also shared his love for Lazarus. They were heartened to hear Jesus say:

"This sickness will not end in death." Jesus paused. "On the contrary, Lazarus' sickness will honor God and manifest His glory. And by it the Son of God will be glorified."

His disciples heard what He said, but did not understand He was providing them with a model of faith they would need when He had left. If He had not spoken His faith they would have been left with the vacuum of the unspoken.

Abi returned to the Jordan to face the two young ladies.

"Tell us about the mission. Did you give Him our message?" At first Abi laughed at their torrent of questions, but soon he turned serious. "I thought the Master was going to cry."

"He has such a wonderful love," spoke Martha with a terror in her voice.

Mary thought back to the many times He had visited their home. Their friendship had grown to where He was perceived of as a member of the family. Martha, Mary and Lazarus knew He was the Messiah, so the essence was conceived in reverence and trust.

Abi sat down at the kitchen table and sipped the cold drink Martha set before him. He looked at Mary's face and saw the exhaustion of caring for Lazarus.

"I thought this was comforting. He said the sickness is not to end in death."

"That's comforting."

"This I also recall. 'Lazarus' sickness will honor God and magnify His glory.'"

Martha let the words of Abi roll around in her mind " ... His sickness will honor God ... and magnify His glory." "I have to be patient. I know He loves us." She fastened her thoughts on the One who was the foundation for her faith.

Meanwhile, in the camp of the Lord, no one prepared to travel to Bethany. Why the delay? This would be His last miracle. Martha and Mary would go through the death of their brother. He would expose Himself and Jis followers to execution. The cost demonstrates the importance that faith meant to Jesus. When His followers learned faith, all things would be possible. The resurrection of Lazarus foretells His own resurrection.

"I think the time has come," Jesus sighed after days of deliberation. "The time has come to return to Bethany."

"You can't do that," cried Thomas. "The place is swarming with people who want to kill you."

"That's true." Peter's eyes were filled with tears. "It was only a few days ago that they wanted to stone you."

Jesus lamented, "Are there not twenty-four hours in a day?"

"That's true," answered James.

"If a person," Jesus enlarged, "If a person walks about in the daytime he does not stumble. He can see where he is going. On the other hand, if one walks at night he stumbles and runs into things. He cannot see where he is going."

Andrew thought to himself, "He has something in mind. He wants us to learn."

John whispered to the disciples, "He's talking about Himself. He is the light of God, and He walks in the light given by the father."

"So," Thomas concurred, "He walks by faith rather than sight."

"What about the darkness?" asked Andrew.

"Darkness," explained Thomas, "means to walk by sight instead of faith. The one who walks in darkness cuts God out of the picture."

"In this indirect way," John explained, "He's telling us He's walking by the light of God as He returns to Bethany."

In the midst of the disciples' search for meaning, Jesus remained preoccupied. In this critical juncture Jesus spoke with great emotion.

"Lazarus, our friend, has fallen asleep."

Peter, the impetuous one, blurted out with optimism, "If Lazarus is sleeping that means he's recovered. That's great. Now we don't have to hazard our lives by returning to Judea."

Peter's hope hung in the air like a question mark.

Jesus brought a sigh from the band when He announced, "Lazarus has died."

"All of us share your sorrow," John spoke from the heart.

"But," Jesus went on, "I am happy I was not there. For this experience will open the door to the secret of how faith works. In light of that, let us set off for Bethany."

Some of the disciples, out of fear, thought it was unwise to return to such a den of hatred.

"Men!" Thomas addressed the disciples. "Let us join the Master in this dangerous journey that we may die with Him."

Jesus learned that Lazarus had been in his tomb for four days when He arrived at Bethany. Many of the Jews from Jerusalem crowded the home of Martha and Mary. Martha learned that Jesus was outside of town and secretly went out to see Him.

"Lord," said Martha, "if you had been here my brother would have not died. I know positively that whatever you ask of God, He will give it to you."

In response, Jesus declared, "Your brother shall rise again."

Martha spoke her faith as she said, "I know for certain he will arise for the resurrection on the last day."

"Martha," Jesus spelled out, "I am the resurrection and the Life and the one who believes in me, even if he die, shall never actually die. Do you believe this?"

"Yes, Lord. I believe that You are the Christ, the Son of God, the One for whom the world has waited."

Martha returned to Mary in secret. "Mary," she whispered, "He's outside of Bethany. He wants to see you."

Mary walked out to the hillside to see Jesus, and a number of her Jewish friends went with her. They thought she was going to the tomb of Lazarus. When Mary met Jesus she fell at His feet, crying. "If You had been here my brother would not have died."

Jesus wept as He saw Mary and her friends weeping, and one said, "Look how tenderly He cared for Lazarus."

Moved with love, Jesus asked, "Where have you laid him?" The entourage walked to the tomb, which was a cave. Across the face, the burial people had placed a stone.

Jesus said, "Remove the stone."

Martha, always the practical one, interposed, "Lord, already there is an offensive odor."

Jesus tactfully replied, "Martha, didn't I tell you and promise you, that if you would believe, you would see the glory of God?"

So they took away the stone doorway.

Jesus lifted His eyes toward heaven and prayed, "I know you always listen and hear, but I have said this for the benefit of those standing around, so they may come to believe I am the Sent One."

Having said this He stepped forward toward the open tomb and shouted with a voice everyone could hear, "Lazarus! Come out!"

The crowd was breathless. Mary's hand covered her open mouth. Martha's eyes revealed the suspense.

Out walked Lazarus. His hands and feet were wrapped in white linen, and a white linen handkerchief covered his face. A hush passed through the crowd.

Jesus said to the grave attendants, "Remove the wrappings so he can move freely." Many of the Jews who had come with Mary became believers, but some of them reported the raising of Lazarus to the enemies in Jerusalem.

Jesus raised Lazarus as a foreshadowing of His own resurrection only days away. He used this miracle to give His followers the faith they would need when He left. If He had stood at the tomb and said nothing, Lazarus would not have emerged. His faith spoke to the problem — death. Just as God spoke to darkness and light came to be, so Jesus spoke to death and life came to be.

He's Not Here

When I shaved that morning I had no inkling of what the day held, for I would see someone take ownership of something God said.

She had grown children, down to earth, impressive with a childlike openness. I had never met Tim's wife, but I introduced myself at his review. His obituary refreshed my memory of a musician who had lived the Christ-like life — a man I had known in another chapter of my life.

Dusk drew its cloak slowly over the city as I entered the hushed funeral parlor.

"I'm here to see Tim," I whispered to a solemn man in a black suit. He pointed to the right. I entered a room where small groups of relatives and friends shared their common bereavement. With head bowed in reverence I tiptoed to the front of the room. I stood before the coffin with my hands folded in front of me. His face aroused memories of experiences we had shared years ago; now he was gone.

I forgot about the huddled groups behind me and listened to my own heart. What does God say to death? I searched the corners of my inner man for an answer. I knew the solution lay in what God said. Out of my aloneness a life-changing fact began to break on me: I was alone.

"You're not here, Tim," my spirit murmured to an invisible person.

"You're not here!" The passing of seconds made the truth clearer.

"Oh, sure, I see your body, but you're not in it! Your body's empty. You've left. You have journeyed elsewhere."

I thought about Jesus and the raising of Lazarus from the dead. "In Him was Life," wrote John. I cast about because I was restless within. I need a revelation from the Lord, said one old man — a sunnier message. I found a Lenten quality to this moment of sacred reflection. I looked for insider knowledge — something that would enable me to say "I understand."

When the words of the apostle came to me I knew the Holy Spirit had witnessed my dilemma: "If I am absent from my body, I am present with the Lord."

That's what Tim is ... absent from the body!

I understand! Tim's not here because he has been escorted into the presence of Christ!

I mumbled the words to myself: "If I am absent from my body, I am present with the Lord."

I hadn't heard a surrealistic voice. No lightning flashed. No grand music. One sentence — a handful of words — that stood in my mind like a billboard.

"Keep quiet!" said the etiquette of the parlor. How can I keep quiet words that should be shouted? "TIM'S NOT HERE!" Shouldn't they be told? What about the man in the black suit? Would he throw me out? I can't bottle up such wonderful news.

"Hi, I'm Tim's wife." My interlude ended with the sound of a woman's voice. Her inquisitive look asked: "Who are you?" I introduced myself and shared why I was here. She stood with a quiet dignity but her eyes betrayed her loss.

"Ya know ... something came to me...only moments ago ... " I broke eye contact and looked at Tim. Am I going beyond respectful condolences?

"Oh, what was that?" I could tell she was looking for answers.

"I've been standing here ... trying to understand ... and this came to me ... He's not here!" I glanced from Tim to her.

She drew back. Puzzlement. Anyone could see he was laying there.

"But ... ?" was all she could mutter as she faced the facts.

I hurried in with words to stop the painful wrestling.

"If I am absent from the body ... " the apostle Paul said this, "If I am absent from the body ... I am present with the Lord."

I took a deep breath and waited. At least I had gotten it out. Assimilation takes time. Let the Word do its work. If I say too much it will bring confusion. I knew God wanted her to see this from His point of view.

"If - I - am - absent - from - my - body ... " Understanding moved across her face as she slowly repeated my words. "How does the rest of it go?"

"I am present with the Lord," we said it in unison.

"You're right. Tim's not here. He has taken leave of his body." God had offered her the seed of His word and she had embraced it. Now it belonged to her. The Holy Spirit had escorted the revelation to her believing heart. "I never knew this," she spoke with new insight. Bereavement's heaviness had disappeared from her face.

I stepped back to leave. "It's been my pleasure ... " my words were cut short.

"Wait. Wait. Wait." she stepped toward me as though jarred from her preoccupation. "You haven't told me where that's found."

"You're right. Second Corinthians, five, verse eight."

"One more thing. See that tall man over there ... " she nodded in his direction, "he's the minister who'll give the eulogy tomorrow. Tell him what you told me and where it's found. I want this to be the anthem of his tribute to Tim."

I did as she instructed and left rejoicing that she took ownership of a truth God wanted her to have.

STEPHEN

He steps on to the stage of history immediately after the resurrection of the Lord Jesus Christ. A scant one hundred and twenty people made up this first church. This changed quickly. Several thousand joined. That's all the people talked about in the city of King David.

One man worked behind the scenes in this theater of panic. He had sold everything he had and joined the communal fellowship. Dr. Luke writes about him in the book of Acts. His task along with six others was the equal distribution of the food. His great miracles came to the attention of everyone.

The Bible tells us little of the person of Stephen. As a Jewish immigrant, he could have been a Roman citizen like the apostle Paul. He spoke Greek and Hebrew. His grasp of the Old Testament was outstanding. Could he have been a priest? Family? Age? Skill? History? Nothing. We know Stephen from the far reaching consequences of his oration before the Sanhedrin. His death became a battle cry, a vivid invocation to an assembly under persecution.

In the sixth and seventh chapters of the book of Acts you find the enlightening story of Stephen. He was a Hellenist, a Jew who adopted the Greek language and part of a throng of Jews who were immigrants. The Jerusalem — proper — Jews looked down on these transient Jews as inferior.

"They're not true Jews," said one Pharisee. "Who knows if they are really Jews or what. Why do they have to talk in a foreign tongue?"

This racism invaded the Christian community. Christian Jews of Jerusalem did not share the offering of the first church with the Hellenists.

"It's the food," said one Hellenist, "our wives are going hungry."

"No need for it," said another, "the donations overwhelm us. Food, money, clothing, property — people give everything they have. Communal living — that's what it is. No one should be left out."

This undertow of complaining and murmuring moved from secrecy into the open.

"Let's tell the disciples themselves." So they did. The disciples recognized they had neglected the fair distribution of food.

"What can we do?" asked Peter. "Everyday people are coming to the Lord Jesus Christ. These need spiritual care. If we spend all our time running the kitchen we neglect these newcomers. Preaching the Word and prayer — that's our job."

"Why don't we select some men to head up this monumental supervision?" said James. All concurred.

"We need men who have a good testimony. Men who are filled with the Holy Spirit, men who know what they're doing."

"I propose Stephen," said one disciple. Six Hellenist Jews and one Gentile made up the mix. These seven men stood before the apostles. They prayed over them and laid their hands on them.

"Now," said the apostles, "we can devote full time to prayer and ministry of the Word." Everyone agreed that this would expedite their ministry.

Though Stephen had been selected to wait on tables, he began to play a significant role as a spiritual leader. He constantly performed miracles among the people and these attested to the testimony that he was inspired of God.

Jewish immigrants, not Christians, who wanted to test their

muscle before the Jerusalem Jews, disagreed with Stephen. These dissenters came from all over the place. Some even from the synagogue of the Libertines. Once known as slaves to Caesar, Rome had set them free. Some were from the synagogue of the Cyrenians. Others Alexandrians. And then there were those that came from Cilicia and Asia. Later we see these as false witnesses and stone throwers.

"I simply testify," proclaimed Stephen, "that Jesus fulfills the prophecy of our scriptures."

"He claims," shouted one Cilician, "that Jesus is our Messiah. What can we do with such a fool?"

Racial impurity lay beneath the surface. If you were an immigrant from Alexandria, you were only part Jew.

"Look at your priests," challenged a man from Cyrenia. "Some of your Jerusalem priests are embracing this nonsense. Why not expose him?"

"He's going to destroy your holy temple. That's what he says this Jesus will do. Yes, and he says He can do it in three days. We didn't rebel against Moses, or Joseph, or Abraham but he says we did."

This Christian movement destabilized Jerusalem. It had to be stopped, so they raised up false witnesses to picture Stephen as a dangerous heretic. The masses, the elders, and yes, those scholars of the scriptures embraced the twisted story.

"We have the crowd with us," they shouted. "Now's the time to move." Without warning they arrested Stephen as a common criminal.

These thugs dragged Stephen before the council of the Sanhedrin — the highest court and council of the Jewish nation.

"This man," shouted the false witnesses, "preaches against the holy place. He preaches against our law. He even says that Jesus the Nazarene will destroy this temple and will change the customs which Moses delivered for us to keep. We cannot forget the solemnity of our traditions."

And all those sitting in the council studied Stephen intently and they saw his face as if it were an angel's face.

"I want to understand the charges," stated the chief priest. "Are they factual? I'm sure no one would say he would destroy our sacred temple. Who would dare to change the customs Moses delivered to us? I've never heard such slander."

Here Stephen stood before the supreme court of the land.

"I couldn't be happier," thought Stephen to himself. "What a glorious opportunity to testify to the authenticity of the Gospel of the Lord Jesus Christ." He could have said the charges are all bunk. He could have brought up the honesty of his accusers. Instead, he took the offensive.

"Your honor," spoke a false witness, "this man says his Lord will destroy our holy temple."

Stephen knew the temple symbolized the faith of the Jewish nation — the very heart of Judaism in the heart of the city of King David.

"He wants," another witness stated, "Jesus the Nazarene to be the King over Israel. Moses lives in our memory. He instituted laws and traditions this sect wants to destroy."

Those sitting in the high council of the Sanhedrin studied Stephen. They saw his face as if it were an angel's face. His argument rang true with scripture. He sought nothing for himself.

This drama of Stephen before the Sanhedrin, in the city of King David — Jerusalem, the nerve center of religion — holds a monumental place in history. Stephen makes the last offer of king and kingdom to the Jewish nation. For Peter had said if Judaism repented, the king would come and introduce the times of refreshing and restore all things.

The take-home point we're all waiting for is found in the phrase "we will not have this man reign over us." *(Luke 19:14:27)*

Israel not only sinned but being under the special care and love of God, they sinned in banishing that special care and love. The Holy Spirit offered them the joyous privilege to enter into a new life — a life of faith and they threw it out.

Acts Chapter Seven gives us a history of Israel. "You are idolaters," preaches Stephen, "and have been so from the beginning of your national history. Your wickedness has culminated in the murder of the Messiah Himself. I extend to you," continued, Stephen in Hebrew, "the opportunity to repent."

"This man," thought the High Priest, "thinks this itinerant preacher from Nazareth was God. That throws aside our law and temple."

Having heard these things, the Sanhedrin was cut to the heart. "Guilty! Guilty!" they shouted. With hatred, they gnashed their teeth at Stephen. Hatred bubbled over roiling passions.

But Stephen, in the Spirit, amid all the shouting, fixed his gaze into heaven. "I see God's glory and Jesus standing at the right hand of God." A roar went through the crowd as they rushed upon Stephen. They dragged him outside the city. The false witnesses, who were to be the legal stone throwers, took off their outer robes and set them at the feet of a young man named Saul.

And they kept on stoning Stephen with fist-size rocks as he continued to call up the Lord. "Lord Jesus, receive my spirit." Then he knelt down and cried with a loud voice, "Do not place this sin against them." Having said this he fell asleep.

And Saul with the rest of the crowd joined in their murder. Not only did he take pleasure in it, but he also applauded it. As the first Christian martyr, Stephen joined other Christians — beaten — jailed — hounded — in rejoicing that they were counted worthy to suffer shame for His name.

Marching orders had already been given: Go into all the world.

Stephen

The first church had enjoyed the wild evangelism in Jerusalem. With the death of Stephen, Christians became fair game. This persecution drove the believers to go into all the world.

Israel had been the apple of God's eye. He revealed Himself to them. The Messiah would come through them. Through their sin you and I can find faith. Stephen spoke his faith when he said, "Receive my spirit."

Pool of Bethesda

If you want a message on the power of the spoken word this is it. In fact, only two words were spoken. It's enough to take your breath away, especially if you're the benefactor of that which was spoken.

Before we get to that we're going to take a side trip. It's a peek into the question: How did the temple in Jerusalem get water? Solomon's pools were located ten miles from Jerusalem. Water from these pools traveled through an open aqueduct to the temple enclosure. Large reservoirs cut in the solid hilltop held the water. No valves controlled the flow of water, so engineers constructed other pools throughout the city to receive the overflow.

You would ask, "What does that have to do with the story?" It takes us to the scene where a helpless man found someone who loved him. The pool of Bethesda, meaning house of Mercy, was one of these overflow pools in the city. If you had sheep to sell you brought them here. So this gate to the city became known as the sheep gate.

If a visitor came to town and asked, "How can I find the Bethesda Pool?" They would reply, "You'll find it by the Sheep Gate."

Five large porches surrounded this pool. Since the pool had become known as a place to be healed, great numbers of people languished in these pavilions. They traveled from far and wide to receive the miracle of Bethesda.

"I have brought my son. He's thirteen. Unable to walk. It took us three days to walk from Nain to this pool."

The porches of Bethesda were like a great waiting room of a

Pool of Bethesda

hospital. Some could not hear. Others could not see. Friends and family brought those who could not walk. All wanted to find instantaneous healing.

Bethesda became known through the activity of angels *(Galatians 3:19, Acts 7:53)*. Without warning an angel would cause the water to bubble as a fountain. The first one to scramble into the water would be healed of whatever disease he had. To buy up this angelic ministry one had to have the strength to be the first one in the water, for only one was healed.

You can picture the scene when one was healed. Shouting. Crying. Dancing. Praising God. Everyone rejoicing.

"It's the happiest moment!" cried one man.

Jesus was drawn to Jerusalem by the feast of the Jews. He had walked southward from Galilee for three days. He could have had John with Him, for he is the one who records the event. This Man who had preached to thousands, now became a Man in a tumbling sea of humanity. He could have preached in the temple; instead He turned to the crowded porches of sickness and suffering.

"What is the story on this man?" Jesus asked a spectator.

"I know that man lying prostrate. He cannot walk. He's been like that for thirty-eight years."

Jesus selected this man: of all the hundreds he was the most miserable, needy and helpless.

"Do you want to be made well?" Jesus asked the man. At first glance this question appears unnecessary, but Jesus did not wish to overrule his will.

The helpless man looked up into the face of Jesus. "Sir," he said, "I have no one to throw me into the pool the moment the water bubbles. I try to get into the pool, but by the time I reach the water someone else steps ahead of me."

"Here's a strong young spectator," thought the helpless man.

"Maybe he'll be the one who would gather me in his arms and throw me into the pool. He'd have to be fast to beat everyone else." No one cared.

"Why waste time on him?" one older man asked, "even the angel can't heal him." Of all the sick on the five porches, he was the most hopeless. Futility etched itself on the faces of a small ring of curious watchers.

"Stand up!" His authority was masked by His questions. "Stand up!"

"That guy's gotta be out of his mind, thought the older man." He said, 'Stand up.' He can't stand."

And the infirm man on the ground looked up. "Did I hear right? I think he said 'stand up.' I can't stand up."

Two or three in the crowd laughed. He didn't throw him into the pool, he only said "Stand up." Who's he kidding?

An imperceptible strength passed through the weak man lying on the ground.

"It's a strength I haven't felt before. It flowed like a river of energy. I think I could get up. I think I'm strong enough to stand." He looked up into the compassionate face of the One who had healed him.

From the look on the face of Jesus he knew he had no choice. He had to stand. He rolled on to his side. He lifted himself to a kneeling position with his hands on the ground. All held their breath. The strength from Christ continued to pulsate through his body. With strength he had never known he stood up. He quivered like a leaf in the wind.

"I'm standing! I'm standing!" He sobbed. Tears ran down his face.

"Isn't this the man from Nain?"

"Who put him in the water?"

"He didn't go in the water!"

Some laughed nervously for joy.

Unforgettable drama! A moment in itself. A moment for thunderous music. No one sang. Everyone was apprehensive. Maybe he'll fall. The voice of Jesus broke the air.

"Pick up your bedroll." The man did.

"Now walk about."

He walked about. He looked at his legs as new-found entities. "I am somebody. I can walk like everyone else." He turned to hug the man who had healed him. He was gone.

"Where is the man who healed me?" he cried. "Where did he go to?"

All this happened on the Jewish Sabbath, so the man walked to the temple to praise God.

"What are you doing?" cried a Jewish rabbi. "You're carrying your bedroll. Don't you understand this is the Sabbath?" In their ignorance they continued to hound the man. "Finally," they pressed him, "did someone tell you to carry your bedroll?"

"Yes, yes." If I say yes, maybe they will stop hollering at me.

"Point him out to us!" shouted the heckler.

"I don't ... I don't know who he is. He disappeared in the crowd."

After this harassment Jesus decided to visit the temple, and there He encountered the one He had healed.

"Here you are, you're doing fine," said Jesus.

"I can't thank you enough for what you have done for me. I have something to live for."

"Yes," replied Jesus, "but do not continue to sin or you will be worse off than you were before."

You could ask what sin was in this man's life? It was the absence of faith. He could have learned of the giants of the Old Testament who persevered, seeing Him who is invisible.

Our story takes a wry turn. You would think that the healed

man would hold a cherished devotion to Jesus. Not so, as soon as he knew the identity of his healer, he scurried to the rabbi Jews.

"His name is Jesus. You will find Him in the temple."

Now we have Him on two misdemeanors; first: he healed the man on the Sabbath. Second: he told the man to carry his bedroll.

Blinded by sin, the Pharisees conspired to murder Jesus, not only for trampling on the Sabbath, but now He announces God is His Father. He blatantly claims deity.

Hot Cross Buns

"Take that pan over there, Stron, they're a lil' bit cooler." Dad's deep baritone voice with the rich Danish accent instructed me where to bag my hot cross buns. Where'd he get that nickname "Stron"? I don't know. It claimed an affection reserved alone between a father and his son. You never heard it when it came time to render discipline.

Over a dozen large pans of hot cross buns dotted themselves about Dad's bakeshop. One on a mixing bowl barrel. Another sat on a black scale. One perched precariously on a stair wall. Long rows of white icing criss-crossed each bun. Dad could ice a twenty-four bun pan in five seconds. I never saw a man who worked so fast. A true master baker. With a hundred things on his mind, he had no time to dawdle.

Here's a situation where a saying really fits: "They sell like hot cakes." Two weeks before Easter, 1935. I had just turned fifteen. Everyone enjoyed hot cross buns during this Lenten season, and we were the purveyors. With their pieces of citron and spicy taste, I thought they were miniature Yulekage "lay-bys" from the past Christmas season.

"Put a dozen bags into yer basket," I was instructed. Door-to-door sales.

"Good mornin', Ma'am, I have freshly baked hot cross buns."

"How much are they, Sonny?"

"Six for thirty cents. A real buy."

Dad's neighborhood bakery sat on the corner of Minnehaha Avenue and Thirty-Fifth Street in South Minneapolis. I think our motto could have been: Anything to earn a living. Depression tremors continued to send shock waves through our lives. Wives held down the home front. Many men rode streetcars to work. Not everyone had a car. Refrigeration? What's that? Water catch-pans under the icebox often overflowed. Housewives welcomed the peddlers to bring them the necessities of life.

Dad had a penchant toward veterans of the Great War. His own age prevented him from serving, so he saw servicemen as heroes who should be honored. It came as no surprise that two veterans worked for him. They did not fit the prototype of a salesman. Tight-lipped gentlemen in their mid-thirties. They could have played the parts of western gunfighters in a Zane Grey novel. Their silence gave them the larger than life aura. I asked Dad to tell me about them.

"I think they were gassed during the Great War." His tone made it sound like an apocalyptic pronouncement — an invocation that called for hushed reverence.

They called Dad "Chris." He called them "Al" and "Marty" — Albert and Martin. Nice lookin' men. Cleanly dressed. Not alcoholics. Always gentlemen. They remained as illusive and secretive as a bounty hunter out of that same Zane Grey novel.

"Are they married, Dad?"

"I don't know," he whispered.

That answer echoed for everything: children, address, all unknown. This mystique painted images in my mind.

"Ya know, Dad," I speculated, "they've probably seen some things they just can't talk about."

"Yer probably right, Stron. War does funny things to people." Like I say, I did know Dad respected them and had a kindred spirit with them. Of course, I knew what they did for Dad. They peddled bakery goods from house to house. We were like the "dead end kids" compared to them. They were the professionals.

Their baskets held everything the bakery offered. No car. They walked. Cookies. Sweet rolls. Bread. And hot cross buns for the discerning.

When they sold out they returned to Dad for another load. Inclement weather restricted their activity. If sales were brisk they could be done in a few hours. Al and Marty saw themselves as self-employed. Nobody to boss 'em around. What they put on their table, they had earned by the sweat of their brow. I was able to watch their comings and goings with Dad for three years.

My brother Lloyd and I were recruited to join their thin ranks in this Lenten season. Out of one "loop" we could gross $3.60. Our commission: 50¢. That came out to two bits an hour for our two hour of sales. That was the going rate for an hour's work in that day. Spending money. Movie money. If the lady of the house asked for a specialty item, we'd go back to the bakery and get it for her. I'll never forget one lady.

"Is this the order I called in?" she asked in a surprised naive manner.

"Yes, Ma'am, thirty cents please." I handed her the bag of hot cross buns.

"Whew! That one almost got away!" I said out loud when I had cleared the house. All the while I prided myself for my ability to think on my feet. I often have wondered what that lady said when her true order came. I can hear her laughing: "That lil' scamp!"

Maybe you're asking the question, "What ever happened to Al and Marty?" I ask the same question. Don't know. They remain on the screen of my mind as mute men. Intriguing. They left as silently as they entered. Like guards at the Tomb of the Unknown, they protected their secret well.

John The Baptist

Everyone wanted to know who this man was. Crowds followed him. He had disciples. Jerusalem knew about him; but he made his home in the desert.

"You have left your towns to hear him," Jesus addressed a vast assembly. "Why? What did you hope to see? Were you looking for a flimsy reed? Were you looking for something soon blown away? A straw?"

"No! No!" shouted one in the crowd. "I wanted to see if this man was a fanatic."

"I repeat," continued Jesus, "were you disappointed in what you saw? You thought he would be a man dressed up in the finest of clothes? Let me assure you, those who wear stylish apparel live in the houses of kings. You made your way out in the desert. Were you looking for something spectacular?"

"Maybe I'll see a prophet," shouted one.

"Yes. A prophet or more than a prophet," proclaimed Jesus. "You look upon One who is superior to a prophet. The Scriptures tell you about Him. Malachi spoke about Him. His recorded record stands to this day. I send My messenger ahead of you. He will prepare the pathway before You."

"Who is this man?" Jesus extolled. "He didn't care for city living. He embraced the solitary life, but people fled out of towns to hear him." His father's name was Zecharias. His mother's name was Elizabeth. She came from a priestly family, the daughters of Aaron. She was a relative of the mother of Jesus. He dressed in goatskins, and for food ate fried locusts and honey.

John The Baptist

The throng who listened to John, looked for change. Roman bondage strained their backs. "Herod the tyrant! Despot! Oppressor! Dictator!" Soldiers everywhere.

Now the victims of this enslavement hear a voice booming on the banks of the Jordan River.

"Repent! Repent! The kingdom of God is at hand!"

"Who listens to this bearded crackpot?"

"People do! They come by the thousands."

"Yes, and he has disciples."

"He says the Messiah will be here soon."

"There is One coming after me Who is preferred before me."

"If he is to introduce a New King you would think he would dress like a courtier."

"I see him as a prophet," said one of his disciples. "Think of the lofty honor: to introduce the Messiah. After all, a prophet speaks for God to tell us what's on His mind. He has been sent from God to unveil for us the fulfillment of prophecy."

This flurry of activity on the west bank of the Jordan River was not going unnoticed.

"What's going on out there?" queried the chief priest of Sanhedrin. "Is this something that's going to get out of hand? Riots sneak up on one, you know."

A young Pharisee addressed the assembly. "I've seen him. I heard him preach. He's a wind-bag. He dresses like a clown. To be honest, I question his sanity."

"I wouldn't do that," charged an older member of the Sanhedrin. "I've heard him also. He talks about the Messiah. He knows our Scriptures."

"This Man I speak of," John looked across the crowd, "all of us have benefitted from His gift. Lay hold of this; He brings the unmerited love and favor of God to man. You understand that through Moses we received the Law. Now comes One to bring us a new truth. Grace will be heaped upon grace through the Person of the Lord Jesus Christ."

"You have often wondered what God looks like." John paused to let the thought set in. "Does He look like the man next to you? You and I would be excited to stand before Him." Again he waited as the crowd mumbled. "He has come!" A gasp rose up from the listeners. "Yes, He has come. He has come from our heavenly Father so you and I can enjoy the privilege of seeing Him for ourselves."

Who were these men who came from the Sanhedrin? In a few years they would crucify Jesus. Jesus called them hypocrites. They love being called Rabbi. They place a detour sign on the road to the truth. They make long prayers, then turn around to steal a house from a widow. They are blind guides who train proselytes to be worse than themselves. "You pay a tithe," said Jesus, "but you leave out judgment, mercy and faith." He went on, "you are sepulchres splashed over with white paint, but are full of dead men's bones." *(See Matthew 23)*

These enemies or emissaries from the Sanhedrin arrived on the bank of the Jordan River. The size of the throng amazed them.

"Where did all these people come from?"

"We underestimated his popularity."

They were out of place in this sea of common people, but John's disciples steered them to John. "Our mission," a fresh-faced young Pharisee spoke up, "is to find out if you are preaching rebellion."

John listened without a word.

His steady gaze flustered the Pharisees.

"We represent the Sanhedrin," one pompous one stammered. Then the questions flew:

"Who are you?"

"What are you up to?"

"Are you a prophet?"
"Would you like to be a king?"
"Are you a Messiah?"

John listened carefully to the interrogation going on before him. He knew his questioners felt out of place, and he knew who these men were, men blinded by their indoctrination.

"You have read Isaiah, Jeremiah and Ezekiel."
"Yes, yes and so ... "
"They predicted a Messiah would come."
"Yes. We knew. Are you that Messiah?"
"No, no I am not the Christ they talked about."
"Well, who ... who are you?"
"Understand, I hide nothing."

"You don't dress like a king." All the Pharisees laughed at this scornful remark. "You dress like Elijah the prophet." Another one joined in, "and you eat like him too." Again they leered. "Yeah!" sneered another, "you could be the reincarnation of Elijah." That was a good one, so they continued their charade. Little did they understand they were in the presence of historical greatness!

John did not mince words, and had no time to spare fools.
"No, no I am not Elijah."
"Then you must be the long promised one Himself."
John quickly spotted their attempt to entrap him with words.
"No, no." he hastened to reply, "my task lies in announcing His presence."

The dress of the inquisitors stood in sharp contrast to the nature-clad of John. On one hand one sees the aristocracy of Jerusalem, and on the other hand we give respect to the man of the wilderness.

"Our leaders in Jerusalem demand a report, you have given us little to say. We'll be in big trouble if we say that we have nothing to report and we don't know who this man is."

"All I can do is repeat myself. I am a voice crying out in the desert."

"A voice! That's all?"

"Yes, I am only a voice. Prepare the pathway for the Lord Himself."

"So, you prepare the way for Someone. Who ordered you to do this?"

"That is right. You must have a superior."

"I can tell you this, I baptize. I do baptize with the waters of the Jordan River. There is One with us. He baptizes also but He does not use the flowing Jordan. He baptizes with the Person of the Holy Spirit. You don't know Him, but I can assure you He will come after me."

"Will He come in the robes of a king?"

"He is majestic. He is far above me. I am not worthy of tying His shoelaces."

"We can tell the Sanhedrin that he talks about another Man, but we don't know who He is."

"How will I know," John prayed, "when He comes?"

"You will see the spirit descend on Him. That's how you can tell."

The next day John saw Jesus walking towards him.

"Look!" he cried out, "The Lamb of God!" (John foresaw the crucifixion.)

"He is the One," John continued, "who takes away the sin of mankind ... as I have said before, He was here before I was." (John shared the eternal nature of the Lord Jesus Christ.) "I have come baptizing with water to hail His arrival. I saw this for myself. I did see the Spirit come down and land on Him, He is the Son of God!"

John and Andrew, fisherman and disciples of the baptizer, heard his testimony and decided to follow Jesus. They left John and trailed behind Jesus. Jesus turned around and studied the two men carefully.

"Why are you following me? Are you looking for something?"

The two disciples looked at one another and then at Jesus. "Yes," they blurted out in their embarrassment, "we were wondering where You are staying."

"Come along, I'll show you."

They walked with Him to the place He made home and stayed with Him the rest of the day. One of the disciples who followed Him was Andrew the brother of Simon Peter.

"I'll never forget," recalled Andrew, "that first evening with the Master. He looked at me steadily. His eyes didn't blink. I knew He could see inside of me. I said to myself, 'I'll go anywhere with this Man.' As I listened to Him I knew I had to tell others about Him. My brother Peter came to mind. I soon found him and said, 'I've found Him! I've found Him!'"

"What are you saying? Who have you found?"

"I've found the Messiah!"

"No! Is this some prank?" snapped Peter. He continued to unload his fishing boat while Andrew pursued him.

"You know the Scriptures, they say the One is coming, the anointed One."

"All right, all right I'll take your word." So Peter followed his brother.

"Rabbi, I want You to meet my brother."

"So," said Jesus, "you are the son of John and your name is Simon."

"That's right."

"You'll have a new name. It will be Peter, which means 'a rock'."

The following day Jesus left the fishing village of Bethsaida and traveled westward into Galilee.

Philip and Bartholomew joined the growing band of men who would join this Man Moses spoke about. Jesus said of Nathanael, "This man is a true descendent of Jacob. I find in him no hypocrisy. He is the kind of man where everything is on the table."

"How can you know these things about me?" queried Nathanael. "I didn't think anyone knew these personal things about me."

"Before Philip spoke to you," Jesus intervened, "I saw you under the fig tree."

"Teacher, You are the Son of God!" cried Nathanael. "You are the King of Israel!"

"You believe," asserted Jesus, "because I saw you before Philip spoke to you." Jesus paused. "This is only the beginning. You shall see greater things than this. The very heavens shall be opened. You shall see the angels of God descending on the Son of Man."

Light of the World

Peli was only twenty-three. He could have been eighty-three. He looked it. He sat by the dusty roadside in Jerusalem. A beggar. He mumbled a few words and extended his cup when he heard someone pass by. He could not see the one who dropped a coin. Peli was blind. He had never seen the face of his mother or his father. Some day. Some day. Friends said he had a rich voice. They often heard him sing songs of praise. His winning smile portrayed his courage.

He had no forethought of change. What a joy it would be to see! He was made this way. A friend had told him about Jesus. "Who is He?"

"Some say He's the Messiah. He will deliver us out of the hands of the Romans. Oh yes, He has healed people. He's like a man on a steeple. Precarious. The other day the Pharisees tried to stone Him. They couldn't find Him." But here He was. He studied Peli. He loved Peli.

"Do you see this blind beggar?" asked Thomas.

"Yes," responded Jesus.

"I was wondering ... "

"Yes."

"I was wondering how he got this way." Thomas paused to frame his question. "Is he blind because of his own sin?"

"Go on."

"I'm struggling to say the right thing."

Jesus encouraged him to continue.

"Did the sin of his parents cause his blindness?"

"Neither," answered Jesus, "he was not born blind because of his own sin, and he was not born blind because of the sin of his dad and his mother."

"There must be a cause," stammered Peter.

"The only cause ... " Jesus paused, "it was a birth defect, however; I will use his blindness to openly show the works of God in him."

"Will someone tell me what's going on?" Peli smiled at the attention.

Jesus informed Peter, "I am the Light of the World. While I am still here I must hasten on with the Father's work of enlightenment. Darkness comes when no man can see or find his way."

Picture this scene. A crowd had gathered around Jesus and Peli. Jesus kneels beside the seated Peli.

"Son, will you do what I ask you to do?"

"Yes, Sir! Yes, Sir!" stuttered Peli.

"I'm going to put a little mud over your eyes."

"Yes."

"So hold still." Jesus spit on the ground. He blended together the spittle and dirt in the palm of His hand.

"Hold still, I'm going to rub this mixture I have in my hand over your eyes."

"Yes, Sir, whatever You say." Peli tipped his face upward.

Jesus carefully applied the creamy mud over each eye of Peli.

"Now I want you to go to the Pool of Siloam, it's by the king's garden."

"Yes, Sir, I know where it is."

"Wash your eyes in that pool. I'll talk with you later."

He followed the Lord's instructions, and he felt the muddy water run down his face. He splashed more water. He opened his eyes and blinked. Then it happened. Light! He saw light. All was blurred. He saw movement but no form. He breathed deeply.

He looked up and saw the blue sky. "I can see! I can see!" he cried. He looked at those around him. He enjoyed the smell of a flower. Now he could see it. His mind flashed to his family. They would be overwhelmed. Gratitude consumed him. "I have lived a miracle!"

"I want to see the Man Who healed me," exclaimed Peli, "I want to thank Him."

"Isn't that Peli the blind beggar?" a man in the crowd expressed.

"Yeah!" said another; "he can see."

Peli spoke up, "You have never known me to have sight, but now I can see."

Everyone clamored to know how it happened. "I'll tell you," he cried. "His name was Jesus. He put mud on my eyes. He sent me to the Pool of Siloam. I washed the mud from my eyes. Now I see!"

"Where can we find this man?"

"I don't know."

So the inquisitors took him to the Pharisees.

Peli related his story to them.

"This man, this Rabbi," said a spokesman for the Pharisees, "He cannot be of God. He healed this man on our Sabbath."

"But, but wait!" cried a young Pharisee, "if He is a sinner, how could He perform such a miracle?" They argued among themselves on this point: How can a bad man do good?

In their confusion the Pharisees decided to question Peli. "Young man, we want a word with you; you say He restored your sight."

"Yes."

"In the light of that, who is this Man?"

"He is a Prophet."

So the Pharisees asked his frightened parents, "Was he blind?

How did he receive his sight?"

They knew they would be thrown out of the synagogue if they professed Jesus as the Christ, so they said, "Ask Peli, he's an adult."

When they turned to Peli he blurted out, "You sound like you want to be His disciples!"

At this they stared at Peli. "We are the disciples of Moses!"

"This is amazing," boldly cried Peli; "a Man restores my sight and you know nothing about Him; who has ever heard of such a thing? If this Man were not from God He would not be able to do such a wonder."

"From head to foot," screamed the Pharisees, "you are a filthy sinner, and you have the guts to teach us!" With that outburst they threw Peli out of the synagogue.

When Peli was excluded from the rights of the synagogue the disciples brought the news to Jesus.

"Peli has been banned from the synagogue."

"How did this happen?" questioned the Lord.

"He said You were a Man of God, but the Pharisees said You healed on the Sabbath. Only a sinner would heal on the Sabbath."

"I want to see Peli again," insisted the Lord. "I admire his courage."

When they met Peli spoke his gratitude — with tears — for his eyesight. And he filled in the Lord on his encounter with the Pharisees.

"There is one thing I want to ask you," Jesus looked at the man He loved.

"Whatever You say."

"Do you believe in the Son of God?"

Peli studied Jesus with his new sight. "I would if I could, but I don't know Who He is. If I knew Who He was then I could believe."

"For starters, you have seen Him."

"I have? I didn't knew that."

"The Son of God is talking with you at this very moment!"

Peli gasped, now his spiritual eyes were opened. "I believe! I believe!" He knew Jesus was the Son of God.

INSIGHT

Jesus showed Peli — a man without sight, that he could see. He exposed the Pharisees — who had physical sight — that they were blind in their spirit as they worshipped the Sabbath. Peli expressed new spiritual sight when he declared His faith in the Son of God.

See John 9.

To a Land

She left no map. Not even a note
So I could follow her route
She lost her way as she disappeared
To a land with no way out.

She whispered words: I'm going home
As she slipped out the door
(A moment when nothing makes sense)
To a land with a distant shore.

No soft goodbye. Not even a wave
When she left her home that day
To journey to an unknown place
To a land that's far away.

Did she take the second star?
As Peter Pan told her to do
Straight through till morning
To a land with a misty view.

Her favorite rocker sits empty now
Where she watched the world go by
Her story from within played out
To a land that's not nearby.

To a Land

Twilight stillness floods her rooms
A hymn to motherhood
Her torch passed before she left
To a land so misunderstood.

Yesterday. Today. Tomorrow
Tumbling fog enshrouds the reef
Her twinkle and smile are not gone
To a land where time is brief.

With bowed head I hold her hand
That seems to cover the bill
Sometimes words get in the way
To a land where a look will fill.

She wraps her love around me
So visible I can touch it
Even tho' she's journeyed far
To a land without an exit.

In love the Father carries her
As a lamb on His chest
She knows He cannot falter
To a land which can be blest.

Written for my wife, as Alzheimer's disease took her away.
Winter 2010.

A Look at Parables

One day the disciples asked Jesus, "Why do You preach to the crowds in parables? Wouldn't it be clearer if You simply gave them the secret meaning?"

"You have been given," answered Jesus, "special insight into the secrets and mysteries of the kingdom of heaven. The masses lack the special insight when it comes down to seeing things with the heart. If one enjoys this spiritual insight he shall receive more of it, even to abundance. If one has a tiny amount of spiritual insight even that miniscule portion can be taken from him."

"I fail to understand," injected John, "who's at fault?"

"Like you," Jesus went on, "they have eyes, but they fail to see. Like you, they have ears, but they refuse to hear the secrets." *(Matthew 13:13).*

A parable is a story with a hidden meaning. It can be said to be a description of one thing under the image of another. In the story or allegory Jesus teaches spiritual insights. He used seeds, the roadside, thorns, stony ground, and the good earth to picture the reception of the Good News.

The first question we need answered is: "Who is the person who sows the seed?" Here's the answer: ... "eye has not seen, the ear has not heard; nor has it entered into the heart of man (through the gate of the senses), the things God has prepared for those who love Him. But God has revealed them to you and me through the Person of the Holy Spirit." *(1 Corinthians 2:9, 10)*

Second; What is the soil? The "soil" is the heart of man. As you and I look at the parable of the sower we have some answers. We understand that the One who broadcasts the seed is the Person of the Holy Spirit. The big question this parable answers is this: What hinders the seed from taking root? What blocks the life in the seed from germinating?

The first enemy to the Word is Satan. He steals the Word out of the heart before the person gets to understand it. The second enemy to the Seed is persecution. This gentleman abandons his faith because he is offended by the gospel. A third enemy to receiving the Seed lies in the love of money and materialism of life. The fourth ground received the Word joyfully and bears the fruit of the life of the Seed.

If we picture the soil with one word:
    Number 1 enemy: Satan
    Number 2 enemy: Trial
    Number 3 enemy: Greed
    Number 4 soil: Faith

One morning Jesus sat by the Sea of Galilee and spoke to the people.

"I can't hear you," shouted a man from the rear of the crowd.

Jesus entered a fishing boat and asked the fisherman, "Can you pull out from shore? More people will be able to hear me."

"No problem," replied the honored man.

"A sower went out to sow," taught Jesus. "He pictures a farmer planting seeds for an expectant harvest. As he broadcasts the seed on to his land some seeds fell by the road-side. The birds spotted the errant seeds and scurried to gobble them up. Some of the seeds the man threw fell on rocky ground where there was little soil. They sprang up quickly, but when the sun rose they were soon scorched and withered away because they had such little root. Some of the seeds fell among thorns but the thorns soon choked them out. And some of the seeds fell on good soil and sprouted to yield grain."

"You have been given ears," shouted Jesus from the boat, "listen to what I say. Strive to understand the meaning."

One man in the crowd commented to a friend; "I don't get it. We need to be a free people. We're under the yoke of Rome. This Man talks about farming. I don't get it."

His friend said, "Maybe He thinks we should all be farmers," at that he chuckled. "He can't be a king if he prattles about farmers and seeds."

In repudiation of these commentators, we ask ourselves, What is a seed? As you see a seed in your hand you realize, "This possesses life! It will multiply itself after its kind. This seed in my hand possesses life-imparting power; it will give bread to the eater and seed to the sower." So, if the seed is for the sower or bread for the eater, the function of the seed is to impart life. You and I step back stage to have a closer look at "soil." Soil carries the responsibility to receive the life-imparting power of the seed.

The Lady From Dallas

"I wonder if you would do me a favor?"
"Sure, be glad to. What do you have in mind?"

Don Waite and I had just crossed paths on the narrow sidewalk of Trailerville. Christmas, 1952, only two weeks away. Dallas Theological Seminary loomed in the background. Now Don, friend and fellow student at the seminary, stopped me and spelled out his need.

"Saturday afternoon I am supposed to talk to some children. She asked for a sem' student. The lady who called. Tell 'em the Christmas story."

"So you want me to take over for you. Give me the address of the church."

"No. No." Don stammered, "It's not in a church. It's in a home."

"How come?" I queried, "Somebody's Sunday School class?"

"No." Don shifted his books. "This lady has invited the neighborhood kids in."

"Good for her."

"Yeah. She wants to share with them what Christ means to her."

"Commendable," I added, admiring the lady's missionary zeal. Don searched in some papers.

"Ah! Here it is. The address. You can have it. Kinda northeast of the city. Glen Oaks or something like that. Some kinda Oaks. Any problems?"

"No, none that I can see. I'll check a map for directions."

"I have to work that afternoon, so you'll be the man to stand in the gap. Von and I will pray for ya, and I appreciate it very much."

I had a few days to mull it over. Felt like I was going in blindfolded. Ten year olds? Fifteen? Or, may be five. Should I call her? Better not disturb her. No notes. Otherwise I'll lose the kids. I'll shoot from the hip. I filled myself with the joy of the Christmas story till my cup ran over.

Saturday afternoon I jumped on the bus. The message joggety-jogged back and forth in my mind during the ride out.

"Here's where you get off!" hollered the driver. I scrambled for the door. Getting out of Trailerville felt like a mini vacation. I knew many affluent Texans comprised the corporate board of directors for the seminary. Perhaps this lady belongs to the auxiliary. As I looked at the palatial homes, I reminded myself that I had forgotten elegance and splendor.

Number 38, Ballantine Drive. Twin brick pillars faced me like open arms to welcome me to her estate. A lone, grand dogwood tree towered like a guard above the entrance. A stone parapet fortress surrounded the base of the tree. Sleeping azalea bushes provided a haven for the busy mockingbirds.

I lingered under the dogwood to drink in my new environment. Then I saw her. She carried herself with dignity — except for now — it was her pace. I think she was running to meet me. I didn't know what to expect. Her right hand was extended and a smile covered her face. She resonated sunshine.

Five foot six. Aristocratic features. Trim. Tastefully dressed. In her late thirties (don't tell her I guessed that). Dignified, but not aloof. She gave me the feeling I was giving a command performance. Like before royalty. I knew instantly I would savor every moment of her company. I thought I had come here to be the blessing. I began to think differently.

She wrapped her hands around my right hand. "You're from the seminary, aren't you." Her smile — from the sunshine within — spoke of something I needed to know.

"Yes I am." We exchanged introductions. Then she said something that etched itself in my mind forever.

"Aren't you thrilled, Norman, at the joy of being a Christian?" Her eyes continued the question. "Oh! language," I thought to myself, "how frail you are. Why can't you convey her feelings?" I knew the word "Gospel" meant "good news." In childlike openness she resonated the "good news." A total sense of well-being enveloped her.

I think it was the joy in her voice that triggered my mind. I soared back nineteen hundred years. People died for this glorious news. I found myself walking in the first century. And this thrilling news of a new life exploded on people. Fresh. Pure. Powerful.

This woman reminds me of you, Lydia. A successful business woman. A seller of beautiful purple fabric. Influential. Respected by all. Yet, no one knew, you cried on the inside. Then one of your employees told you about Paul. She said he talked about a Person who could change your life. You went. By that riverside in Philippi the Lord opened up your heart. That brief encounter changed your life forever. You received Christ into your heart. Inward tears turned to outward tears of joy. You insisted the apostles make your home their home. They did, and you put your life on the line.

My need to answer her question brought me across the centuries to the moment. Briefly I expressed my own joy at being a Christian. I had to confess to myself privately that I had never told someone I was thrilled at the joy of being a Christian.

She led the way into her home. "I think there are a dozen children. We've been singing songs and getting acquainted with one another."

"I'm happy to be here." A large red-leafed poinsettia plant — on polished brass pedestals — graced either side of the entrance. I spoke, in passing, on how much I enjoyed her home. I stepped into the foyer. Original artwork adorned the walls. A grand staircase on my left curved upward to the second floor. I reached into the atmosphere. Love flooded over me.

"This way," she gestured to my right. Laughter and chatting met me in a King Arthur room. A fireplace stabbed flickering shafts of warm light about the room. Heavy oak beams criss-crossed the ceiling. Wood-grained paneling framed the walls. Laughter ceased as the children appraised their guest. After my hostess had introduced me I shared with them the breathless beauty of the Christmas story. We had punch and snacks. I shook hands with each of the well-mannered children.

I lingered after the children had left. Cryptographic words sandblasted themselves to the wall of my mind. "Aren't you thrilled at the joy of being a Christian." An unfinished portrait painted by Reubens. I went directly to what was on my mind.

"You said you were thrilled at the joy of being a Christian."

"I certainly feel very blessed," she said modestly.

"I take it that it wasn't always this way."

"Why's that?" a smile swept across her face.

"It's so new. So fresh. Something I've rarely encountered."

"Up until a couple of years ago I think I was a cloud Christian."

Both of us laughed heartedly.

"A 'cloud Christian'?" I chuckled.

"God's like a cloud. Ya know, not a person. Hazy. Vaporlike."

"Something happened," I thought of my own life, "where you needed to identify with a Person."

"Exactly. I had to have surgery. Terrified. Scared to pieces. Couple years back. Desperately I turned to the Bible."

"You must have been stirred by God's personal commitment."

"Under no circumstance would Christ leave me or forsake me."

"He had now become a Person," I interjected.

"His presence engulfed me. Fear disappeared. Even the doctor commented on my new-found courage." She paused. "I entered a whole new world." She searched the fire for words. I waited.

"I discovered for the first time in my life that spiritual life comes out of what God says in His Word. Up to that point I think I had always tried to do things to be a Christian. Do you get what I mean?"

I shared with her that the Spirit had changed my life simply through the reading of the Word. That was ten years ago, I told her.

"So often today," I had to confess, "you have reminded me of that delightful lady, Lydia." I started toward the front door.

A quizzical expression crossed her face.

"Lydia," I clued her in, "in the book of Acts." I stood under the dogwood.

"Oh!" She exclaimed as I moved to waving distance. "What chapter?"

"Sixteen!" I hollered back with a wave.

I passed between the brick pylons that had welcomed me. "I had come to give," I mused to myself, "but I had received. I have to tell the bus driver what this lady said: 'Aren't you thrilled at the joy of being a Christian?'"

The Hidden Treasure of Faith

"Who is He? Who is He?" Shoutings from the crowd reverberated up and down the narrow winding streets of Jerusalem. Excited anticipation rushed through the sea of people like a tidal wave.

"Something's brewin', something's brewin'," could be heard on lips in the uneasy air. "Just say it's the rumblings of revolution," said a passerby.

Sunday Before Passover

"It's the Emperor himself," someone shouted. People stood on their tiptoes. Others craned their necks to catch a glimpse of this man of the hour.

"Nobody's at home. They're out here on the streets," observed a scribe, "thirty-five thousand people have come out to see a present-day David." Two frightened dogs barked at the sight of two donkeys.

"I can't see a thing!" screamed a distraught child, fearful that the excitement would pass him by.

"He's a great prophet," hollered a woman, "I've heard Him preach."

A cluster of shopkeepers roared in derisive laughter, "He's riding a donkey. Ha ha ha."

One lifted a glass as a mock toast, "Hail to our new king! Ha ha ha."

A Little Past Noon

He rode a donkey. A bewildered colt followed. Jesus moved

in a tight circle formed by His closest disciples. Celebrants laid palm leaves as a path for Him and spread their clothes as a picture of their allegiance. He turned a corner to enter a new street. At the sight of Him, His worshippers rose en masse and sang and chanted with joy.

"Hosanna! Hosanna! Blessed is He who comes in the name of the Lord! Blessed is He who comes in the name of the Lord!"

"Our King David talked about this day a thousand years ago," proclaimed a man who wore the robes of a priest.

The Year: 33

"Hosanna! to the Son of David. Hosanna! to the Son of David."

"What's goin' on? What's this parade all about? I've never seen so many crazy people. Who's the Man on the donkey?" Two Roman soldiers wedged in a doorway vented their confusion as they were overwhelmed by the clamor.

Jostling women on a side street screamed, "Messiah! Messiah!" Husky Galilean fisherman, shepherds from the Mountains of Ephraim, merchants from Capernaum — Jerusalem teemed with pilgrims eager to commemorate the Feast of Passover.

A gang of laughing young toughs on a roof cupped their hands around their mouths and yelled sneering rebukes with shameful mocking.

"Hail to our new king! Ha ha ha."

"What a joke! Ha ha ha."

"Get a horse! Ha ha ha."

"Get a goat! You're a silly sight!"

One young embarrassed teenager stuttered, "Ya know, guys, this time I think we're on the wrong side."

A familiar threesome from Bethany waved to Jesus from a raised porch. "It hardly fits." Martha spoke to Mary.

"What's that?" asked Mary.

"Your washing His feet last night. He must reek of the ointment you put on Him. It's like you were getting Him ready for burial."

"You're right, Martha," sighed Mary, "it doesn't make much sense. We'll have to wait and see what happens. Things are moving faster than I can keep up with them."

"You wouldn't be here, Lazarus," asserted Martha, "if He hadn't brought you back to life."

"I know. I know." affirmed Lazarus with tears in his eyes.

"Do they see," asked Mary pensively, "who He is?" A faraway look came over her face. "How can they possibly grasp what He has to offer?" His identity was no secret to her. She had pored over the arresting revelation of the Messiah in Isaiah fifty-three. No longer could she simply admire the picture, now she had to step into it.

"Oh yes," she had voiced, "the confused multitudes want nothing more than temporary political freedom."

Sunday Afternoon: 1:45

"A dangerous man. A dangerous man." Mutterings came from a band of rabbis gathered near a fruit stand. They used their position to help themselves to dates from the merchant's display.

"He's a real trouble-maker," grumbled one in a raspy voice.

"He's going to bring Pontius Pilate down on all our heads." cited their leader who spoke with furtive glances at the crowd.

"He's the Messiah of Israel!" defiantly shouted Nahum, a fearless old shepherd.

"Aw shut up, you old fool!" yelled a red-faced young rabbi seeking to make points with his superiors.

"I won't shut up!" shot back Nahum. "He healed me." he countered. "He healed me. I was blind. Do you hear me? I was blind.

Now I see. He gave me my sight. That's what you need. You're blind. You need your eyes opened."

A very old rabbi embarrassed by the verbal brawl went, "Shush. Shush. Shush." with his forefinger over his lips.

Nahum wouldn't let up. "Seven hundred years ago Isaiah told us of this day. 'Say to the inhabitants of Israel, behold your King is coming to you, lowly, riding on a donkey, and on a colt, the foal of a donkey.'"

"We offer a lamb in our Passover Feast," explained the Mayor to a Greek visitor, "to commemorate God's deliverance from bondage in Egypt. I presume this young Man will liberate us from our present enslavement just as Moses did fifteen hundred years ago."

Celebration Ends: 2:45

"He'll put Herod on the run!" hollered a father with a small child perched on his shoulders.

Jesus received the plaudits with kingly dignity. He neither smiled nor frowned, but it was obvious He loved the people. He looked like an ordinary man — older perhaps than His thirty-three years — His cropped beard and shoulder-length hair suggested this. He rode with purpose. His bearing conveyed an unmistakable aura of power that inspired immediate respect, awe and devotion.

"I think it's in His eyes," said an attentive teenager, "like He's from someplace far away — someplace different from Judea."

"I pick it up when He talks," commented his friend. "It's as though He was reaching out for you."

"Now's the hour!" shouted a man by a tent booth with a drink in his hand. "Now's the hour!"

With this threat intoning in their ears a squad of armed soldiers arrived to put an end to the demonstrations. Jerusalem — "pos-

Insights

session of peace" — had its day in court. It had slammed against Rome its anger against enslavement.

Jesus Goes to the Temple of Solomon: 3:25

"You have no place here!" Jesus flipped over the table of the money changer.

"Are you people blind?" With that aside Jesus threw the chairs of those who sold pigeons.

"All of you! Out of here! Don't you know what the Scripture says? My house shall be called a house of prayer. What have you made it? A den of thieves. That's what you have done. Robbers!"

A Little Past Four: Jesus Heals the Blind and the Lame

"Who is that man stumbling along the wall of the temple?" asked Jesus.

A doctor looked in the direction that Jesus pointed, "He is blind, Master. There are some lame there with him. They have been trying to see you for days," he said in an excited voice. "They thought they might find You here in the temple. They have been here all day."

Jesus seated himself on a carved stone bench and waited for the entourage of blind and lame people. The crowd provided a corridor for them to get through.

"What do you want Me to do for you?" Jesus wanted him to speak his need. His friends had led the young man to Jesus, and he fell on his knees before him. Jesus cradled the man's face in his lap. Sobbing softly he looked up at Jesus.

"I can't see, Master. I have never been able to see, and all I've heard the past year is Your name. People kept saying, 'He can heal you. He can heal you.' I would like to look into Your face."

Jesus laid His fingers over the blind man's eyes. No one spoke or stirred in the temple. Jesus lifted His hand from the man's face surrounded by an imperceptible outpouring of power. "You can see." He stated simply.

With repeated blinking a smile spread across the face of the man.

"Blessed is He who comes in the name of the Lord!" shouted an old woman who spent her days in the temple.

"I can see You, Lord! I can see You!" excitedly proclaimed the young man. He arose to see his friends for the first time. "Come," he shouted, "Come, and meet the God of our salvation." And Jesus continued to heal the blind and lame there in the temple.

4:50: Jesus Uses the Scriptures Like a Sword

"A fake! A fake!" intoned some youths in monotone.

"That's the street gang," observed Peter, "we ran into at the procession."

"I remember them," answered John, "they were on the roof by the market place."

"Ha. Ha. Ha."

"He will lead us to the promised land!"

"Ha. Ha. Ha."

"He's going to blow Herod away."

"Ha. Ha. Ha."

"What a joke!"

Some priests by the doorway joined in the chanting and mocking.

Peter turned to John, "I know the Master will have just the right answer."

"It is evident," responded Jesus in a strong and authoritative voice, "you don't know the Scriptures. Have you never read, 'Out of the mouths of children God has provided perfect praise.' "

"He sure put those priests down," said Peter. "Where's that found?"

"I think it's a Psalm," replied John. "One thing those priests fear, and that's the Scriptures." John glanced at the face of Jesus. "Peter, I think the Master looks tired. I think it's time we go back out to Bethany."

Early Monday Morning: 5:35

"Are you hungry, John?" Jesus asked one of His disciples as the band of two dozen men walked westward toward the city of Jerusalem. They had spent the night in the town of Bethany with Mary, Martha and Lazarus.

"I'm thinking of You," replied John, "You're the One who should be hungry after the exhausting day You had yesterday."

"What about that lone fig tree on that hillside?" Jesus pointed off to his right. "It does have leaves on it."

"We know it should have figs seeing it has leaves," asserted John. "You surely will find something to eat there."

"I can't find a single fig." Jesus and John examined the tree closely.

"I'm surprised, Master," responded John, "can you beat that?"

Jesus stepped back a few feet and sized up the tree. After a moment he answered and spoke directly to the tree for the statement it had made.

"From this day forward and forevermore no man shall ever eat fruit from you again."

His disciples heard Him talking to the tree.

"It's not the fault of the poor tree that it had put out leaves," stammered Andrew.

"That's the funniest thing I've ever seen. It's not even the season for figs. It's way too early." whispered James to Peter.

Jesus offered no explanation as they continued their trek westward through the valley of Kidrin. They could see the three hills of Jerusalem as the sun broke behind them over the valley. Little

The Hidden Treasure of Faith

did his disciples know He was teaching them a life-changing and last minute lesson on faith.

Tuesday 5:50 a.m.: Jesus Arms His Disciples for the Days Ahead

Jesus and his disciples left Bethany for another day in the city of Jerusalem. They had almost cleared the Kidrin valley when John pointed.

"There's that lone fig tree. The one we checked out yesterday morning."

"That's right." Everyone followed Jesus to look at the tree.

"You can see the tree's dead. The leaves are shriveled." Peter faced Jesus as he spoke. "It's just as You predicted."

"Let's get going." Judas tried to get them on their way. "We can't waste time over a dead tree."

Jesus paused for a full minute before the tree. It was obvious He had thrown Himself into this episode of the tree. No one spoke or moved.

"I used this tree to demonstrate how faith works." Jesus spoke deliberately. "I want you to have in your life the same kind of faith I have in My life."

"All You did was kill a tree without figs." Hard-breathing Thomas spoke without thought.

"Because of Who I am My words are alive and filled with power." Jesus continued with his lesson on faith. "For you to have faith you have to use God's words. Remember, God always does exactly what He says He'll do."

"So when You condemned the tree you used God's words?" inquired Andrew.

"My words are God's words." Answered Jesus. "Not only do you use My words," Jesus went on, "you speak to the problem just as I spoke to the tree."

John sought clarification. "I use God's words and address the prob-

379

lem before me." He paused. "Don't I need a certainty inside me?"

"You have spoken God's words so you know in your heart that what you say will come to pass."

"But what if I doubt in my heart," shot back Peter, "that it's really going to happen?"

"If you doubt in your heart," continued Jesus, "then you are saying that God does not keep His word."

"From your smallest problem ... " Jesus continued.

"A fig tree's a small problem" interrupted Thomas.

"From your smallest problem, like this tree, whatever it might be, talk to it. It could be mountainous to you — impossible to overcome. I would say to that mountain: 'Mountain, get yourself up and throw yourself into the sea.' Now, if you have faith in the power of God's words that what you say will come to pass the mountain will get up and throw itself into the sea!"

"Wow!" cried out Thomas. "No one can throw a mountain into the sea."

"You have doubt in your heart, Thomas," Jesus made plain, "you fail to believe in your heart what you say will come to pass."

Peter jumped in excitedly, "If I don't believe in my heart what I say will come to pass, even in the face of impossibility, then I don't have faith. It's that simple."

"It's that simple," responded Jesus.

Writer's Epilogue

You can read the details of this story in Matthew 21 and Mark 11. Hebrews 4:12, John 6:63, 1 Thessalonians 2:13, and Romans 10:8. It brings out the truth more fully — that the believer speaks God's Words. What He says sets limits on what I can say.

We can see the urgent entreaty of the message. Three days after this scene in the Kidrin valley Jesus was crucified.

Letter to Ted

Hi Ted,

I read a startling truth the other day that I felt compelled to share with you. It's one of those insights that walks up to you and asks, "Would you like to travel in the opposite direction?" I had felt overwhelmed, so the timing was perfect.

This breakthrough flip-flops my old horse and buggy reactions to tough trials. These invaders, my problems, threaten to take me hostage. They laugh when they taunt me to throw in the towel. I've got news for these vexing troublemakers.

Here's what my revelation uncovered: When these problems converge on me I don't run for cover, I recognize them as a visitors. I am learning that life brings these trials to serve a purpose. The source for my new directions comes out of the book of James (1:2,3). Here's what it says:

> Count it a matter for pure joy when you are surrounded by trials. You can prove your faith is genuine by how you react. That's why these tests came your way in the first place, to see what you would do about it.

You can see why I was excited to share this verse with you for it empowered me to take control of the circumstances of my life. As I ruminated on this verse I asked myself this question: How can faith raise to wield such authority?

I found the answer to that question in 1 Corinthians 10:13. This verse declares that God is faithful to His Word. When I say from the heart what He declares in His Word, then I am exercising genuine faith. This I know for sure, He always carries out what He says He'll do.

If you see me doing cartwheels in the parking lot, don't be surprised.

Love,

Norm

One Word Can Make Your Day

A Peek Into Meditation

It doesn't take a lot to generate a time of meditation. Seclusion. Quietness. An uncluttered mind. A listening heart. And words. Yes, I need words to stir into the pot of my reflection. Look at these four words: *accepted in the Beloved.* They are found in Ephesians 1:6. *Accepted in the Beloved.* I pause to think on the word "Beloved." Where have I seen that? My mind tumbles back to a mountain scene. Jesus is transfigured. A voice booms out of heaven: "This is my Beloved Son ... " The Father gives Jesus another name, "Beloved."

I go on. I remained focused on the four words: *accepted in the Beloved.* Now rumination mulls over the word "accepted." I look for synonyms. I think of the idea of "born into." "Welcomed." Welcomed into the Beloved. That doesn't tell the whole story, so I mutter the words again — *accepted in the Beloved.* I listen to my muttering. I sense I am beginning to hear the truth in the verse. I say different thoughts. I have been washed from my sin. I have been made a king. I have been made a priest *(Revelation 1:5,6).* Back to my four words. These words say a lot. How about embraced in the Beloved? Do you think these insights shine some light on the phrase? So I ask myself, Am I alone? No, the Beloved is here. His arms are wrapped around me in tenderness. I rest. Then my heart says, Yes, Norman, you are *accepted in the Beloved!*

Let me chat with you about meditation. Set aside a time when you can be alone. Yes, Jesus drew apart to talk with the Father.

Insights

Embrace quietness. Leave life's clutter outside the door. Listen. Question. Ponder. Savor. Gratitude and praise well up in my spirit.

Give this some thought: meditation finds a cousin in the word "medicinal." In the original language the word "meditation" carried with it the sense of "to mutter." You and I know mutter means to speak in low tones. So if I have a Bible verse before me, I mutter it. In low tones I verbalize the words before me. In slow muttering I am reaching out to understand what is said. Faith comes by hearing *(Romans 10:17)*. I take a step backward and listen to the words I speak. When I mutter a verse my ears listen to what I say. I engage the verse with my speech, and my ears weigh in to what is muttered.

The writer in the Book of Hebrews says the Word is sharper than a sword *(Hebrews 4:12)*. It pierces its way into the deepest recesses of my being. It draws a clear line of distinction between what is of the mind, and what is of my spirit. The Word possesses the inherent divine power to expose and judge the secret intents of my heart.

Let us say you have decided to meditate. Where do you start? Set up a time when you can draw apart from your day. When you close the door to your closet, leave the baggage outside. Your mind says, "I am free to listen to the Holy Spirit." You will need a Bible you can write in. Why write? It could be an insight. A prayer. A name. A lesson learned, or simply praise. You'll always enjoy reading these in the future. I also use a fluorescent highlighter.

After I have selected the verse I read it. Then I mutter the verse. I listen to its message. How does it fit into my life? I want to carry it into my day. Meditation moves the truth into the fabric of my daily life. My spirit is like a blank slate on which the Holy Spirit can write. You'll need starter verses. Here are a few.

        Joshua 1:8

Psalm 104:34
Psalm 1

Here is an extended list.

Thirty-three verses you can use in meditation:

Joshua 1:8   18. Psalm 37:4
Psalm 104:34   19. John 3:16
Psalm 120   . I Peter 1:23
I Corinthians 2:12,13   21. Mark 9:23
Hebrews 4:12-16   22. Isaiah 40:31
Ephesians 1:16-21   23. Proverbs 4:23
Ephesians 3:14-19   24. Romans 4:20,21
Psalm 23   25. Isaiah 46:11
Mark 11:22-24   26. John 15:1-7
Matthew 7:24-27   27. Hebrews 11:6
Proverbs 3:5,6   28: Zechariah 4:6
John 14:21   29. I Kings 8:56
Isaiah 26:3   30. Isaiah 55:10,11
Jeremiah 1:9   31. Ezekiel 22:30
Matthew 4:4   32. Job 23:12
Romans 10:17   33. Isaiah 65:24
2 Corinthians 5:17

My words tell you who I am.

Your words tell me who You are.

God's Words tell you and me Who He is, and what He does.

Meditation spills over into one's daily life. Words can give us the joy of walking on clouds or regretting what we said. How often have you reflected: I wish I had never said that. Me too. The Psalmist wrote that he had put a watchman on his lips. It's a tough guard. James, in his own book, said a man who keeps his tongue is a perfect man.

Words are thoughts out in the open, where everyone can see them. Look at these revealing words:

Love	perfect	irrevocable
Hope	certify	revelation
Faith	verify	pledge

Insights

Forgiveness	friend	guarantee
Eternity	reify	name
Epiphany	Gospel	magnify

Oh! There are thousands of thought-provoking words, but their significance is seen in this declaration. He has magnified what He says even above His own name *(Psalm 138:2)*.

Think of this: words are like the weather. Lightning. Thunder. Winds that tear down everything in their way. Breathtaking days that make the flowers grow. Rains that give us nourishment, but also floods. So the spectrum goes.

Words can be a sunrise when I delight in something I never saw before.

A carpenter uses a hammer. A plumber uses a wrench. A painter uses a brush. God uses Words to exercise His power. He upholds, maintains, guides, and propels the universe by His mighty Word of power *(Hebrews 1:3)*. He said, Let there be light! And there was light. He has bequeathed to you and me His Words in the Bible. What a gift! Here we discover Words filled with divine life and awesome power.

There are some who have not found the way. One man said faith is only an opinion. Another held that faith was an attitude. Some put faith and hope in the same boat. But meditate on this: faith is a container, like a can or a jar; it packages a material. Hebrews 11:1 says faith is a substance. Faith has matter. You could say faith could be compared to a box with supplies inside. So what are the supplies in this box of faith? This box, my faith, contains the Words, which I find in the Bible. The Holy Spirit can infuse these Words of life and power into my living through the door of meditation.

He Had Never Walked

"That's all they're talking about," exclaimed the busy mother, "he talks about a young Man Who now lives even though He was crucified."

"Who's talking?" asked her son.

"A young man by the name of Paul."

"I never heard of him," answered the son.

"He's a rabbi from Jerusalem."

This dialog took place between a mother and her adult son, Nicolus. He had been born with an impediment. Due to weakness in his feet and ankles, he could not walk.

"But we have a goddess," argued the son, "Ashtaroth. Do we need other gods?"

"Pshaw!" Spit the mother. " Filth! Idolatry! Lies! Money! We need truth. We need action."

Everyone in the farmer's market loved Nicolus where he sat on a stool in the family's stand. An affable smile. Ears that listened. Eyes that flashed with hope and a ready laugh. No wonder the market business thrived.

"What does this preacher say?" Asked Nicolus.

His mother answered, "The Man who was crucified lived south of here, around Jerusalem."

"Was He a teacher?" asked Nicolus.

"I don't know, but this man says He healed a lot of people. Here's where you come in, Nicolus. We're going to hear this Paul."

"I knew where you were heading." A warm smile crossed the

Insights

face of Nicolus.

"We'll go together."

While Nicolus and his mother made arrangements to hear Paul, the writer Luke fills us in on the ministries of Paul and Barnabas. Crowds spill out of the crowded synagogues onto the packed streets.

Some shouted, "These men talk of a God of love!"

"They challenge us to believe in our hearts," confessed many.

Not everyone in this crowd was happy. The rebellious Jews, on seeing the riotous acceptance of Paul and Barnabas, were filled with envy and rage.

"Who are these people," enquired one young scribe.

"You can't trust strangers," incited a member of the Sanhedrin.

"Money! The old story. One has to look behind the facade."

"They have invented lies to tear down our ancient laws and traditions. Heresy! Where is the respect for Moses? Tell them to read our Scriptures."

When the Jews left to draw up a new plan, Paul had a word for the departing Jews. "You have fanned the flames of hatred!"

Paul shouted, "You aren't judging us! You are condemning yourselves. Sure! This message was extended to you first. You have thrown the Good News into the gutter. You will be judged by the words of your mouth. You have no place to hide. You have made yourselves unfit for eternal life. There's one thing left for us. Turn to the heathen. That's right. The heathen." Paul and Barnabas left the synagogue for the sunlight outside. It seemed like the whole city was there.

"We want to hear more!" shouted the crowd.

The Gentiles were delighted to learn that Paul and Barnabas would now direct their work toward them.

"Praise God for his Word!" They shouted and many trusted

He Had Never Walked

Jesus as their Savior. So the Word went from mouth to mouth in different directions throughout the whole country.

"This is the downfall of Judaism!" shouted one indoctrinated rabbi. Outstanding women joined the resistance against the Gospel. Rabble-rousers were stirred up by moneyed men to kill these heretics. Paul and Barnabas learned through informants that a plan was underfoot to stone them.

"We'll have to move on," they concluded, so they set out for the town of Lystra.

A story of warm human interest takes place here in Lystra as these men of God meet the young man, Nicolus, who had never walked. He was seated in the front row by his mother, who encouraged him to attend.

"Now you listen carefully," she directed. "He'll be talking about this young Man who healed many. It's a story we've never heard before, but everyone is talking about Him now."

"I'll listen," assured Nicolus, and he did.

Paul spoke about the fulfillment of prophecy about Moses, Abraham and David. Jesus is the heralded Messiah these men spoke about.

A wild man was healed.

Another was raised from the dead.

A cripple man by the pool of Bethesda, handicapped for thirty-eight years. Jesus told him, "Get up!" He was healed.

Nicolus grasped the words to his bosom. With rapt attention the words moved to his heart.

"Seeing He healed that man by the pool, there's no reason He can't heal me."

Paul read the face of Nicolus.

"I can see," Paul thought, "that he has the faith to be healed. He has more than hope." He stopped preaching. He walked back and forth. He waited for the prompting of the Holy Spirit. Then he did something which caused the crowd to gasp. He stopped in front of their beloved Nicolus. He looked into the believing face and with a loud voice of command he ordered,

"Stand up!"

Thoughts swirled about in the young man's mind. "I have never stood. I have never walked like people do. The man by the pool of Bethesda stood up. He's talking about divine power. I believe! Why not stand?" With that he stood up.

"I'm standing!" He looked at Paul in amazement. Then he looked down at his feet. That smile of discovery crossed his face.

Why not walk?

He took a few steps. He thought he'd fall, but he caught his untested balance. "Nicolus! Nicolus!" They cheered. They thundered applause.

Now he understood why Paul called Him the God of love. No idols. No sacrifice. A free work of grace. "All I had to do was believe."

INSIGHT

Before we go on, and there is more to tell, I want to ask this question: What can you and I learn from Nicolus? What is the Holy Spirit saying?

<u>*He acted on what he believed!*</u>

He could have said to Paul, are you nuts? Can't you see I'm a cripple?" He said nothing. He could have listened to his body. You can't stand up. His spirit said, "You can stand."

Nicolus heard what Paul preached. Faith comes (Romans 10:17) by hearing. He <u>acted</u> on the knowledge of the Word Paul preached.

What ever happened to Nicolus? We don't know. You and I know God had something in mind when He healed him. We already know he brought a lesson to the world on acting on his faith, but he had a future in Lystra to share the Good News.

So the story continues. When the crowds saw that Nicolus had been healed they shouted, "The gods have come down to us in the form of men!"

They called Barnabas 'Zeus' and Paul 'Hermes' and they sought to sacrifice bulls.

Paul and Barnabas roared into crowd shouting, "You can't do this! We are simply men sharing with you the Good News of the living God."

While Paul sought to reach the idolaters, Jews arrived in Lystra from Antioch and Iconium. With stunning effect they turned the vulnerable crowd against Paul so that they stoned him. They dragged his body out of town, all the while assuming that he was dead. His disciples formed a circle around him and he stood up, and returned to town. The next day he and Barnabas left Lystra for Derbe.

See Acts 14.

I Need a Watchman

King David prayed, "Set a guard, O Lord, before my mouth; keep watch at the door of my lips." *(Psalm 141:3)* He saw that the words in his daily living were as important as the words he prayed. I have to be reminded that the words I speak reveal who I am. Words are far-reaching.

> God speaks to you and me with words (in the Bible).
> We eulogize God with words.
> We profess our faith with words.
> People fall in love with words.
> They marry because of what they speak.
> Children are raised with words.
> Divorce happens because of words.
> Wars start and end with words.

The apostle James said that the child of God may stumble in many ways, but if he never says the wrong thing, he is spiritually mature *(James 3:2)*. God-fearing Job said to his detractors, "How long will you drive me crazy, torment me, and break me to pieces with your words?" *(Job 19:2)*

> In the beginning, before all time, was the Word, Christ, and the Word was with God, and the Word was God Himself.
>
> And the Word, Christ, became a Person in the flesh, and lived among us and we actually saw His glory, the glory as an only begotten Son, full of grace and love. *(John 1:1, 14 amplified)*
>
> The Words that God speaks contain divine life and are filled with His power. *(Hebrews 4:12)*
>
> Every Scripture is given by God's inspiration. *(2 Timothy 3:16)*

God tells us Who He is through what He speaks.

The Father has willed to us the utilization of His words. Think of it: He has bequeathed to us His Words. You and I can say His Words in our daily lives.

His Words contain the power to move mountains.

His Words are seeds, seeds containing spiritual life.

I see my faith as a pilgrimage to a far country. Each town along my journey calls for a unique faith because the challenges are different. Picture with me the following scenarios. In town Number 1, I received eternal life. We could name the town New life. My faith was grounded in John 3:16. I move on.

I arrive at town Number 2, "Worry." That's the name of the town. From town Number 1, I learned the mechanics of faith: I'll need a verse from the Word, and I'll have to act on it. As you can see from the name of the town, the new challenge is worry. I am unaware of what the Bible says about worry, so I am helpless to exercise my faith.

As a horse eats hay and oats, so faith gets nutrition from information, I'll have to do my homework. What does God say about worry and anxiety? When I find this, I'll have the hay and oats — the information — to back up what I believe. I understand that faith is based on knowledge, so I need the information from the Word.

I spot 1 Peter 5:7:
> Casting the whole of your care (all your anxieties, all your worries, all your concerns, once and for all) on Him, for He cares for you affectionately and cares about you watchfully. (amplified)

Aha! I'm delighted to find such a verse here in Worry Town. Take your worries I am told, and put them like a backpack on to Jesus. I can do this for one reason: He affectionately cares about me. Gone! I see them as no longer existing, replaced by His love.

How can I internalize this truth? How can I make it a part of

Insights

myself? I understand His Word is a seed and I plant it by saying it out loud.

> You tell me in Your Word
> To throw all my worries
> On the back of the Lord Jesus
> Because He cares
> About me affectionately.

Faith comes by hearing what the Spirit has to say about worry, but in saying it, I also hear myself reaffirming the truth. (I can write it in a journal or on a flashcard.) The seed is sown in the soil of my heart.

"Here's my problem," says one reader: "I settle my worries on Wednesday, but on Thursday they're back. What do you do about that? Do I go back to Wednesday and re-believe?" *(1 Peter 5:7)*

If you do that, you are saying — I found no answer — the faith you first declared was counterfeit faith. Genuine faith has received once and for all the promise in the verse (when he first states it).

So what do I do on Thursday when worries resurface in my life? I remind myself of a fact that *has* taken place in my life.

Kenneth Wuest taught New Testament Greek at Moody Bible Institute. In his expanded translation he brings joyful enlightenment on the power of what I say.

> I have not received the spirit of the world system but the Spirit Who is of God, in order that I might know (if I know not, I can't believe) the things which the Father has bestowed on me in grace, which things I also put into words, not in words taught by human philosophy, but in words taught by the Person of the Spirit Himself, fitly joining together Spirit revealed truths with Spirit-taught words. *(1 Corinthians 2:12, 13)*

It takes a spiritual being to impart spiritual life. Seeing my eternal life came out of the creative power of God's Words, when I change my words I change my life. I live on Holy Spirit power because I use Holy Spirit Words. The joyous realization of my faith comes about through the creative power of what God says.

Singers Go Before the Army

As I read this amazing story of the battle in the wilderness of Tekoa, I am challenged to practice in my own life the mind-boggling faith King Jehoshaphat had. I can see with clarity the steamroller enemy armies poised at the Dead Sea. Listen to them. They shouted at Israel:

"We're taking your land!"

"You're dead!"

I try to capture in my mind how the king felt. How would you feel? Fearful, O yes!

General Eliada speaks up. He hails from the tribe of Benjamin.

He rallies the troops of Israel. "Stand and fight!" I hear his voice vibrate with authority.

Then I see Jehozabad stand up. He's also a general. He pauses before I hear him say,

"Send in spies to assess the strength of the enemy."

I can hear the king respond, "Gentlemen, thank you for your input." His voice is steady. He goes on, "I will seek the mind of the Lord with all my being." He paused to emphasize the announcement. "Immediately we shall begin with a fast throughout all the cities and towns of Judah."

I can see the people streaming into Jerusalem.

Our King will lead us in prayer.

We'll find him in the temple.

Many cried and fell on their faces as they heard the king beseech the Lord to intervene on their behalf.

Singers Go Before the Army

I think of the difference one man can make, when I hear one man speak up:

"This is God's battle, not yours! Take your positions. Then stand still! Watch what God does!"

I want to know who this man is. He's a radical. He speaks about future things as though they had already happened. Oh, sure. Someone would call it prophecy. No. No, it's not prophecy, it's faith.

Jahaziel. That's his name. Jahaziel, who was he? He was a priest of the tribe of Levi. He spoke his earth-shaking insights under the sanction of the Holy Spirit. God spoke through Jahaziel.

But, who would believe this crazy man? I find here further attestation of the work of the Holy Spirit: Everyone did! The King. The Priests. The masses. They all embraced the revelation: stand still, watch what God does!

Three mighty enemy armies stood at Engedi. The Moabites, the Ammonites, and the men of Mount Seir *(2 Chronicles 20)*.

They shouted, "We will take the land of Judah! We will overrun the Israelites! Men, women, and children will be slaughtered!"

This terrifying news of annihilation was brought to King Jehoshaphat in Jerusalem.

"Three armies have amassed themselves at our border!"

"What do they want?" enquired the king.

"They want Jerusalem and the half of Judah. They come from beyond the Dead Sea, from the land of Edom."

Fear paralyzed the king. "I have soldiers, and they are courageous, but ten to one ... that's ridiculous. They will run off with our women. What will happen to our children?" From the deepest part of his being, out of the hour of despair, the king set his face to seek the Lord. "We have to know what God thinks. He can see the enemy poised at our border. He performed wonders in the lives of Joshua, Moses, and Samuel, and now, our backs are against the wall."

"We will fast. We will fast, not only in the Jerusalem, but throughout the land of Judah. Our fast will say to God, 'We yearn for You with all our hearts.'"

"O Lord," Jehoshaphat prayed in the temple in Jerusalem, "God of our fathers, are You not God in heaven? And do You not rule over all the kingdoms of the nations? In Your Hand are power and might, so that none is able to withstand you."

"Did not you, O our God, drive out the inhabitants of this land before Your people Israel and give it forever to the descendants of Abraham Your friend?"

"They dwelt in it and have built You a sanctuary in it for Your Name, saying, 'If evil comes upon us, the sword of judgment, or pestilence, or famine, we will stand before this house and before You — for Your Name is in this house — and we cry to You in our affliction, and You will hear and save.'"

"And now behold, the men of Ammon, Moab, and Mount Seir have come to drive us out of the possession You have given to us to inherit."

"Our God, will You not exercise judgment upon them? For we have no might to stand against this great company that is coming against us. We do not know what to do, but Your eyes are upon us."

Jehoshaphat met with his advisors after the prayer in the temple. "In my prayer I talked about the power of our God."

"Yes," said Amariah the chief priest, "you reminded Him that He gave us this land in the first place."

"The symbol enlightened the king — of His presence lives in our Jerusalem temple."

Amariah continued, "you prayed well when you said that the only solution lay in God's intervention. You said so much when you spoke from the heart; our eyes are upon you."

Singers Go Before the Army

All Judah stood as one before the Lord, with their children and their wives.

How will this supplication by the king be answered? "I know," said one man, "we'll all go back to Egypt."

"No. No." replied another, "they would chase us down."

"I know," replied a listener, "they will be struck down by a plague."

In the midst of this fearful speculation God had heard the prayer of the king. The Spirit of the Lord came upon Jahaziel a priest of the tribe of Levi.

He said, "Listen to this you inhabitants of Jerusalem, and you King Jehoshaphat, and all Judah: Throw out not only your fear and these invaders, for the battle is not yours, but God's! Go down to them tomorrow and you will find them at the end of the ravine, but you shall not fight, take up the position for the battle, and then stand still! I want you to see for yourself My deliverance."

Without hesitation Jehoshaphat bowed his head with his face to the ground, and all the people fell down before the Lord in worship.

Many Levites stood up and shouted their praise and their volume was indicative of the joy in their hearts. So the people arose early on this fateful day of battle and went out to the wilderness of Tekoa.

"Believe in the Lord," spoke the king, "Believe and you will not retreat."

"Put out singers!" responded the people.

"Put out what?" asked the king.

"Put out singers to go before the army!"

The king appointed choirs to sing! "Give thanks to the Lord, for His mercy and loving-kindness endure forever!" Their priestly robes enriched the dignity of their joy.

"Foolishness! Foolishness!" Said an elderly priest. "The Moabites will hear our singers and say, 'we'll kill the singers and take the land.'"

Jahaziel spoke up, "No! No! You are not listening. Unplug your ears. God has said this is His battle. You have your eyes on the Moabites. Look at the Words God speaks."

The general for the army of Mount Seir spoke up. "Here is the plan: we'll occupy Jerusalem and take the land all the way to the sea."

"Wait! Wait!" Replied the Moabites and Ammonites, "That plan will give us the left-overs." The negotiations escalated into hatred. War broke out and the army of Mount Seir was the first to be annihilated by the Moabites and the Ammonites. But the panic of confusion continued in a field of blood, and all the while the Israelites sang, the remaining enemies slaughtered themselves.

"This is the field of battle." Jehaziel showed Jehoshaphat where the battle had taken place. From the watchtower in the wilderness, as far as they could see, dead bodies littered the fields. There were no survivors to draw a picture of what happened.

Jehoshaphat instructed his people, "To the victor go the spoils." They found cattle, goods, clothing, and precious jewelry, which they scoured from the enemy's battlefield. The spoil was so great it took the Israelites three days to complete their plundering.

"As you read this astounding story of faith," says King Jehoshaphat, "I'm sure you will ask how it came about. First, I sought to walk in the hallowed ways of my father and of David. Secondly, I removed any idolatry I found among my people. Thirdly, I sent out teachers. Many were princes and Levitical priests — men like Elishima and Jehoram — and I told them, teach my people the Word of God. In every town and city my people studied about Abraham, Isaac, Moses, Joshua, and David. The testimony of our spiritual strength brought great respect from our neighboring nations." *(2 Chronicles 17).*

"You will want to know if we celebrated after victory. Everyone came to Jerusalem. There we had the parade of parades. Harps, lyres, and trumpets sounded out our joy in the faithfulness of our Lord."

Letter to Larry

Words that Live

It has been a couple of weeks since I took you to the airport. At the time you mentioned your interest in a truth found in the Bible. It says that the words God speaks are alive *(Hebrews 4:12)*. This affirmation, that words can be alive, began to tumble around in my mind like a cement mixer. I kept asking myself, how can words be alive?

Does it mean that they are alive because the Holy Spirit wrote them? After all, I reflected, they are only black marks on white paper, so, where is the life? I asked myself, If I simply "read" a verse in the Bible, does that make it alive? I have heard of some people who read through their Bible each year. Very commendable, but did that cause the words to come to life? I continued my quest. How can written words be "alive"?

In my trek I thought about memorization. If I memorize a verse, does that make it come alive? Someone could ask, "If I store it away in the memory, how has it come to life?" I agree; if it has an end in itself, it does not bring words to life.

I felt like an archaeologist in my search. I dusted away the sand to unearth my discovery. There are those who say, "The words come to life when you meditate on them." They go on, "close your eyes, say the verse slowly, and allow the words time to slosh around in your mind." So we have some who "read" the words, still others "memorize" and then others "meditate."

Another approach is a group who shout this question: "What Would Jesus Do?" They shorten it to "W W J D?" In this scenario they say they copy Jesus. "I'll be kind," "I'll be forgiving," "and I'll be long suffering." "I'll behave like Jesus would in any given situation. Jesus lives through me," they say. They seek to affect spiritual realities with physical means. The apostle Paul condemns this in the Book of Romans.

I have to tell you this story. A while back I was caught up in some problems that seemed to overwhelm me. You know what I am talking about. All of us experience that. It was a time when there didn't appear a way out. Gloom took up squatter's rights in my life. Answer blew out the window. My journal spoke of my anguish and the desperation of being on a one-way street to panic land.

In the midst of this "lost weekend," John 3:16 came to mind. I recalled that the margin in my Bible said it was "the most precious verse." Sunday School children often memorize this verse. Someone said this verse is "the Bible in a nutshell."

My gaze changed. No longer was I focused on my problems, but a ray of light shined in my spirit. My feelings were mixed. On the one hand I was ashamed, ashamed for words like, "there's no way out." On the other hand — gratitude. Yes, gratitude, gratitude for His love. That's right, His love. Four words from John 3:16 paraded across my spirit — *God so greatly loved.* These words burned their way into my heart. I was filled with ardent thankfulness for His love. I wanted to immerse myself in His love.

The apostle Paul prayed for the believers at Ephesus *(Ephesians 3:19)* ... might you know the love of Christ, which passes knowledge.

I have gone full circle. I am back to the question you ignited in my mind. How can the words God speaks be alive? In the parable of the sower Jesus talked about "the good soil." He said that the good soil is a person who hears the words from the Bible. He understands what God says. Not only does he understand, but also the words interlock themselves with his spirit so that they "bear fruit" in his life *(Matthew 13:23).*

God's words in the Bible lie as dormant seeds. They are alive, but inactive. When you and I act in return to these words they possess the power to transfer their life to you and me.

In closing, Larry, I am reminded of the words of the apostle Paul " ... the love which Christ has for me presses on me from all sides, holding me to one end and prohibiting me from considering any other, wrapping itself around me in tenderness." *(2 Corinthians 5:14, Wuest's translation)*

Christian love,
Norm

A Soldier Learns About Real Authority

Men would give their lives because of his words of command, but he learned someone had power with God.

He strode briskly down the army post street on his morning walk from his base home to the command center. Thirty-two years old, ram-rod posture, shoulders squared, Capernaum's most powerful man was on his way to work as usual, early, but this morning a furrowed brow gave away a numbing problem.

Captain Percel, six feet tall, athletic build, walked with a purposeful stride. Brown hair was almost hidden by his officer's cap, tanned from the Mediterranean sun, set jaw, but compassionate brown eyes contradicted the tough-willed man. An occupational soldier from a strange land, he returned a crisp salute and smile to men he met on his way.

A sign above the door read:

Roman Detachment

332nd Infantry Company

Capernaum District

Captain Percel, Commandant

He swung through the door that opened magically with a corporal's assistance. Young Lieutenant Cheval greeted his superior as he entered the office.

Captain Percel leaned back in his office chair with the sigh of a man in pain. His shoulders dropped. The ever-listening lieutenant knew the senior officer had to unburden himself, for life and death lay in his words. If a suicide charge was necessary, then his charges followed what he said to their deaths.

405

He had thrown himself into his five-year assignment, but this morning he faced a personal life-and-death crisis — his servant boy, a Jewish slave, lie critically ill. Getting that child away from death's door had become the object of his life. Against his background of authoritarianism the love of the lad engulfed him.

"Have you heard from the doctor?" He asked dejectedly.

Lieutenant Cheval paused to answer, "Josh, of course, suffers from some sort of mysterious paralysis. This we know."

He wanted to be exact. "The doctor wants to know how to treat something when he doesn't know what it is." He glanced at some notes on his desk, shuffled some papers, "He doesn't know how to stop the downward spiral."

"I even give him a fatherly hug," the captain voiced his thoughts out loud, "before he goes to sleep at night." In another world, he pursed his lips with the forefinger and thumb of his left hand. An image of the eleven year old who lived in his home passed across the screen of his mind.

"My transient lifestyle has deprived me of a wife and a son. So, I guess, or you might say, I've kinda adopted him. All the guys like him, I know."

" ... Kind of a company mascot," sided in Lieutenant Cheval. "It's got to be his disposition. I've never seen a cheerier kid."

"I looked in on him before I left home," the captain continued with hands tied in a knot, "His aunt's with him. She's acting as his nurse. As I was leaving he slid his feeble hand into mine — soft as a sparrow. Right now, I'd say, he doesn't have the strength to lift a rose. 'Captain,' he whispered, 'you'll know what to do!' I have to admit that threw me."

"Yeah," blurted the lieutenant in masculine embarrassment, "that's the way he is, smiling in the face of troubles."

Compassion — endless, tireless, quenchless — that was what distinguished the captain here in Capernaum. A product of a

406

close knit military family in Naples, both he and his father had graduated with honors from the prestigious Aversa Military Academy. Personal warmth gave him a circle of friends among the officers. Openly sentimental, anyone could get his ear. No wonder so many liked him.

He was, however, living on a collision course with his superiors for his fraternization with the Jews.

"These people," voiced a few, "are nothing more than slaves. We have to act as an army of occupation in an enemy land."

"I've studied their history," answered the captain, "They know we have no business here. The land belongs to them. Along that line, what do you know about this Man Jesus? Everyone's talking about Him. I hear He's healed many like Josh."

"I'm afraid Josh is too far gone to be moved," said the lieutenant with his palms extended in hopelessness.

From his south-facing office window the captain gazed futilely at the Sea of Galilee in the distance. He mused in faint tones, "Could He help? I don't know."

"You could see if He could come here."

"No. No. No." hurriedly interjected the senior officer, "have you seen the hordes around Him? A human stampede." Captain Percel chuckled lightly for the first time that day. "People tumble over one another. Dust? One can hardly breathe."

"He's been up on Mount Hermon the past week with His disciples," observed the younger man. "They say He's east of town, somewhere over by the Jordan River."

Early in the afternoon the two soldiers hiked eastward. A carnival atmosphere filled the air with people talking excitedly — expectantly.

"I think He's a sorcerer or a magician," eagerly speculated one.

"You haven't seen what He does," testified another.

407

"I think," shouted the lieutenant over the crowd, "He's at the base of that hill. You can tell by the turmoil." He pointed northward.

"There He is! There He is!" the two men shouted as they stood on their toes to see over the crowd.

They saw a young Man the age of the captain. Unpretentious. An unspeakable magnetism captured the allegiance of the captain. An unmistakable aura of power — something up the captain's alley — inspired respect, awe and devotion.

"Someone's lying on the ground in front of Him!" a girl yelled.

A leper, nothing more than a wreckage of a man, had thrown himself on the ground before Jesus. Pitifully he cried out, "If You wanted to heal me, You could!" Tears streaked his cheeks. The agony was utter, crippling.

Captain Percel, holding his breath, riveted his eyes on Jesus with careful intensity. He saw love. Slowly Jesus reached down and touched the contemptible outcast.

"I will," He said with pointed words.

"He's not supposed to touch a leper," grumbled a rabbi.

"But he's healed!" shouted another. "His leprosy's gone!"

"Josh could be healed," screamed the captain, "if we'd had him with us!" He stared in disbelief at the calamitous change in the leprous man.

"Did you see how he did it?" laughed the lieutenant excitedly. "He used words. Just two little words — 'I will'."

"That power comes from who He is," quietly stated the captain.

People, moving like minnows in a pail, eddied them along, and the two dumb-stricken military men made their way through the sick and afflicted.

"You know, Lieutenant," cited the captain on their trek home, "these people are more mystical than we are. We're so orderly, so logical — I swear," he chuckled at the observation.

Captain Percel had learned that successful people are often mavericks, who allow their minds to roam out of prescribed paths of thinking. He knew he himself had the strength to go against the grain.

Inside their base the lieutenant suggested, "Send a committee to Him. You helped them build their synagogue. That's the least they could do."

"I know. I know. They see Him as a radical. A fanatic. They're legalistic. He's not."

An aid entered to hand the captain a note.

"It's from the doctor. He says," the captain hesitated, "he says Josh has slipped into a coma."

It didn't take the captain long to get home.

"Could he last twenty-four hours?" he asked the doctor with distress in his voice.

"Well ..."

"What I want to do is take him to the itinerant preacher. I saw Him heal a leper today. He's a powerful man."

"Oh, Him. I'm surprised at you, Captain, that you would grasp at a straw. Anyway, you can't move the child. It would kill him."

Sleep was impossible for this weary warrior from a faraway land. As he tossed, there was no debate, only certainty.

"I know He can heal him."

"I know He can heal him."

Darkness still blanketed Capernaum when the captain confronted the nurse. "I'm going to see the preacher. He'll heal him." She smiled faintly, knowing he was almost out of time. He hurried into the night.

He knew this was not something to be tried. This was a miracle to be received. There were those who came to be reassured. Not him. He was like the leper, he knew the Preacher could restore Josh to full health.

"I'm not certain I'll be able to find Him. Could He have gone back to Mount Hermon? Maybe the crowd will keep me from seeing Him. He wouldn't see me as an enemy? No. He's too large a Man for that. I know, He'll see Josh as his kin. That could help. Again, Josh's time is running out. Hold on, Josh. Hold on, Josh. 'You'll know what to do, Captain.' Will I? I'm going the only route I know, Josh."

Dawn had trouble pushing aside the night. The captain's thoughts were like a great river running into the sea. "A new day. New life. That's what this sunrise means — life. Should I be embarrassed? What about shame? I don't care about the detractors. I care about life — life for one who hasn't seen puberty."

He heard the clamor in the distance. Ah — a little more to the left. In the semi-darkness he left the road and crossed a sandy rise. "I'm so glad He hasn't left. He's my only hope." He heard the uproar, and broke into a run. Already the crowd engulfed Him. They're squeezing Josh out. Love threw his anger aside. His anticipation made him breathe deeply. False pride had no place in a last ditch struggle.

This is as close as he can get. Too many people. Full light now. He's a stone's throw away. How could He see the soldier in this sea of faces?

"It's my servant boy!" he hollered. It disappeared into the dust.

"My servant boy. Near death!" he shouted in a frenzy. Again he thought of the leper.

Suddenly Jesus stopped. A hush went through the crowd near the captain. Yes, He had heard the captain's cry. Now Jesus looked at him. People moved aside as the soldier obeyed His summons. He stood before Jesus. As their eyes met the soldier saw authority

A Soldier Learns About Real Authority

he had never seen before.

"My servant boy." He was not his articulate self. "My servant boy. He's at home. Near death."

Jesus saw inside the foreign oppressor of His people. Everyone watched. A chill of quiet shuddered through the crowd. A moment passed. He wanted what belonged to Israel. How could this heathen have faith?

Then Jesus spoke. "I'll go with you to your house and restore the child to health." His voice wrapped itself around the beleaguered officer. Everything the officer wanted lay before him, but he had to refuse it.

"But, Lord," stammered the humbled soldier, "I ... I am not worthy to have you enter my house. I know nothing of Your kind of power. Your words — all You have to do is speak them, and Josh will be healed.

"I, too, understand authority, but only as a man. For example, I say to a soldier, 'Go,' and he goes. I say to another soldier, 'Come,' and he comes. I say to a slave, 'Do this,' and he does it."

Jesus was surprised at the faith the soldier expressed when he said: "Your words; all you have to do is speak them and Josh will be healed." Behind these words He heard the soldier saying: "I, too, understand power and words, but I would never dream of having any kind of power to heal a sick child, but You do. I live in the human realm. You live in the supernatural. I serve the Emperor. You are of God."

So Jesus declared, "I have not found such faith in all my travels. Even Israel has not exhibited such faith."

Jesus paused a moment looking at the ground. He raised his eyes to look with compassion on the desperate soldier, "Go, it shall be done for you just as you have believed."

Jesus was swept away before the captain could say thank you. Captain Percel stood transfixed. He knew the lad he loved had

Insights

been healed. He took a deep breath. "Thank God this is not a dream." His feelings were mixed. He wanted to rush back and see Josh. But, then again, he wanted to savor the moment.

"Do you think the boy's healed?" A straggler, an older man, questioned him softly.

"Oh, yes ... yes, I know he's healed," testified the captain. A sense of knowing came out of his faith. All was well with the world. He hadn't felt so good in weeks.

He turned his back slowly on the hallowed ground where the miracle had taken place. Tracing his own footsteps he took the same route back into town. The same sandy knoll. The same road. They looked different now. He wanted to share with everyone his wonderful news.

"I told them the Preacher had the power to heal Josh. You'll know what to do, Captain," rumbled through his mind again and again. "But it wasn't me, Josh. I didn't do it. God did it. Thank Him. The Preacher is the one who had His power. I was able to stand to one side and watch Him work."

See Matthew 8:5-13 and Luke 7:1-10.

Illusions

Charles Steinmetz, the great scientist, was once asked which field for future research offered the greatest promise.

"Prayer," he replied instantly. "Find out about prayer! Find out about prayer!"

Why study prayer? I think of the singular pleasure that successful prayer gives. Or of the enormous power it adds to one's life. Think of a dimension where I am constantly receiving what God wants me to have. No other activity gives me such authority to live above the circumstances of daily living.

Successful prayer belongs to the skilled craftsman — the one who has learned the art of prayer. Through training you and I can learn the mechanics of prayer. No investment will pay greater dividends — beyond what I can dream right up front — than achieving mastery in prayer.

Some live a lifetime, pray daily, and never see one answer to prayer. Think of it. What's wrong? This frightening void of unanswered prayer rests on the fallacy that proficiency need not be acquired. As long as I put up walls around myself I'll forever be doomed to lifeless prayer.

A deeply personal look into a mirror helps to reveal the cause for a dead prayer life. Could it be that I am the most formidable opponent of a prosperous prayer life? Self examination might uncover the blindfold of indoctrination saying, "I have turned my thinking over to someone else." Here's self deception: How can I answer the wake up call when someone else does my thinking for me? My mind has the capacity to resist new ideas with startling energy. How often have I argued against a challenging teaching before I have the facts?

My breakthroughs in prayer will not come out of the laboratory. What we need to "find out about prayer" has been under our noses all along. God's not adding anything new. He's done everything He's going to do. Now it's up to me. God's revelation — the Bible — houses the secrets. Our job lies in panning for the gold in the stream of His Word.

We'll need a role model for our prayer study. Let's say that my daughter drives from Chicago to Minneapolis. How do I pray for her? I want my prayer to be effective for her. "Effective" means to produce the intended result, and the intended result for her trip would be that she arrives safely. How can I know God has heard me? Has God altered her day? If my prayer lacks the power to affect the consequence, I've got to go back to the drawing board and learn what went wrong in the architecture of my prayer.

As I pray I see several obstacles ahead of me. I've called these barriers "illusions." Why illusions? An illusion can be defined as a false idea not based on fact. Illusion, they tell me, mocks the truth. How can I have illusions in prayer? The illusions that follow ridicule the basics of prayer. Usually I'm unaware of these illusions, but these detours put my prayer in the category of dead prayer. It's a very dangerous thing to give oneself to illusions in prayer — a matter of life and death.

Illusion Number 1

I deceive myself when I picture God shaping the answer to my prayer in His workshop.

What's wrong with that? After all, doesn't God fashion an answer for every prayer?

I am misleading myself when I think God has a workshop and

creates the answer on the spot. In this scenario God scurries about to construct a response. He has no workshop. Our inheritance says He has (past tense) given to you and me everything which pertains to life and godliness *(2 Peter 1:3)*.

Notice these verses:

> ... Your father knows what things
> You have need of before you ask Him.
> *Matthew 6:8*
>
> ...Before they call, I will answer.
> *Isaiah 65:24*

Long before my daughter starts her trip, the Father has crafted an answer. But someone asks, does it really matter? Isn't this nit-pickin'? No. This illusion of a workshop keeps me from finding out what God has in store for her trip. A critical difference exists. Rather than stand like a question mark at the door of His workshop, I ferret out the provisions He has made beforehand for her trip. I know He has the response in His vast treasure house, so it becomes accessible, user friendly. My faith couples naturally with what God has said, for faith, after all, locates itself as a creation of God.

Now that I know I receive what God wants me to have, I need not come as a beggar. I come boldly, and a new adventure begins in my life. I find the promise, or promises, that belong to her traveling. Once found, I unearth what God has done in His love for her. I lock on to His pledge, His guarantee, and His unflinching faithfulness behind the declaration gives me a living faith.

Where does dead prayer come from? It comes from an ignorance of what God says in His Word. When I know the mind of God for my daughter's trip, as revealed in the Bible, I can pray with certainty. I say what God says about the need. When I pray what God says, my prayer breathes with divine spiritual life. I receive the answer immediately for I know God never fails to do what He says He'll do. I can rise from prayer knowing a foolproof formula is in place.

Illusion Number 2

I'll ask God till He answers.

In this deception I kid myself into thinking that it takes a lot of prayer to get the job done. I make prayer a work. I try to get the task done by my own muscle. This false impression, along with the others, comes from a failure to grasp the mechanics of faith.

Let's take a closer look at this brow-sweating error. I pray for my daughter's trip, but an hour later I repeat the same request. I say in essence, that my first prayer failed so I'm back with a support prayer. My second prayer exposes the fact that I did not have faith in my first prayer. I didn't receive what God wanted me to have in my first prayer. True faith receives the answer at the moment of the request.

Once I have prayed and simply accepted what God has lavishly given in His Word, I have no need to make the request again. For I have already received. Why would I pray a second time when I have inherited by faith what I desired in my first prayer? Additional prayers should be prayers that reflect my faith — thanksgiving and praise for what I have been given.

The fact that I do not pray twice for my need demonstrates the authenticity of my faith. For faith shouts, "I have received!" A second prayer of begging declares, "I have not received!" Is this presumptuous? No. God expects me to have faith when I pray.

Illusion Number 3

God will give me what I hope for.

Hope. Here we have another illusion.

Ninety-nine percent of all prayer roots itself in hope.

I deceive myself when I pray with hope alone. My confusion lies in replacing faith with hope. Hope says, this is what I desire.

This is what I'd like to have. On the other hand, faith says, this is what God has bequeathed to me. Faith has received. Hope has not received. Hope ever wishes — remains expectant. But hope precedes faith. Hope locks its arms with faith, but hope cannot usurp the place of faith. Hope brings me to faith — brings me to what God says. There I find the kind of faith God wants me to have. Faith goes the distance that God expects.

Hope achieves greatness when its steps lead to what God has to say on the subject. Hope lacks the certainty of reception which adorns faith. Hope crawls like the caterpillar. Faith flies like the monarch butterfly. Hope never says after the amen, "I have received." Hope forever goes on hoping. Hope ignores God's bounty and God's Person.

Why have so many of us been bogged down in dead prayers of hope? No one had told us the secret. We would think faith ranks as classified information. God has marked the trail well. I take my first step when I say, I'm sick and tired of unanswered prayers. I want to cross the chasm to a thrilling new life.

Illusion Number 4

I can go by my inner voice.

My gut feeling gives me the assurance my prayer will be answered. What do I feel like inside? What about the gut feeling? Can I go by feelings? Does a hunch get the job done? Do I get my marching orders to the mission field because of feelings? As a pastor can I accept a call to a new church based on my feelings?

Too often the tragedy in the feelings-illusion lies in pushing aside what God has to say on the matter. Feelings alone are unreliable. Getting-the-job-done faith builds on the foundation rock of knowledge. If the feelings bear the testimony of what God has to say on the matter, then they are reliable.

My "inner voice" cannot throw faith out in the dumpster. But

Insights

let us not throw feelings into the dumpster either. For feelings follow faith. Ecstatic feelings of joy can splash forth like a geyser from the breakthroughs of faith!

Illusion Number 5

I don't need to know the will of God.

I have a friend who ends his prayer with this phrase, "If it be Thy will." "Take care of so and so 'if it be Thy will.'" Now, what's wrong with that? After all, some would counter, if you don't know the outcome, you have to conclude, "if it be Thy will."

"If it be Thy will" parades the fact that I do not know the will of God. Do I have to know the will of God? You and I have to know the will of God if we want to have faith.

What you are saying then is this: "if I pray 'If it be Thy will,' I do not have faith. What would faith say? Faith would say: I know Your will. I find it in Your Word. I know You cannot lie, so I pray Your will with certainty; You will do what You say You'll do."

I pray what God thinks. I pray what God says. When I have done that, then I can have faith.

One says, "I never knew I needed to have faith when I prayed." If I have no faith when I pray, then I am outside of God's will. Prayer expresses the faith life. The just shall live by faith *(Romans 1:17)*. Inherent to the Christian life lives the faith principle. As a result, prayer without faith equals dead prayer.

"Find out about prayer." It boils down to this: Find out what God has to say about your daughter's trip. Then you'll have what God thinks of her travel.

"I love her," He says, "with a love that never lets me stop thinking about her." *(Ephesians 2:4 see Amplified translation)*

"Because I love her with such intensity I'll never be away from her for even a second." *(Hebrews 13:5)*

"I'll be at work in her life far above what you can

think, or ask, or even dream." *(Ephesians 3:20)*

What do I do with these pronouncements: His love, His presence, and His power? He has bequeathed to me His Words so I say His Words for my daughter. I pray His Words out loud. For a prayer to live it needs to be uttered. My spirit listens in, so I seal what God says with my spirit in an audible voice. Any further prayer rejoices in what I have already received.

Are there other verses one can use to undergird her as she travels? Oh, yes. There are dozens of them. I've selected the three above. They lift me out of all worry as she travels today. The Father wants me to enjoy His rest *(Hebrews 4)*. I do have it! Plus the thanksgiving and praise.

We have captured freedom and industry, equality and technology. Now you and I need to appropriate the life of Christ in prayer — and then, for the second time in the history of the world we'll discover fire — spiritual fire!

About the Author

When one goes forth a-voyaging,
he has a tale to tell.

Norm Sorensen is at once a story-teller and a philosopher; one with a seemingly bottomless store of tales — amusing, inspiring, and sometimes heartbreaking. He relentlessly draws from the amazing array of books, papers, magazines, and eclectic reading material that he always needs to have close at hand. And fortunately for us, he is generous in sharing his insights.

The son of immigrants, he went to public school in Minneapolis, Augsburg College, the University of Minnesota, and on to Dallas Theological Seminary. There he got his Master's Degree in Theology, and subsequently served as a minister. The Second World War took its staggering price on his generation; during its course he landed on the shores of Normandy and survived the Battle of the Bulge.

For most of the rest of the century he had a small sign-painting business while he continued his loving service to God and neighbor, work he continues to this day, encircled by his children, grandchildren, and wife of 63 years. Now, at age 93, Norm has collected his lifetime of wisdom to share with others. *Insights* is a fascinating, inspirational guide for Christians, the faithful, and all others on a spiritual quest.

He is currently working on his next book.